New Pathways for Sock Knitters, Book One

8 new forms of sock architecture
28 individual designs
8 Master Patterns
and all the elements needed to
empower you to knit with freedom
and joy in a new world of sock knitting

by

Cat Bordhi

Also by Cat Bordhi:

Socks Soar on Two Circular Needles

A Treasury of Magical Knitting

A Second Treasury of Magical Knitting

Treasure Forest *(a novel, with knitting)*

Book design: Cat Bordhi
Illustrations: Cat Bordhi
Photography: Michael Hopkins
Front cover photos: Kathy Ballard
Cover design: Bruce Conway and Cat Bordhi

Passing Paws Press, Inc.
P.O. Box 2463
Friday Harbor, WA 98250

Email: cat@catbordhi.com
Web site: www.catbordhi.com

Printed by Friesens in Manitoba, Canada

Dedications

To my beloved daughter, Jenny -
without you, this book would have taken ever so much longer. Since the day you took over as my business manager, I've been able to immerse myself in the creative side of my work. Thank you for handling everything so gracefully and professionally, and for living in a way that shines with compassion, integrity, and intelligence. *And to your newborn son, Charlie Pepper Johnson,* who has been inspiring his grandma to knit baby socks since he was the size of a peppercorn . . . may you always be filled with awe for the beauty, innocence, and mystery of this world, and know you are loved wholly.

And to the other "yarn babies" who've been born to friends in the knitting industry during the past year: *Marcelo Loring Jones*, grandson of Susan Druding of Crystal Palace Yarns; *Etta Mae,* born to Handmaiden's Jana Dempsey; *Rowan Margaret*, born to Jana's sister Emily Dempsey of Fleece Artist; plus an honorary yarn baby, *Max*, born to my niece Nona Lynn Haydon. I've designed a baby sock to honor each of these bright new beings.

The golden heart of my dear friend Sivia Harding casts a glow on every page of this book. Sivia, your steady radiance and knitterly intelligence, creativity, and wisdom are always present though we are miles apart, and your test-knitting of several challenging patterns has helped me immeasurably.

To all the knitters in my workshops . . . thank you for your soulful camaraderie, corrections, and the many thoughtful questions and suggestions that have steered me to make the book as user-friendly as possible.

As I work on book design, I often feel grateful to book designer extraordinaire Val Speidel, who allowed me to learn so much from her and who one day handed me a book she had designed, *Spirit of Siberia: Traditional Native Life, Clothing, and Footwear.* Its timeless beauty haunted me, eventually led me to the Bata Shoe Museum in Toronto, and slowly blossomed to become the inspiration for this book and the two that will follow.

Table of Contents

4 The Inner Light of Knitting

6 Chapter One — Knitting Along New Pathways

24 Chapter Two — Sky Architecture
Charlie's Seeded Heart Socks, Bartholomew's Tantalizing Socks, Robin Hood's Fireside Boots (Elf Toe option), Master Sky

34 Chapter Three — Cedar Architecture
Max's Springy Ring Socks, Veil of Leaves, Cedar Dancing Socks, Ocean-Toes, Slipstitch Rings, Master Cedar

50 Chapter Four — Coriolis Architecture
Charlie's Dragon Socks, Tibetan Coriolis, Master Coriolis

60 Chapter Five — Foxglove Architecture
Marcelo's Seven-League Boots, Simple Socks with a Slant, Bubble Trails, Fountain Foxgloves, Master Foxglove

68 Chapter Six — Upstream Architecture
Etta Mae's Bootikins, Philosopher's House Socks, Dove Socks, Milkmaid's Stockings, Master Upstream

80 Chapter Seven — Riverbed Architecture
Rushing Rivulet, Margaret Rowan's Silken Slippers, Clematis Vine, Cables & Corrugations, Master Riverbed

92 Chapter Eight — Ridgeline Architecture
Home & Hearth Eyelet Anklets, Charlie's Wiggle Socks, Soft-Hearted Socks, Woven Ridge, Master Ridgeline

100 Chapter Nine — Sidestream Architecture
Charlie's Sheriff Boat Socks, Sunrise Socks, Jeweled Steps, Master Sidestream

109 Chapter Ten — Master Numbers Make You a Designer

120 Chapter Eleven — Master Heels, Toes, & Cuffs

134 Resources, abbreviations, and technique and pattern indexes

The Inner Light of Knitting

I share these new forms of sock architecture with deep reverence for all who have preceded us and made this evolution possible. I could not be opening the doors I am opening today were I not standing on the rich threshold built by generation upon generation of knitters whose hands performed the miracle of pulling loops through loops to clothe the bodies of kin and strangers alike. My gratitude and reverence reaches all the way back, thousands upon thousands of years, to the earliest individuals all over the world who first twisted fragile fibers into something strong and useful. They stand at the evolutionary origin of yarn, and their pleasure and astonishment at what they made must have been akin to ours. I suspect we both light up in exactly the same way. We are one.

Five hundred years, two styles of socks

For about five hundred years, hand-knit socks have been dominated by two architectural styles: one with a heel flap and side gussets, the other with an inserted heel. In North America and Europe, the heel flap and gusset were dominant until about a decade ago, when Priscilla A. Gibson-Roberts published *Ethnic Socks & Stockings* detailing the Eastern inserted heel, and later added her *Simple Socks*, which introduced the short-row heel, architecturally (but not procedurally) similar to the inserted heel. Her introduction has spawned numerous variations and today in North America the short-row heel is nearly as common as the heel flap and gusset. Priscilla's scholarly work on Eastern methods, and Nancy Bush's pattern collections and meticulous research on traditional Western methods in her books, including *Folk Socks, Folk Knitting in Estonia*, and *Knitting Vintage Socks*, immeasurably enrich the lives of countless serious knitters.

Recent innovations

Over the years, a few free-thinking knitters have designed and published socks with unusual architecture. Elizabeth Zimmermann's Wearable Art Stockings and Refootable Moccasin Socks come to mind, as well as Debbie New's unbelievable Maple Swirl Socks and Better Mousetrap Socks. I too have come up with new ideas, and have done my very best to develop each one into a friendly and clear method which invites you to make it your own and take it far beyond what you see in this book if you wish. Basically, I've discovered that we never needed to limit ourselves to the two primary architectural styles. Most sock knitters and designers, myself included, have spent years assuming that what was familiar was necessary, when it was only one of an infinite number of options.

A surprise

There was a moment in June of 2006 when this truth was brought home to me. I was between workshops, enjoying several peaceful days in a cabin on a lake in northern Indiana. Sitting in the dappled shade of a giant cottonwood tree a few feet from the water, my toes wiggling in the grass, with a toe-up sock for this book (well, for what I thought was this book - that single book was about to explode into three) on my needles, I was soaking up the sweet, soft, balmy air, entirely unlike the bracing atmosphere I'm used to in the Pacific Northwest. Twice that morning I'd glimpsed the scarlet streak of a cardinal swooping past, the only time in my life I've ever seen one.

I finished the arch expansion and pulled the sock onto my foot (I knit with two circular needles, which allows me to try on a sock quite naturally because the cable wraps the foot without interference, or what I am about to tell you would not have happened) and began rotating it around to see if there were any new positions the expansion triangle might like to occupy other than instep and sole.

I had no idea that my curiosity was about to topple me into a discovery that would alter the entire course of the book I'd been working on for the past year. One moment I was relaxing in the shade, and the next my mouth was hanging open because suddenly it seemed that the half-done sock and my foot were in cahoots, playing tricks on me. *Every* position I rotated the expansion triangle into worked. Impossible! How could it be, for instance, that the triangle could be entirely on one side of the foot without skewing the other side?

I still don't quite understand why that didn't skew the sock, but it doesn't, and you'll find a sock architecture in this book called Sidestream that proves it works. Through some mysterious affinity of foot and knitting, the necessary increases are happy to be randomly scattered, meticulously organized, or anything in between. In the months that followed, I could hardly sleep because I wanted to jump out of bed and try something to see if that too would work. I finally chose eight forms of sockitecture, leaving an infinite number of untried and thrilling possibilities for you to play with on your own.

The formula revealed beneath the cottonwood tree

Luckily the formula is simple. Here it is: after knitting the first section of the foot (if knitting toe-up), or completing the leg down to the anklebone (if knitting top-down), work increases at the rate of *two every three rounds*. You may put those increases *anywhere*. As you work your way through the different kinds of sockitecture in this book, you'll realize this is true. In fact, *all I have really done is to liberate the increases that used to be unnecessarily confined in side gussets in the Western architectural style* (I still incorporate a heel flap, although it never flaps, since it is integrated into the continuous knitting). But this liberation changes the world - just have a look at Coriolis Architecture on page 50, for instance. As you journey through this book, you'll find individual patterns, ready to follow, as well as a Master Numbers chapter which empowers you to use each Master Pattern for the eight styles of sockitecture to knit and design socks to fit anyone, in any yarn at any gauge, using double-pointed or circular needles - your choice.

There are a few other details, of course. For instance, sometimes the total number of increases is smaller when knitting top down, and you'll learn how to truly conceal wraps, and there are tricks for custom-fitting various and sundry feet.

Learning to knit along new pathways

Please slow down to read and digest the following chapter, and knit both little learning socks. I designed the chapter and the little socks expressly to enable you to move through the book with ease. They are your passport to sock happiness.

Once you learn the new pathways, they're yours

I hope that over the years to come, this book and the next two will become an evolutionary springboard for knitters with inquiring minds. I think of myself as having plowed a field, grown a good crop, and I can see there is plenty of space for everyone to farm in the field I happened to discover. Please let this book nourish and kindle your creativity. Once you understand how the socks are proportioned, how the heels flow, and most of all, how completely free you are to organize the increases in artistic ways, you too may be jumping out of bed in the middle of the night to knit up your latest idea.

Like our oldest fiber ancestors, we light up at the miracle of fiber transforming in our hands. May this inner light that knitting carries so well be awake in you always.

How to use this book well

Please read the next chapter, knit the little socks, and become familiar with the techniques. Then jump wherever you like! You might knit all eight baby socks (there's one for each architecture), or fully explore one architecture at a time. Relax and enjoy the adventure - there is a lot here, and it could take you years to try everything.

Chapter 1 - Knitting Along New Pathways

This entryway chapter takes you by the hand and teaches you new ways of knitting around the foot. The techniques you'll need appear in easy-to-spot yellow panels. Please read every page in this chapter until you come to the two little socks near the end. Then pull out some leftover yarn and knit them both - hopefully a pair of each for better learning - and you'll be ready to travel happily along brand new pathways of sock architecture.

Here are some signs you'll soon recognize

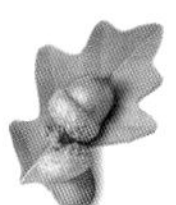

The acorn cluster invites you to take a few moments to learn something worthwhile. From how to avoid ladders, to tips for sending designs along new sock pathways, these explanations encourage you to understand what you are doing and take matters into your own hands. Like this child's verse, *In the heart of a seed, so deep, so deep, a dear little tree lies fast asleep,* I hope my acorn explanations grow inside you to become mighty oak trees, with branches of understanding, skills, confidence, and inspiration.

Master Numbers - The large sock circle reminds you to collect your master numbers, like Ⓐ, which allow you to knit along any of the sock pathways, creating a custom-fit sock! If you'd like to keep a notebook of master numbers for yourself and other favorite feet, you'll find a reproducible form on page 109.

Green letters like A and B refer to letter stitch markers. "Knit to A" means "knit to marker A." These friendly markers map your sock and let you knit with confidence. You might also make your own (like those shown here), or use markers in different colors, assigning letters to colors. Addi Turbo is also making letter markers - see page 134.

Companion rows or rounds **stay together like good friends**, are repeated together, and appear like this:
Rnd 1: Knit to A, p3, repeat **k1, yo, ssk** 3x, p to B, k to end.
Rnd 2: Purl to A, k to B, p to end.
Repeat companion rnds 1-2 another 4x.
A repeat within one row or round (see Rnd 1 above) looks like this: repeat **k1, yo, ssk** 3x.

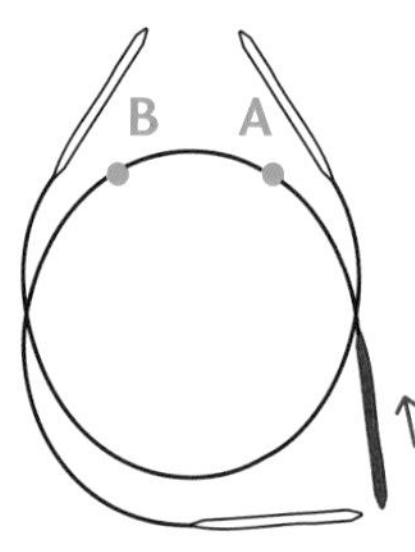

You may choose 2 circular needles, 5 double-pointed needles, or 1 long circular needle. Instructions and schematics are given for 2 circs and for 5 double-pointed needles (dpn's). If you'd like to use 1 long circ (Magic Loop), simply follow the two circ directions, placing a cable loop at each needle intersection. The small red arrow indicates the direction of knitting. The red starting needle is the "delivery" needle in your left hand. It delivers loops to the "stitch-producing" needle in your right hand. Green dots beside A and B indicate marker placement.

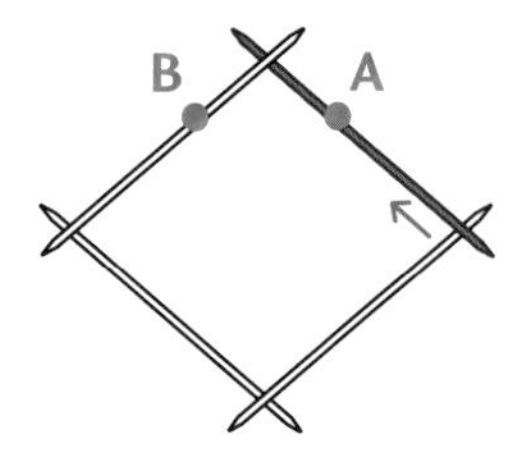

Knowing your needles' names

Think of the center space in needle schematics as the inside of a sock - imagine sliding your foot right in. Then it's easy to remember that in the drawings, the top circ or top 2 dpn's always represent the instep and the lower circ or lower 2 dpn's always represent the sole.

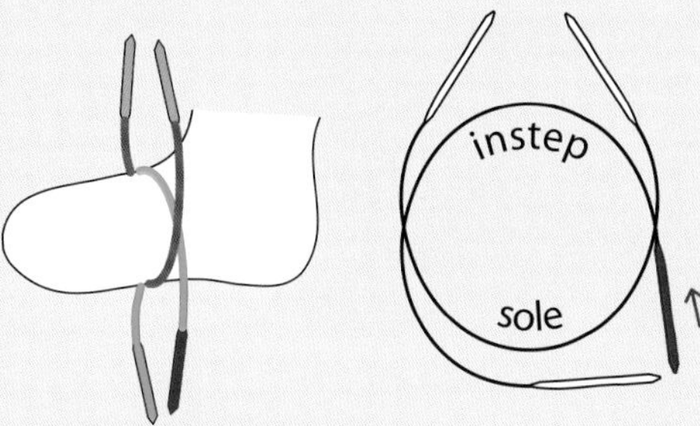

Compare the foot and the 2 circ schematic above. The **blue needle** hanging over the foot's instep is the instep needle. Since its left **tip** is red, it's also the **starting needle** (the needle in your left hand). The **green needle** is the **sole needle**. Don't be confused by the way the **sole needle's** tips point up, and the **instep needle's** tips point down. Look at the cables. They hold either sole stitches or instep stitches. This is how you know their identity.

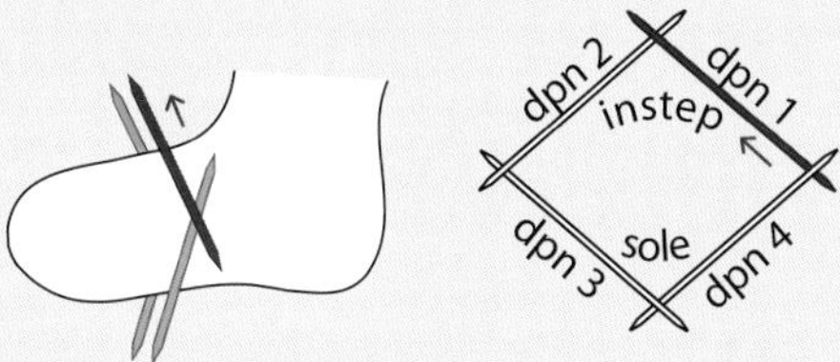

Now compare this foot and the dpn schematic. The 2 top dpn's are instep needles, and the **red dpn** is the starting needle. The **green dpn's** on the bottom are **sole needles**. The **red dpn** is **dpn 1**, followed by **blue dpn 2** and **green dpn's 3** and **4**.

Sock parts

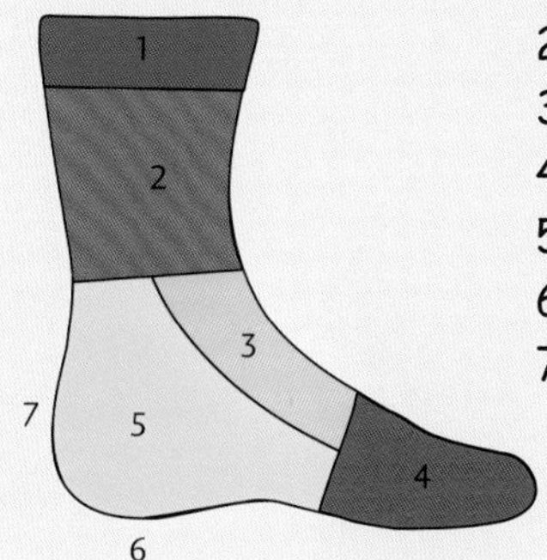

1. cuff
2. leg
3. instep
4. toe
5. rear foot
6. base of heel
7. back of heel

Instep stitches ride the instep needle(s), and sole stitches ride the sole needle(s).

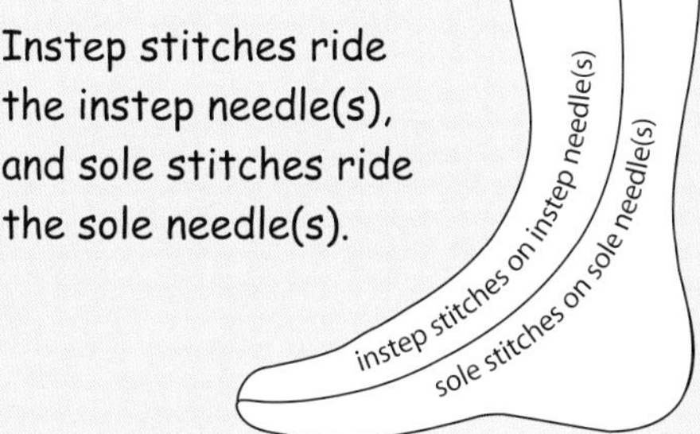

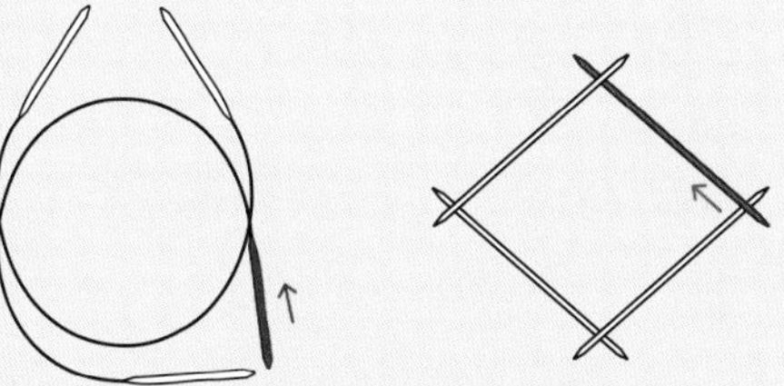

The drawings show the needles as they would look if you laid them flat on a table, with the sock growing towards you. The **starting needle** is always the one in your left hand. As you knit around, imagine the picture rotating with your knitting.

Knitting with 2 circular needles

To start a sock cuff, cast on to 1 circular needle. Divide the stitches evenly on 2 circular needles (I prefer 24" length), and join (page 10).

The **instep needle** (with the **red tip**) knits its own stitches, as if it is the only needle in the world. Then it slides its stitches to the middle of its cable, so the tips hang down out of the way. The circle of needles **rotates clockwise**, right side facing you, and the **instep needle** passes the yarn to the **sole needle**.

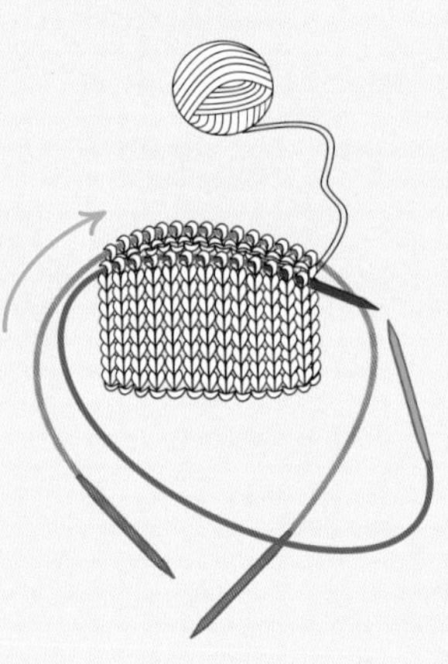

The sole needle now knits its own stitches, as if it is the only needle in the world. Then its stitches slide to the middle of its cable, its tips out of the way, and it passes the yarn to the **instep needle**. Around and around they go, sharing yarn but nothing more.

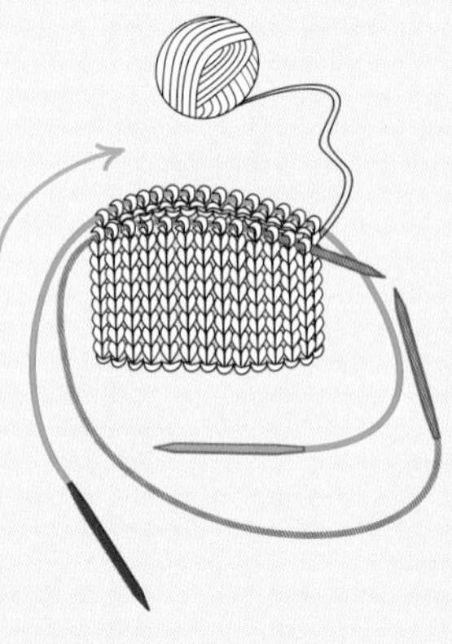

The 2-circ rule: "Knit or nap"
One needle knits its own stitches while the other needle naps. **To be sure you always have both ends of the same needle,** tug at both ends before proceeding. You'll know right away.

Knitting with 5 double-pointed needles

To start a sock cuff, cast onto one dpn. Divide the stitches evenly among 4 dpn's and join (page 10). Use the **free dpn** to knit across the **starting needle, dpn 1**. The circle of knitting rotates clockwise.

(Each newly freed dpn knits across the next one.) The **freed dpn** knits across **dpn 2**. When **dpn 2** is freed, it will knit across **dpn 3**. Once it is free, **dpn 3** knits across **dpn 4**. And round and round they go.

Important:
Unless a pattern specifies otherwise, dpn's 1 and 2 hold instep stitches, dpn's 3 and 4 hold sole stitches, and knitting begins at start of instep. As your tube of knitting grows, push the right side to face out.

Knitting with 1 long circular needle

This popular method, called Magic Loop, uses one 40" or longer circular needle, and was introduced by Sarah Hauschka. Magic Loop knitters can follow the directions and schematics for two circular needles by locating their two **cable loops** at the circular needles' two intersections.

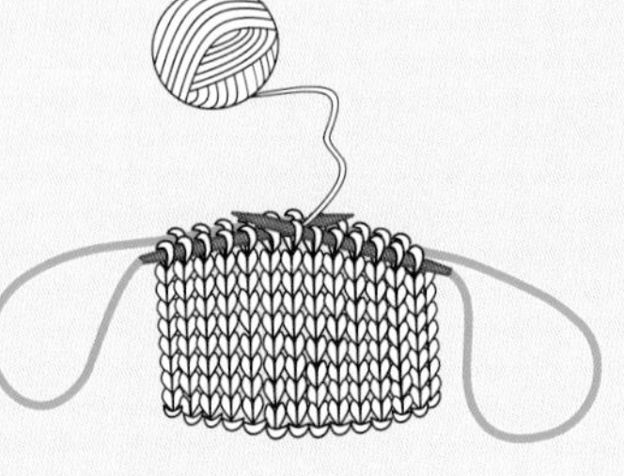

Gauge really does matter!

Please don't be a foolish sock knitter.
Just as your handwriting differs from that of others, so does your gauge. When a pattern suggests a particular needle size, it does NOT mean you should use that size - not unless that size gives YOU the required gauge.

See these two little socks, which you'll knit with your own choice of yarn and needles in a few pages? Each was knit by a different knitter. Both used the same yarn (Socks That Rock), and the same needles (size 5 /3.75 mm Addi Turbo circulars), and worked the exact same number of stitches in the same order, on a drizzly February day, while sipping the same lavender rooibus tea in my living room. But one variable was different. Yes — the individual knitters. The socks are not the same size. Luckily, gauge doesn't matter on a little sock which is bound to fit someone's little foot. But it matters very much indeed when you are knitting a sock for a specific individual who likes to walk around in shoes.

Sock knitters have to swatch in the round, not in rows, because most people knit at a tighter gauge in the round than in rows. I'm going to teach you a quick way to make an educated guess about the gauge you'll get with your yarn and needles, followed by a way to take that information to a very precise level. Mysteriously, round or row gauge varies among knitters even when stitch gauge is the same. In this book it matters only for toe-up socks, and you'll learn to measure it while your sock is underway, on page 112.

Begin by reading pages 22-23 to learn Judy's Magical Cast-on (JMCO). Later you'll use it for everything from toes to a Cobblestone Cuff. It is truly magical.

Step 1: Use the JMCO to cast on enough stitches to each needle to make a swatch a little over 2" (5 cm) wide. Knit in the round for about an inch. (You end up with this tidy little rectangular pouch, with no flare at the base like you'd have if you'd cast on and joined to knit in the round.) Measure a row of stitches 2" (5 cm) wide and divide by 2. This stitches-per-inch gauge is likely within 90% of the real thing. If it matches the pattern's gauge, go on to step 2. Otherwise, adjust as follows: Purl 1 round to mark the needle change you're about to make. If you have more stitches-per-inch than the gauge calls for, go up a needle size. If you have fewer stitches, go down. Knit another inch. Measure again, and either go on to step 3 or purl another round and adjust size again - until you have the required gauge.

Step 2: Experienced knitters know that the best way to get an accurate gauge is to make a big one . . . like the entire garment. Sock knitters can take advantage of this sad truth, because socks reveal gauge early on. Simply begin your sock with the needle size you think will work (see step 1). After about 2" (5 cm), measure your gauge. Just right? Continue on. If not, don't be in denial and don't unravel. Work a purl round to mark the change, then resume with a larger size needle (if you had more stitches than the gauge called for) or a smaller size needle (if you had fewer stitches). Work another 1" (2.5 cm) and measure again. Repeat if necessary. Before unraveling, record the gauge from each needle size in this yarn, so you have a record to refer to later.

Stitch Mount

Stitch mount is how a stitch sits on the needle. Here the **front legs** are closest to the needle's tip. If the legs were racing to the tip, the front legs would be the **winning legs**.

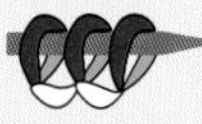

Sometimes the winning legs hide behind the needle. Back legs can also be winning legs.

Here's the rule:
Go with the winner, the leg that's ahead! Always knit or purl into the winning leg unless a pattern instructs you to do otherwise (for example, twisted stitch patterns).

Slipping stitches correctly

To keep stitch mount the same, slip tip-to-tip. Slip stitches as if sliding them along a clothesline. The legs will maintain their winning or losing positions.

To reverse stitch mount, slip knitwise. Insert right needle against the **winning leg**, as if to knit. Now on the right tip, the **former loser** is in **first place**, and the **leg** that thought it was a champion now trails to the **left** of the **winner**. If instructions say to put the stitch back on the left tip, do so tip-to tip to maintain mount reversal.

Managing markers

Markers ride along the needle (and cable, if using circular needles) as if it is a clothes-line. A marker keeps track of the same point in a line of stitches, no matter what happens in front of or behind it. These 'signposts' help you map your knitting.

If you are instructed to knit 6 and place A, just place the marker after knitting the 6 stitches. At other times, you may be instructed to place markers before knitting to their location. Some markers can be clipped in place, or you can slide stitches from needle to needle to access the placement locations.

To mark rounds as you complete them, use a short length of contrasting color yarn. Lay it between stitches on the first round so 1 end hangs to the front and the other to the rear. Flip it to the other side when you meet it again. It leaves a little "dashed line" of yarn on the right side every 2 rounds.

Joining in the round

This method requires **1 cast-on stitch** more than is needed for the cuff. Be sure your **cast-on edge** is not twisted. Notice how the **cast-on edge** stays inside of the needles, with the stitches to the outside. It works just the same way on circular needles.

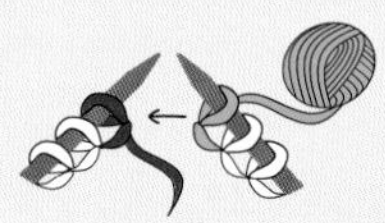

Transfer the **extra stitch** to the starting needle. Knit the **extra stitch** together with the **next stitch**. This eliminates the **extra stitch** and joins the circle. There are many good ways to join a line of stitches into a circle. This particular method is simple, secure, and gives smooth results after the end is woven in carefully.

Increases (used in most patterns)

LRinc ("La-Rink") and LLinc ("La-Link")
I use these paired increases almost exclusively in the book. They are more invisible than most and are easy to work. In knitting references they appear under a confusing assortment of names, so I'm giving them new, descriptive names, in hopes they will stick. Visualizing three generations of stitches helps you see which strand of yarn to lift up onto your needle when you work the sleek and fluid LRinc and LLinc increases. Say their names out loud like this: "La-Rink" and "La-Link," as you learn them, and more parts of your brain will store them.

The **daughter stitch** is the top stitch. The **mother stitch** is beneath the daughter stitch, and the **grandmother stitch** is beneath the mother stitch.

LLinc ("La-Link") is a leaning-left increase. Lift the **left side** of the grandmother of the last stitch knit, place on left tip, then knit into its back leg.

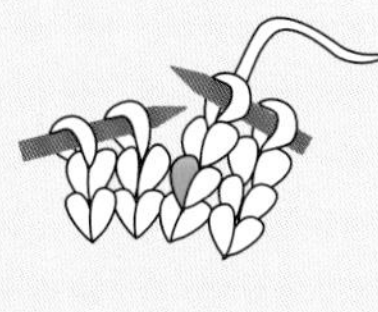

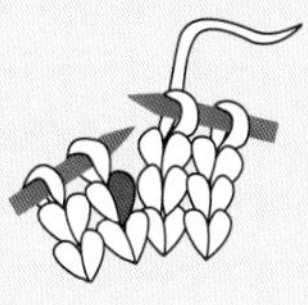

LRinc ("La-Rink") is a leaning-right increase. Lift the **right side** of the next stitch's mother, place on left tip, then knit into its front leg.

Other Increases

Knit into front and back of a stitch (k1f&b)
Knit into the **front leg** of the next stitch as usual but do not remove the stitch from left needle. First knit into the **back leg** of the same stitch. Then remove it from the needle. This increase appears as a knit stitch with a purl bump to the left.

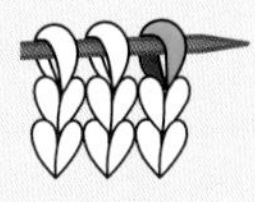

k1f&b

Purl into back and front of a stitch (p1b&f)
Purl into the **back leg** of the next stitch but do not remove the stitch from left needle. First purl into the **front leg** of the same stitch. Then remove it from the needle. This increase appears as 2 purl bumps on the side it is worked, and on the other side as a knit stitch with a purl bump to the right.

p1b&f

Decreases

Slip, slip, knit (ssk)
Slip the next 2 stitches 1 at a time knitwise, reversing their mount (see page 10). Then slide them tip-to-tip back to the left needle. Insert the right needle into the **back legs** as shown and knit them together. This decrease leans to the left. **Helpful hint for a smoother line:** As you come back around to the ssk stitch on the next round, knit it through the back leg, and it will lean a little to the left as well, creating a much smoother decrease line.

ssk

Knit 2 together (k2tog)
Insert the right needle into the next 2 stitches on the left needle, first through the **second** one and on through the **first**, as shown, and knit them together. This is a right-leaning decrease.

k2tog

Moving stitches between circs

(Note: This method also works if you need to knit some stitches from the other circ.) Sometimes you'll need to transfer stitches from one needle to the other. On double-pointed needles this is simple because the ends are always close enough to trade stitches. Here's an easy way to move stitches between circs.

Pull the **needle which will receive stitches** out until a length of its cable emerges. Now point this **needle** at the **donor needle** and slide the stitches (as if along a clothesline) from **donor tip** to **receiving tip**. Then gently pull the **receiving needle's** far end so the cable slides back into place.

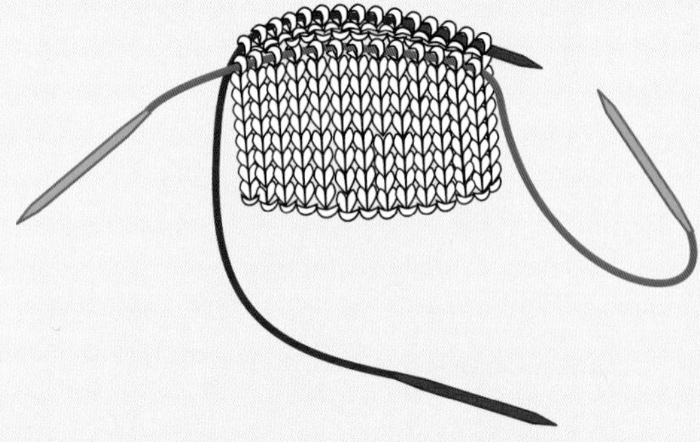

Sometimes after moving stitches, the working yarn becomes temporarily inaccessible, located among stitches instead of between tips. (This will happen after moving wing stitches - as you'll discover when you knit the first little learning sock.) Just bring the needle's right tip around to meet its left tip, and transfer the stitches that are in the way. Now the yarn is between tips again, ready for knitting.

Little Sky Sock - your first learning sock

This is your first project. Knit a pair, and you'll learn twice as well, and have a little pair of socks to fit a baby. I knit this sock in Fleece Artist's Blue-Faced Leiscester Aran, at a gauge of 5.5 sts per inch (2.5 cm). *The foot is* 4.5" (11 cm) *long and the mid-foot circumference is* 5" (13 cm). *I used* size 6 (4 mm) *needles, but as you know from reading page 9, your gauge may be different than mine. The time you spend knitting this small learning sock and the next one will reward you later with a feeling of "I've been here before!" and teach you the new skills you'll need to travel the pathways in the book. So relax, pay attention, and enjoy yourself!*

Yarn: about 3 ounces worsted weight
Needles and gauge: Worsted weight yarn, with the size needle that gives *you* 5 or 6 sts to the inch (2.5 cm) knitting in the round. See page 8 for the 3 needle methods to choose from.
Markers: A and B
Slip all stitches tip-to-tip (see page 10)

Start leg at top
Cast on 32 stitches plus 1 extra for joining (page 10).
Join, and repeat **knit 1, purl 1** for 3 rounds.
Next round: Repeat **knit 2 together, knit 1, purl 1** 8 times. (At end of round, 24 stitches remain.)
Repeat **knit 2, purl 1** for 8 rounds.
Knit 8 rounds.

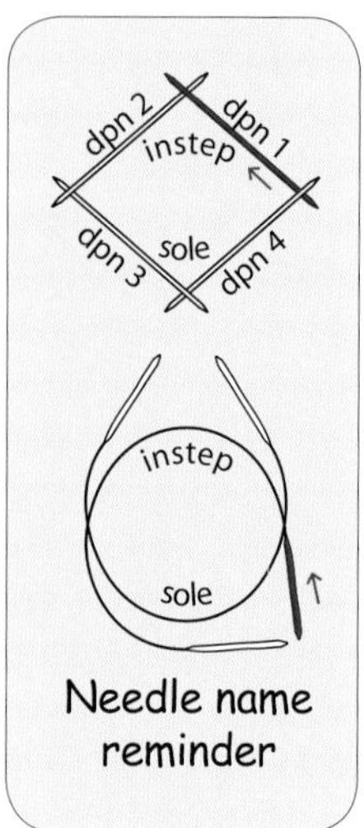

Needle name reminder

Panel 1

Two circular needles (circs)

The instep needle is the starting needle. The other one is the sole needle. The **red arrow** indicates the starting needle's **tip** (the end that is in your left hand as you knit).

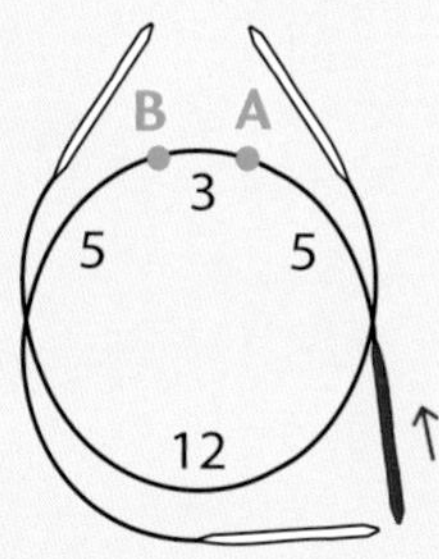

Knit 5, place A, knit into front and back of next stitch (k1f&b), knit 1, place B, knit to end of round. There are 3 stitches between A and B.

Panel 2

Double-pointed needles (dpn's)

The **red arrow** indicates **dpn 1**, the starting (lefthand) needle. **Dpn 1** and dpn 2 (the next needle) are instep needles. Dpn's 3 and 4 are sole needles. The fifth dpn will begin knitting from **dpn 1**.

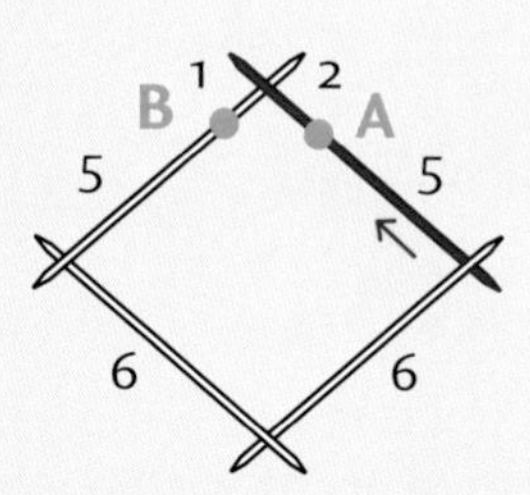

Dpn 1: Knit 5, place A, knit into front and back of next stitch. (k1f&b). Now there are 2 stitches between A and the end of dpn 1.

Dpn 2: Knit 1, place B, knit to end of dpn. There are 3 stitches between A and B.

Dpn's 3 and 4: Knit to end of round.

Sky arch expansion (panels 1, 2, and 3)

First see panel 1 or 2, according to your needle choice, and follow all directions in that panel.

Knit 2 rounds.

Arch Expansion Companion Rounds

Round 1: Knit to A, knit 1, make a leaning-left increase (LLinc), knit until 1 stitch remains before B, make a leaning-vright increase (LRinc), knit to end.

Rounds 2-3: Knit.

Repeat companion rounds 1-3 *another* 4 times.

Work a partial round 1, stopping at end of instep. There are 37 stitches total - 25 on instep, and 12 on sole. See panel 3.

For dpn's only: Put all 12 sole sts on dpn 3, setting dpn 4 aside for now. See bottom of panel 3 for *before* and *after*.

Panel 3

After arch expansion

During the companion rounds, 12 stitches were added between A and B. You stopped knitting at the end of the instep needle(s), so the yarn comes from that intersection. The starting needle is now the sole needle or dpn 3. Move all sole stitches to dpn 3 (see below for before and after).

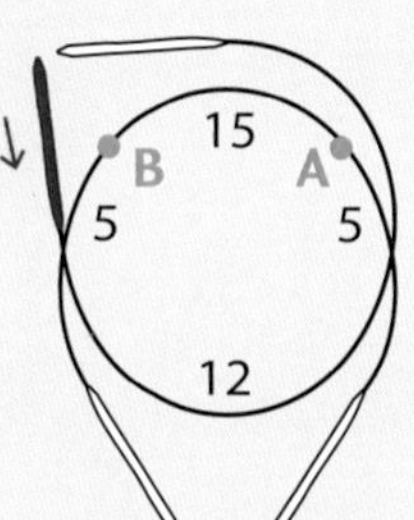

Sole stitches are already on 1 circ.

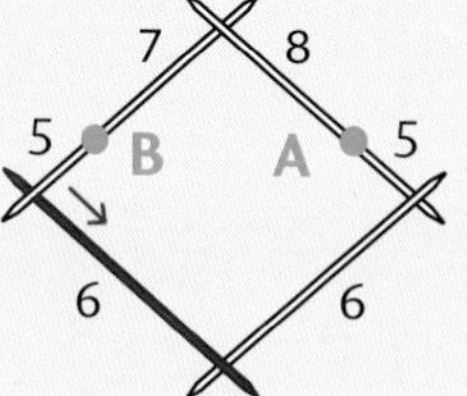

Before: sole stitches are divided on 2 dpn's.

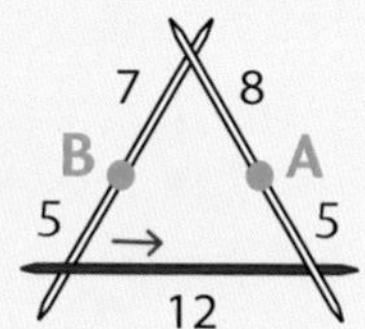

After: all 12 sole stitches are on dpn 3.

Heel turn (panels 4, 5, 6, and 7)

The heel turn is worked back and forth in short rows on the 12 sole stitches alone. The instep needle(s) rest while you work the heel turn and base of the heel. When you resume knitting in the round, the instep needle(s) will work again.

If you've never worked short rows, you may wonder why the directions stop short of the end of the needle. Well, that's why they're called short rows! See what they look like in panel 5.

Before continuing, read panel 6 to learn how to wrap and turn (w&t) knit and purl stitches. *Always use the knit method for a knit stitch, and the purl method for a purl stitch.*

Row 1: (sole needle) Knit 10, (2 sts remain on needle) wrap and turn (w&t). The slipped stitch is unworked and is wrapped with a necklace of yarn (final st is also unworked).
Row 2: Purl 8, (2 sts remain on needle) w&t. The slipped stitch is unworked and is wrapped with a necklace of yarn. (Final st is also unworked.)
Row 3: Knit 7, (3 sts remain on needle) w&t.
(final 2 sts remain on needle unworked)
Row 4: Purl 6, (3 sts remain on needle) w&t.
(final 2 sts remain on needle unworked)
Row 5: Knit 5, (4 sts remain on needle) w&t.
(final 3 sts remain on needle unworked)
Row 6: Purl 4, (4 sts remain on needle) w&t.
(final 3 sts remain on needle unworked)
Panel 5 shows the heel at this stage.

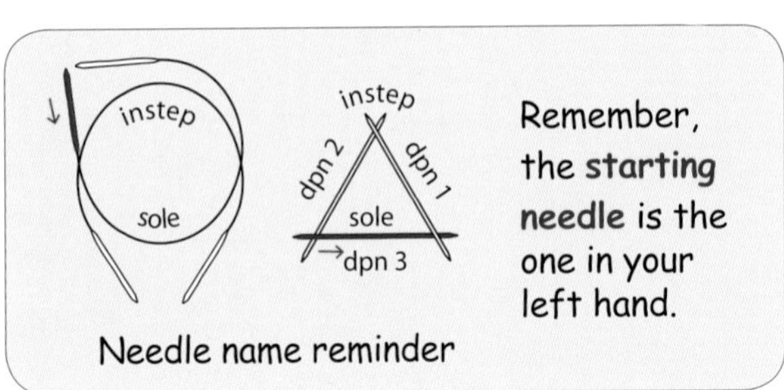

Needle name reminder

Panel 5

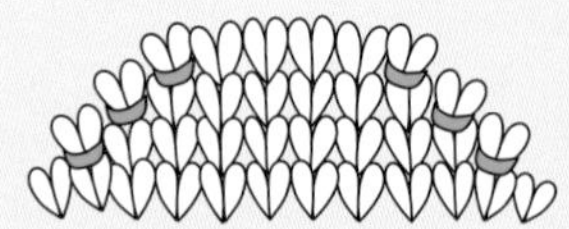

The heel turn after completing row 6. There is 1 unwrapped stitch at each end, **3 wrapped stitches** on each side, and 4 unwrapped stitches in the center. (The first 4 stitches are on the right needle and the remaining 8 stitches on the left after turning.)

Panel 6

w&t wrap and turn

For a knit stitch:
Bring **yarn** between the needles to the front. Slip next stitch **knitwise** (see page 10). Move **yarn** between the needles to the back. Slide the **wrapped stitch** from the right tip back to the left tip, and turn to the purl side.

For a purl stitch:
Bring **yarn** between the needles to the back, slip next stitch tip-to-tip, move **yarn** between the needles to the front, slide the **wrapped stitch** from the right tip back to the left tip, and turn to the knit side.

Panel 7

cw conceal wrap (this **totally** conceals a wrap)

Always lift wraps from the public (knit) side of the knitting, up and over the st they wrapped, then release them to sit on the needle to the left of the stitch they had wrapped. Don't worry if the wraps seem to stretch - they will be fine. The drawings show wraps already moved.

On the knit side: Insert the right needle under the **wrap** to lift it from the public side, up, over, and to the left of the **stitch** it wrapped. (See the **blue wrap** sandwiched between the red and white stitches?) Now knit **stitch** and **wrap** together from right to left through the back legs, like an ssk: go through the **stitch**, then the **wrap**. The wrap is now hidden on the 'private' side of the sock. The drawing shows the **wrap**, already relocated and ready to be concealed, and **2 more wraps** waiting in line. (Note: if you forgot to slip the wrapped **stitch knitwise** when wrapping it earlier, slip it knitwise before the ssk).

On the purl side: Insert the right needle beneath the **wrap** on the public (knit) side to lift it up, over, and to the left of the **stitch** it wrapped. Then purl **wrap** and **stitch** together just like a purl-2-together (p2tog) decrease. The drawing shows the relocated **wrap** ready to be concealed, and **2 more wraps** waiting in line.

cw/ssk or cw/p2tog

Prepare to conceal the final wrap as usual, sliding the right needle through the stitch and the relocated wrap, then keep sliding it right on through the final stitch on the left needle. Decrease the first stitch, the wrap, and the final stitch all together like an ssk (on knit side) or like a p2tog (on the purl side).

Before continuing, read panel 7 to learn to conceal wraps.

Row 7: Knit 4. The next 3 stitches are wrapped. You will conceal the wraps as you knit the stitches. Use the right needle to lift the wrap's *bottom edge* from the *knit side* of the sock *up and over* the stitch it wraps. Drop the wrap to the left of that stitch, *sandwiching it between the first 2 stitches on the left needle*. Knit the stitch and wrap together through the back legs, inserting the needle from right to left like an ssk. Conceal the next wrap the same way. Prepare to conceal the final wrap, and slide the right tip through the stitch, the wrap, and the final stitch on the left needle and knit all three together like an ssk (cw/ssk). Turn to work the wrong side.

Row 8: Slip 1 stitch. Purl 6. The next 3 stitches are wrapped. You will conceal the wraps as you purl the stitches. Use the right needle to lift the wrap's *bottom edge* from the *knit side* of the sock *up and over* the stitch it wraps. Drop the wrap to the left of that stitch, *sandwiching it between the first 2 stitches on the left needle*. Purl the stitch and wrap together. Conceal the next wrap. Prepare to conceal the final wrap, and slide the right needle through the stitch, the wrap, and the final stitch on the left needle and purl all three together like a purl 2 together (cw/p2tog). (10 sts remain on sole)

A wrap resembles a necklace. This knit stitch wears a blue diamond necklace, with the diamond on the knit side. Lift the diamond up over her face (if purling, you must reach around to the opposite side - the knit side - to lift the diamond over her face), and pull it over her head onto the needle behind her. When our stitch and her necklace are joined with an ssk or p2tog, the necklace (wrap) remains tucked behind the stitch, out of sight on the purl side.

Base of heel (panels 8 and 9)

Before continuing, see panel 8 or 9 to rearrange stitches.

Base of heel companion rows

Unworked stitches will remain at ends of companion rows.

Row 1: Slip 1, knit 8, ssk, turn to purl side.

Row 2: Slip 1, purl 8, purl 2 stitches together (p2tog), turn to knit side.

Repeat companion rows 1 and 2 *another* 3 times, working back and forth on sole needle(s) alone. (12 sole sts remain)

Foot

Now you return to working in the round *with all needles.*

(There are 11 sole sts on left needle (or 2 dpn's) and 1 on right needle.)

Round 1: (sole) Slip 1, knit 8, ssk, (go on to instep) knit 15.

Round 2: Knit 2 together, knit to end of instep. (25 sts remain)

Knit 8 more rounds.

Panel 8 - Two circs

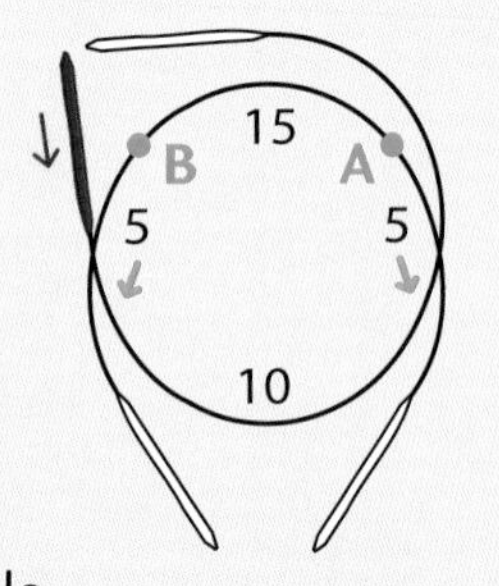

(Review page 12 on moving stitches.) Move the 5 instep "wing" stitches before A to the adjacent end of the sole needle, and the 5 instep "wing" stitches after B to the other end of the sole needle. After the moves, 15 stitches remain on the instep needle and 20 are on the sole needle. Put A and B away. The **working yarn** is attached to the 6th stitch on the sole needle. Slide the first 5 stitches onto the other tip of this needle so the 6th stitch becomes the 1st one on the left tip. The result is shown to the left.

Star Toe

Round 1: Repeat **knit 3, knit 2 together** 5 times. (20 sts)

Rounds 2 and 4: Knit.

Round 3: Repeat **knit 2, knit 2 together** 5 times. (15 sts)

Round 5: Repeat **knit 1, knit 2 together** 5 times. (10 sts)

Round 6: Repeat **knit 2 together** 5 times. (5 sts)

Cut 8" tail, thread tapestry needle, and weave end through remaining 5 stitches. Pull snug and weave in all ends.

Panel 9 - Dpn's

Dpn 4 returns, taking half of dpn 3's 10 stitches. Now dpn 3 and 4 each have 5 stitches.

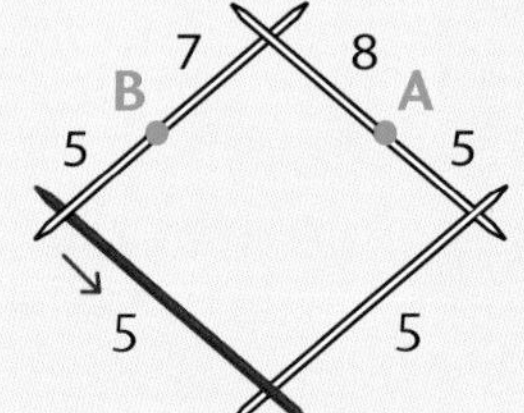

Move the 5 instep "wing" stitches before A down to dpn 4. Remove A. Dpn 1 now has 8 stitches and dpn 4 has 10 stitches.

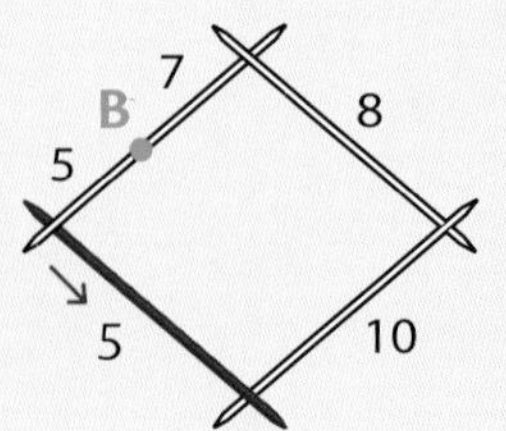

Move the 5 instep "wing" stitches after B to the 5th (working) dpn. Put away B. Now 15 instep stitches remain (on 2 needles), and there are 20 sole stitches (on 3 needles). The **yarn** is coming from the 1st stitch on the starting needle.

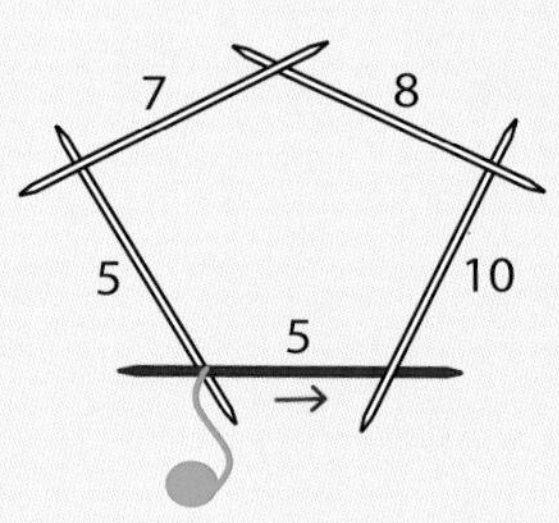

Little Coriolis - your second learning sock

Here's your second project, a toe-up sock. The Coriolis is a particularly magical form of sock architecture, with a right and left version. I knit this little pair in Louet's Merlin, 70% merino and 30% linen.

Yarn, needles, gauge, and markers - same suggestions as the Little Sky Socks (page 12).

Start with Whirlpool Toe (panels 10-11)
Follow all instructions in panel 10.
Then return here to continue with toe instructions. You should have 6 stitches total, 3 on each needle. If using dpn's, add the other needles in as soon as it is comfortable for you, probably after round 1. *(The figure-8 cast-on is easier to manage on circs, because the unused needle is not in the way.)*
Round 1: Repeat **LRinc, knit 1** 6 times. (12 sts total)
Round 2: Knit.
Round 3: Repeat **LRinc, knit 2** 6 times. (18 sts total)
Round 4: Knit.
Round 5: Repeat **LRinc, knit 3** 6 times. (24 sts total)
Knit 8 more rounds.

Panel 10

Figure-8 Cast-On

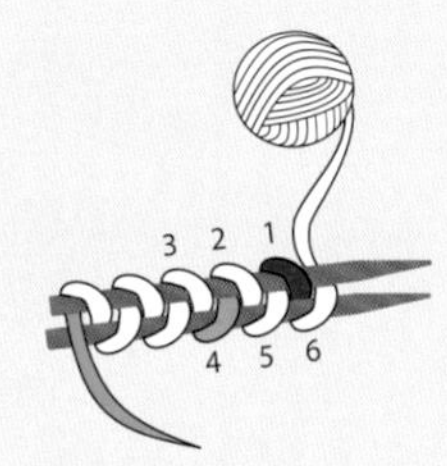

If using dpn's, use just 2 needles to start. Hold 2 needles parallel as shown. Pull the **tail** from front to back between the needles and begin snugly wrapping the yarn around the 2 tips in a figure-8, so the 2 tips fill the holes in the 8. (Try pointing 2 fingers at yourself and drawing 8's around your fingertips. Now do the same thing with yarn and needles.)

Always cast on a few extra stitches, as shown. Since end stitches tend to be sloppy, you avoid them by knitting tidy stitches and pushing the extras off. Here, 10 have been cast on, but only 6 will be used.

Notice how stitch 6 is wrapped around the lower needle. The yarn tugs **upward** from that position when you begin. This is important.

If using circular needles, pull the bottom needle so its stitches rest on its cable - this gets it out of your way. Using both ends of the upper circular needle or, if using dpn's, a free dpn, knit the **first stitch** (stitch 1) on the upper needle and then stitches 2 and 3.

Push off the extras, letting them fall off the other needle as well. Keeping the right side facing, turn the needles clockwise so you can knit across the other needle. The stitches on this needle are mounted with their right legs behind the needle. Knit into the right legs of **stitch 4**, 5 and 6. Rotate again with the right side facing, and knit the 3 stitches on the first needle. Now both tail and working yarn are at the same end. If the cast-on isn't snug, tighten it by tugging at each stitch, working from the other end toward the tail.

Knit 1 more round, placing marker A as shown in panel 11.

Coriolis arch expansion (panels 12-13)

(For dpn's, shift sts between dpn's 1 and 2 as needed, to keep stitches more or less balanced between the dpn's.)

Arch expansion companion rounds

Round 1: Knit to 2 stitches before A, k2tog, k1f&b, knit to end.

Rounds 2 and 3: Knit to A, k1f&b, knit to end.

Repeat companion rounds 1-3 *another* 5 times. On final round, place B 12 stitches after A, and slip final sole stitch of the round tip-to-tip instead of knitting it.

See panel 12 for result.

Move the slipped stitch from the sole needle (or dpn 4) to the start of the instep needle (or dpn 1), and move 1 stitch from the end of the instep needle (or dpn 2) to the start of the sole needle (or dpn 3). For dpn's, put all 12 sole stitches on dpn 3.

See panel 13 for result.

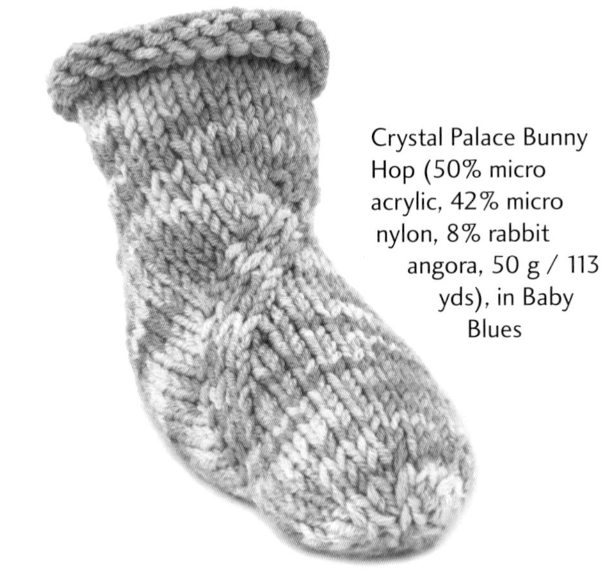

Crystal Palace Bunny Hop (50% micro acrylic, 42% micro nylon, 8% rabbit angora, 50 g / 113 yds), in Baby Blues

Panel 11

Place marker A 1 stitch before the end of the instep (starting) needle. The other needle is the sole needle. On the instep there are 11 stitches before A and 1 stitch after A. There are 12 stitches on the sole.

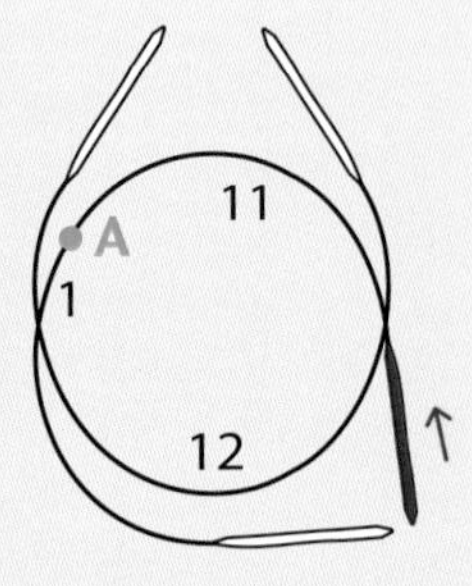

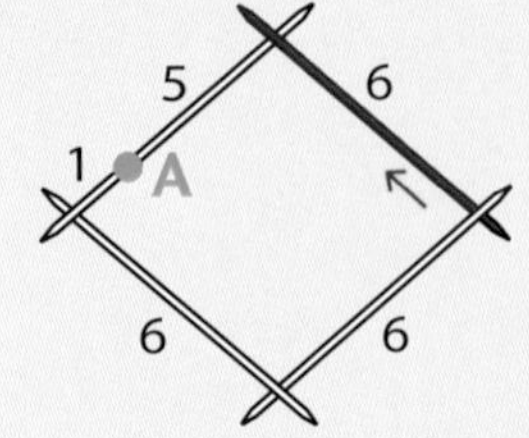

Place marker A 1 stitch before the end of dpn 2. Dpn's 1 and 2 are instep needles. Dpn's 3 and 4 are sole needles. There are 6 stitches on dpn's 1, 3 and 4, and 5 stitches before A and 1 stitch after A on dpn 2.

Panel 12

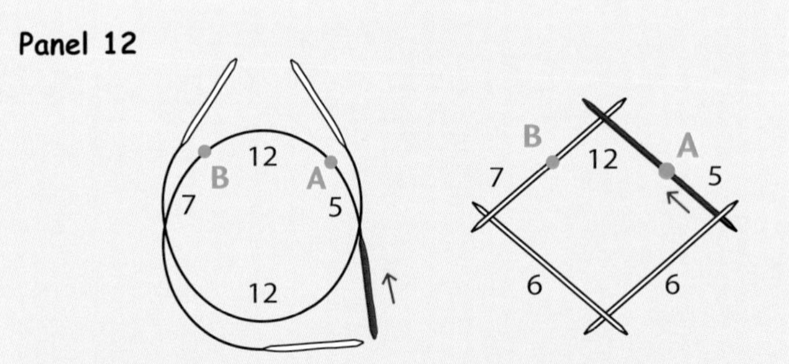

After final arch expansion round, the instep has 5 stitches before A, 12 between A and B, and 7 after B. The sole has 12 stitches.

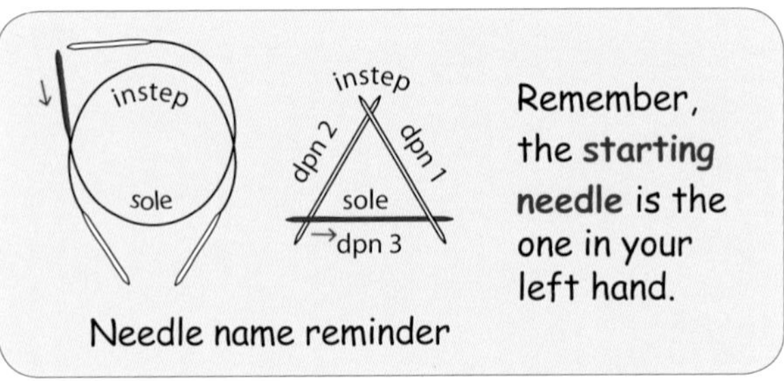

Needle name reminder

Crystal Palace Bunny Hop, in Fall Herbs

Louet Gems Merino, (100% merino, 100 g/ 225 yds) in Willow

Increase wing stitches

Working across instep needle(s) only: Knit 1, LRinc, knit 2, LRinc, knit 1, LRinc, knit to 2 stitches past B, LLinc, knit 1, LLinc, knit 2, LLinc, knit 1, *stop here.* See panel 14 for result.

Panel 13

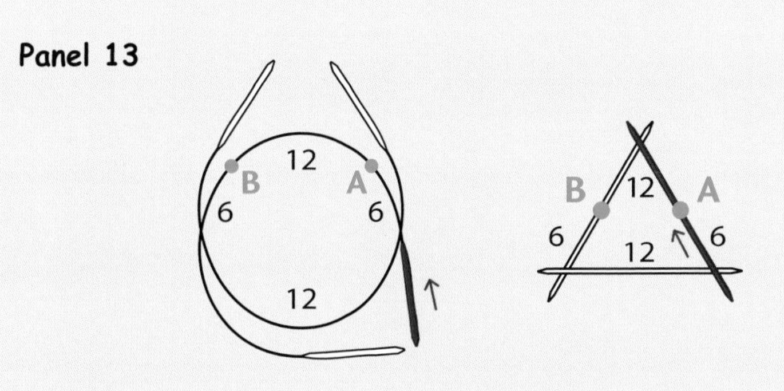

After moving stitches, the instep has 6 stitches before A, 12 between A and B, and 6 after B. The sole has 12 stitches. For dpn's, put all 12 sole stitches on dpn 3.

Panel 14

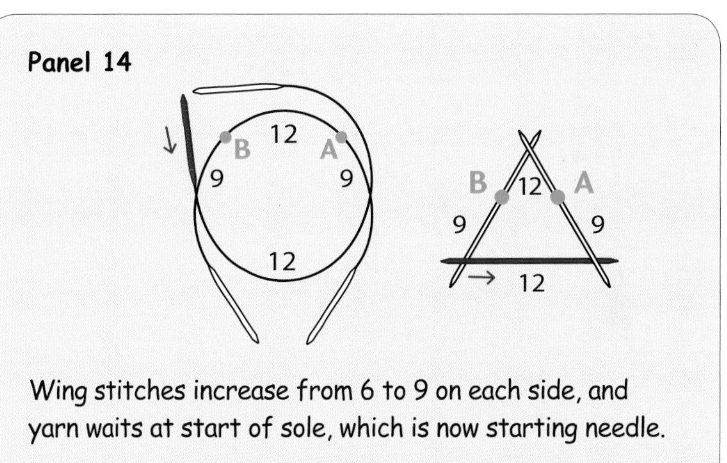

Wing stitches increase from 6 to 9 on each side, and yarn waits at start of sole, which is now starting needle.

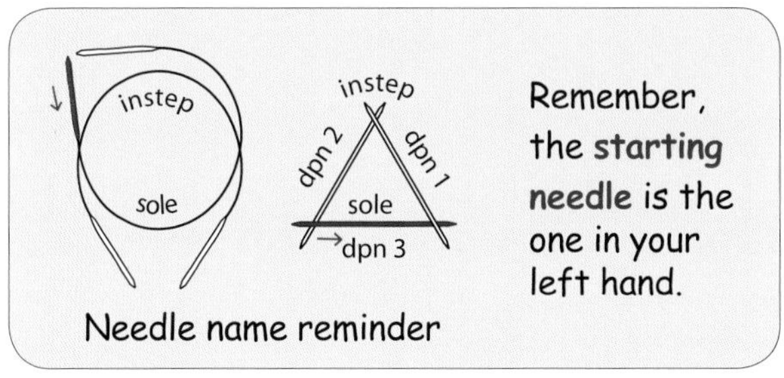

Heel turn

The heel turn is worked in heel stitch, back and forth in short rows on the 12 stitches of the sole needle alone. Slip stitches tip-to-tip. You may need to review wrapping stitches and concealing wraps in the previous pattern - see pages 14-15.

Row 1: Knit 1, LRinc, k1, repeat **slip 1, k1** 4 times, (2 sts remain before end of needle), w&t. (13 sts on sole needle)

Row 2: Purl 9, (2 stitches remain before end of needle), w&t.

Row 3: Repeat **k1, slip 1** 4 times, (3 sts remain before end of needle), w&t.

Row 4: Purl 7, (3 sts remain before end of needle), w&t.

Row 5: Repeat **slip 1, k1** 3 times, (4 sts remain before end of needle), w&t.

Row 6: Purl 5, (4 sts remain before end of needle), w&t.

Row 7: Repeat **k1, slip 1** twice, k1, repeat **cw** twice. Prepare to conceal the final wrap, and slide the right tip through the stitch, the wrap, and the final stitch on the left needle and knit all 3 together like an ssk (cw/ssk). Turn to work the purl side.

Row 8: Slip 1, p7, repeat **cw** twice. Prepare to conceal the final wrap, and slide the right needle through the stitch, the wrap, and the final stitch on the left needle and purl all 3 together like a p2tog (cw/p2tog). (11 sts remain on sole needle)

Panel 14

Move 8 of each set of 9 wing stitches to adjacent sole needle, leaving 1 stitch behind in each wing. After the move, there are 14 instep stitches and 27 sole stitches.

Back of heel (panels 14 and 15)

If using dpn's, divide sole stitches between 2 dpn's before continuing. The back of the heel will be worked on sole needle(s) alone.

Follow all instructions in panels 14 and 15, then continue:

Back of heel companion rows

Row 1: Repeat **slip 1, k1** 5 times, ssk, turn. (unworked stitches remain on needle)

Row 2: Slip 1, p9, p2tog, turn. (unworked sts remain on needle)

Repeat companion rows 1 and 2 *another* 6 times, continuing to work back and forth on sole alone. (13 sole sts remain)

Leg

Resume working in the round on all needles, putting away A and B as you come to them.

Round 1: (sole) Slip 1, knit 9, ssk, (instep) knit 14. (26 sts total)

Round 2: Knit 2 together, knit to end of instep. (25 sts total)

Knit 10 rounds. Bind off loosely and weave in all ends.

Panel 15

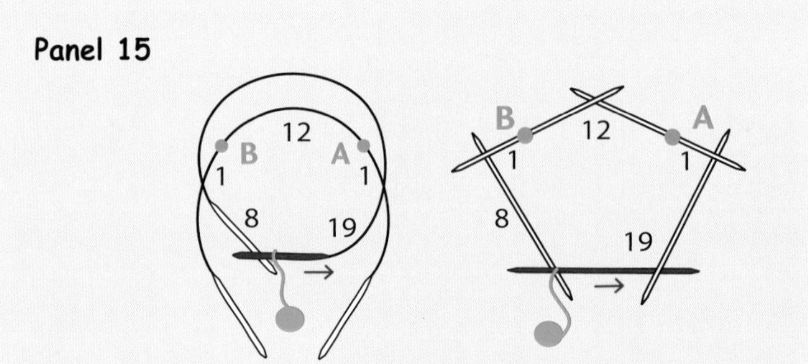

After moving wing stitches, the yarn is coming from the 9th sole stitch. Slide first 8 sole stitches to other tip of sole circular needle (or a free dpn) so yarn now comes from 1st stitch on sole **starting needle**.

Abbreviations and a list of technique lessons can be found on pages 134-136.

Second sock - a mirror image of the first (panels 16-18)

Incorporate these changes to the pattern:

After final round of Whirlpool Toe: Place B 1 st after start of instep needle. See panel 16. *On the first sock, you placed a marker near the end of the instep and it moved toward the beginning. This marker moves in the opposite direction.*

Second sock arch expansion companion rounds:

Round 1: Knit until 1 st remains before B *(first time around, there is only 1 st before* B), k1f&b, k1, ssk, knit to end.

Rounds 2 and 3: Knit until 1 st remains before B, k1f&b, knit to end.

Repeat companion rounds 1-3 *another* 4 times, then repeat rnds 1-2 once more.

Final round 3: Knit 7, place A, knit until 1 st remains before B, k1f&b, knit to end. See panel 17 for result. Yes, the wing stitches are out of balance - we'll fix that. Move 1 st from start of instep needle (or dpn 1) down to end of sole needle (or dpn 4), where the yarn waits, and knit this 1 st, to bring yarn back to end of sole needle. Move 1 st from other end of the sole needle (or dpn 3) up to adjacent end of instep needle (or dpn 2). Now there are 6 wing sts on each side, with 12 sts between the wings on the instep, and 12 sts on the sole. See panel 18 for result. For dpn's, put all 12 sole sts on dpn 3 before continuing. See panel 13 (page 19) for result. Continue as for first sock from heading (page 19), "Increase wing stitches," to end.

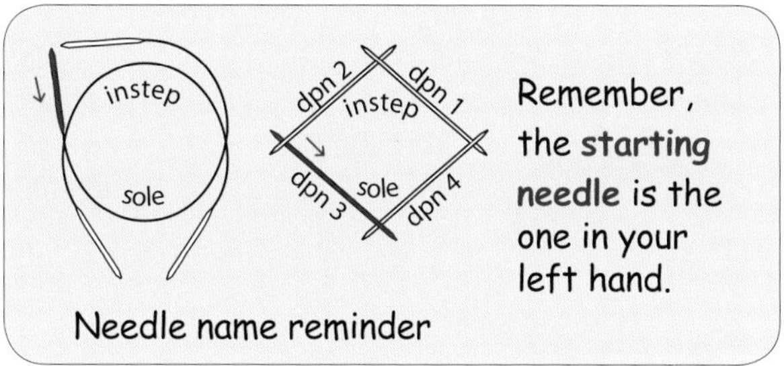

Needle name reminder

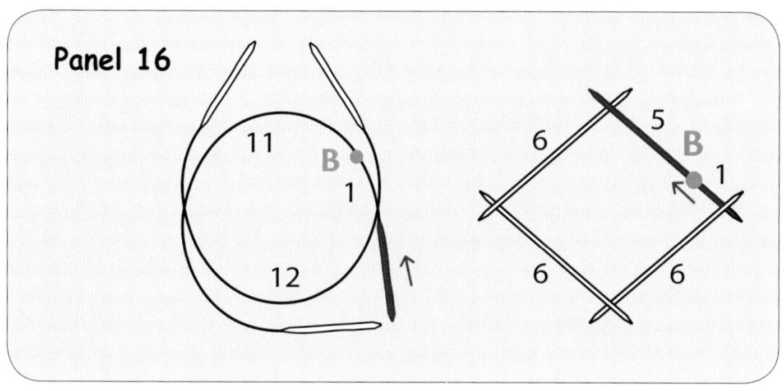

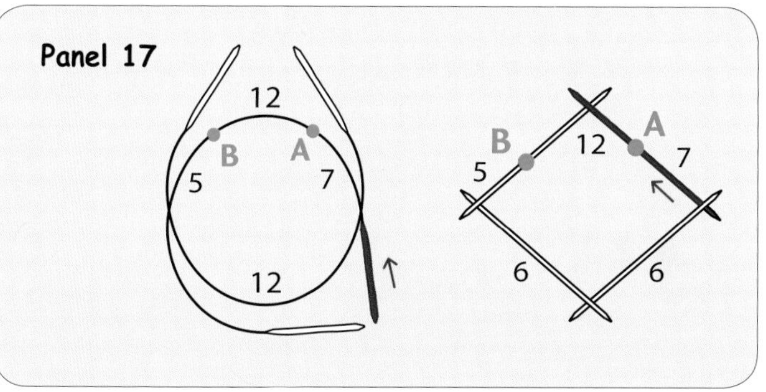

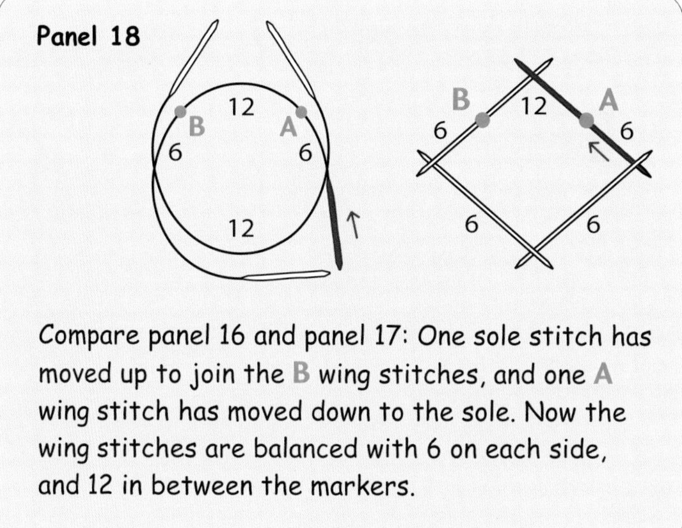

Compare panel 16 and panel 17: One sole stitch has moved up to join the B wing stitches, and one A wing stitch has moved down to the sole. Now the wing stitches are balanced with 6 on each side, and 12 in between the markers.

Provisional cast-ons

My hands love the cast-on you see to the right so much that the moment I even whisper *cast-on*, they start Judy's magic dance, as if it's the only cast-on in the world. It's a provisional cast-on, meaning that it places stitches alternately on two parallel needles, so the knitting can grow in either direction, and it is used to birth most of the toe-up socks in this book, as well as several cuffs.

Grafting, Kitchener stitch, weaving . . .

These words all refer to the same technique, which seamlessly joins one line of stitches to another. If you can duplicate stitch along a row (and you can - just follow the path the yarn takes), you can graft. It's the same path. Here's how: Have an equal number of stitches on 2 parallel needles, with the yarn coming from back needle. Thread yarn on a tapestry needle, and insert through 1st stitch on front needle as if to purl, pulling yarn through. Insert tapestry needle through 1st stitch on back needle as if to knit, pulling yarn through. Continue with:

Companion steps

One: Insert tapestry needle through 1st stitch on front needle as if to knit. Remove stitch from needle. Insert tapestry needle through 2nd stitch as if to purl, but do not remove stitch.

Two: Insert tapestry needle through 1st stitch on back needle as if to purl. Remove stitch from needle. Insert tapestry needle through 2nd stitch as if to knit, but do not remove stitch.

Repeat companion steps one and two, pulling up the slack and keeping the working yarn beneath the tips of the needles. Here's your grafting mantra:

"Knit off, purl on ~ purl off, knit on."

When done, neaten the seam by tugging at the yarn until the tension is just right, and weave in end.

Judy's Magic Cast-On

This splendid cast-on, developed by Judy Becker, an ingenious designer from Oregon, was first revealed on Knitty.com. She is generously allowing me to include her discovery here. I would've gotten down on my knees to beg if she'd said no. Thank you, Judy, for inventing the best provisional cast-on in the world! (By the way, she explained to me that she invented this one day when she was home too sick to read or knit . . . I am speechless.) Her cast-on has perfect tension, uniformly mounted stitches, and a sturdy row of purl stitches on the back, which comes as a happy surprise the first time you turn to find it there. Note: This cast-on is far easier on circs, because once you begin knitting, the stitches on the second needle can be pushed out of the way onto its cable. If using dpn's, try putting the second needle's stitches on a circ, then knitting them off onto a dpn.

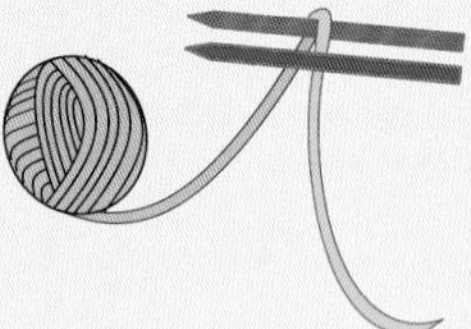

Step One:
Hang a long tail of yarn between 2 needles (2 dpn's, the ends of 2 circs, or both ends of 1 long circ). How long your should your tail be? Designer Sivia Harding of British Columbia suggests winding the yarn around your needle as many times as the number of stitches you'll need, then adding a few extra inches. The **blue tail** hangs between the needles and the **taupe working yarn** falls over the back of the top needle. The colors are just to make it easier for you to learn - your yarn may be one color.

To make learning really easy, knot 2 colors together and use 2 distinct needles, as shown.

Step Two:
Pull the **tail** to the back, from the right side of the **working yarn**. Hold the yarn with the tail over the index finger and the working yarn over the thumb. The other fingers tuck the ends against your palm. Note there is now **1 stitch** on the **top needle**.

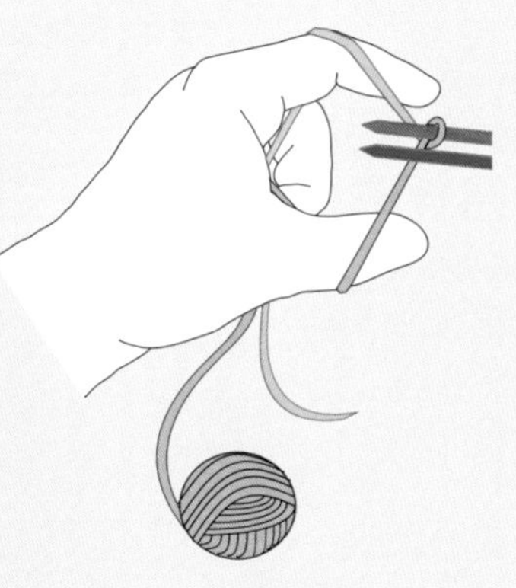

Step Three:
The **bottom needle** needs a stitch, so it reaches upward, over and behind the **blue yarn** on the index finger, and pulls a strand forward between the needles, wrapped across the front of the **bottom needle**.

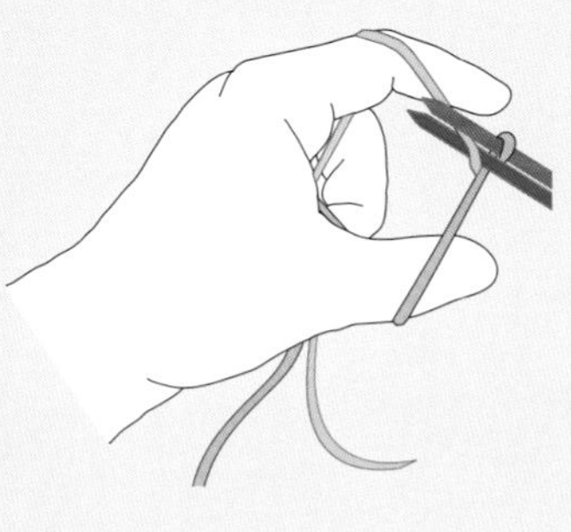

Step Four:
Now it's the **top needle's** turn. It reaches down, slides behind the **taupe yarn** on the thumb, and rises with a strand between the needles, wrapped across the front of the **top needle**.

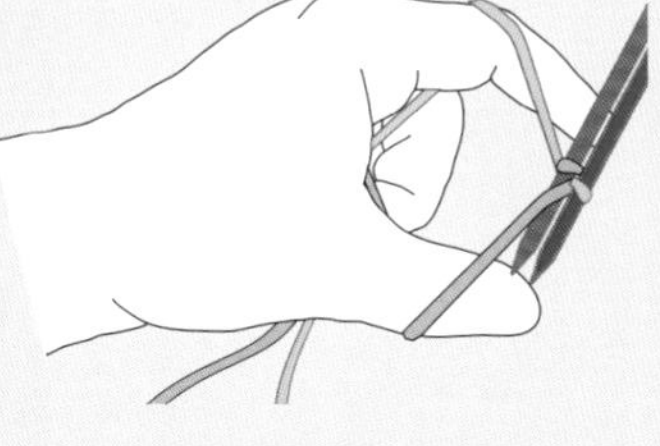

Repeat steps 3 and 4 until an equal number of stitches are on each needle. The last stitch taken is a **blue one**.

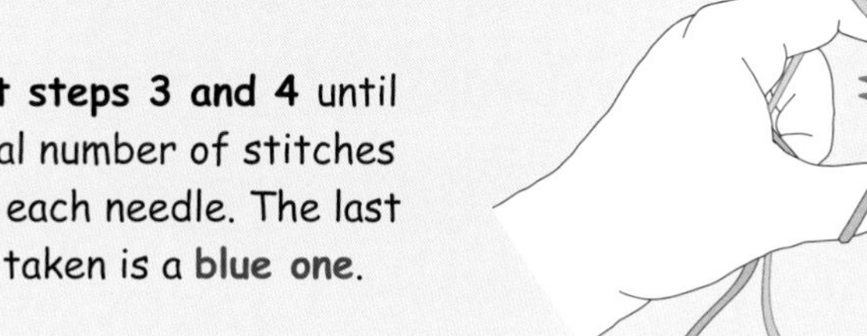

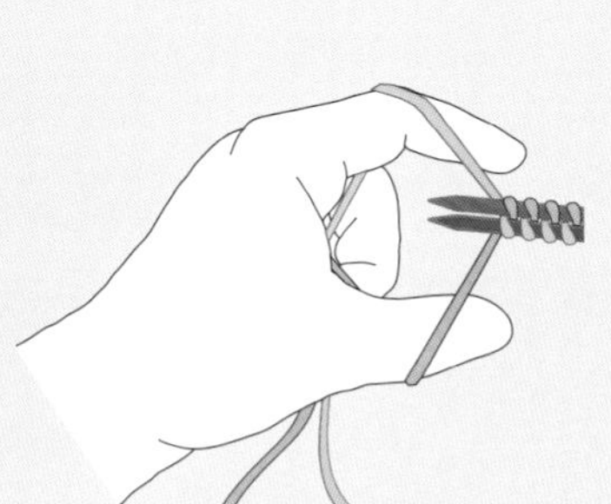

Step Five:
Secure the last stitch by pulling the **tail** down over the **taupe yarn** and behind the needles up to the back.

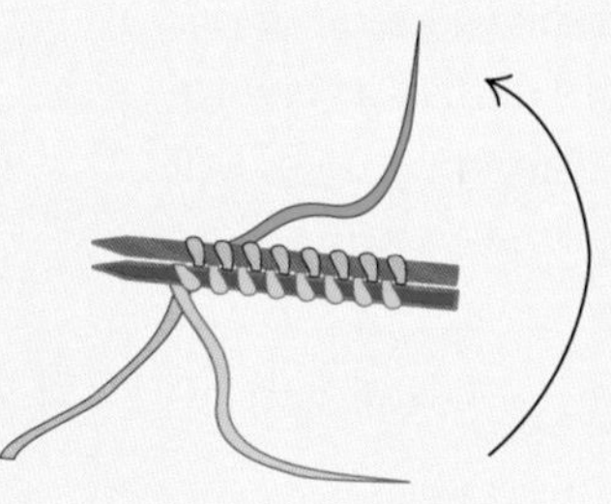

Step Six:
Rotate the needles clockwise, keeping the right side facing, so the **blue needle** is on top. Now the **tail** is tucked down below. The needles have switched positions, and the last stitch you cast on will be the first one you'll knit.

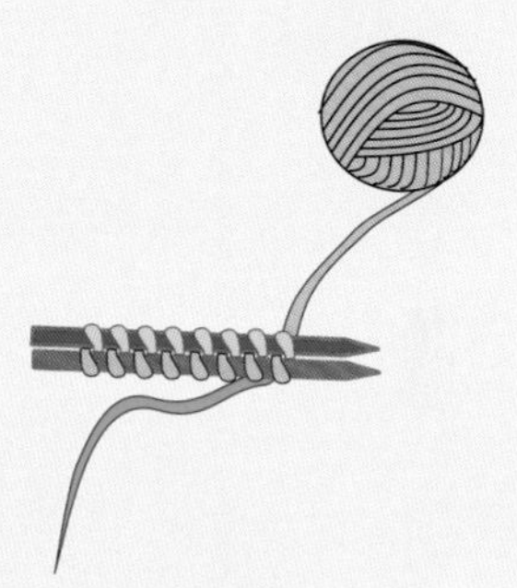

Step Seven:
Begin to knit: use the other end of the **top circular needle** (push **bottom needle** out of the way by sliding its stitches to its cable) or a free dpn (if using dpn's) to knit across the **top needle**. Now rotate clockwise, with the right side always facing, and use the other end of the second circular needle or a free dpn to knit across the second needle. You've knit the first round. On the back side, you'll find 3 purl rows - the central purl row happened during cast-on!

Chapter 2 - Sky Sock Architecture

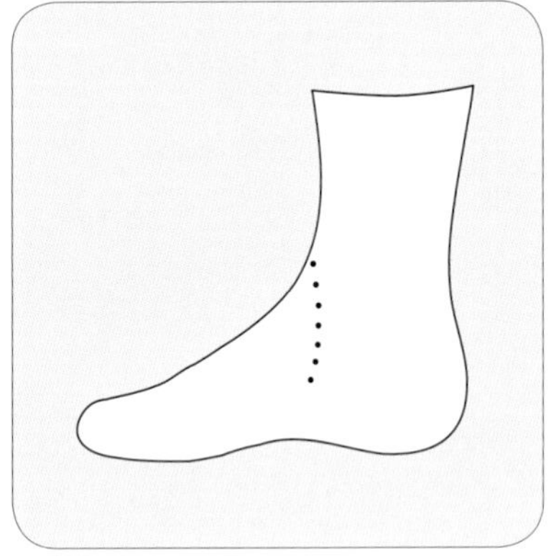

Sky architecture was inspired by a collection of hauntingly beautiful traditional outer footwear from above the Arctic Circle, which I was able to study at the Bata Shoe Museum in Toronto, Canada. This museum is a paradise for an inquisitive sock knitter, because the displays of seemingly endless ways in which humans have sheltered and decorated their feet with leather, fur, fabric, and other materials suggest new avenues for knitting around the foot as well. I was extraordinarily fortunate to be able to spend several mornings in the museum's artifact storage rooms (which had the most heavenly fragrance of sweetgrass and caribou) examining and photographing their sock collection (which is not on exhibit) as well as hundreds of examples of native footwear. The third book in this series, *Knitting Around the Foot: Ancient Pathways*, will reflect those inspirational hours.

Sky architecture expands over the arch from the point where the leg flexes at the top of the instep. Heel stitch may be worked on the back of the heel as well as through the heel turn and base of the heel. In the example you see here, I worked ribbing on the back of the heel for a decorative effect.

The Joys of Sky Architecture

- The sides and back of the ankle are smooth and free for design
- The instep triangle may be filled with a decorative element
- Learn this pathway, and you're ready for Cedar architecture

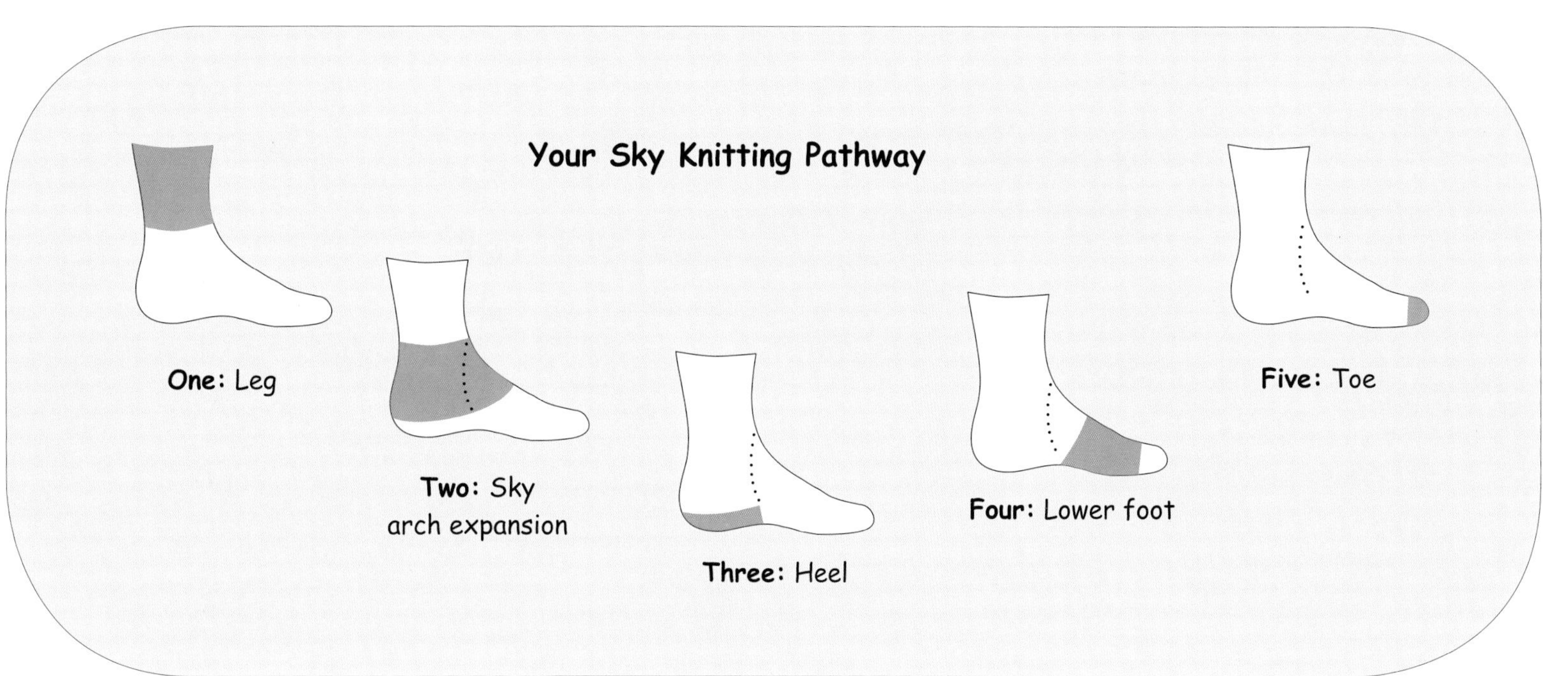
Your Sky Knitting Pathway
One: Leg
Two: Sky
arch expansion
Three: Heel
Four: Lower foot
Five: Toe

Charlie's Seeded Heart Socks

These are my grandson's first socks, with soft ties to keep them on tiny feet as they grow. The seed stitch hearts, upside-down on the instep, gaze at the baby.

Yarn: Heirloom Breeze (30% wool, 69.6% cotton, 0.4% Lycra, 50 g / 95 m), 1 skein Light Blue
Needles: 5 (3.75 mm), or size you need to get gauge
Gauge: 5.5 sts = 1" (2.5 cm)
Size: newborn - 3 months
Markers: A, B, C and D

Cuff and leg

Make Cobblestone Cuff (page 132), casting on 30 sts to each parallel ndl. Knit 5 rnds. Next rnd: Repeat **k2tog, k3** 6x. (24 sts total) Knit 3 rnds.

Arch expansion - picture ①

Rnd 1: Knit 5, place A, k1f&b, k1, place B, k to end. (25 sts)
Rnd 2: Knit to A, k1, p1, k to end.
Rnd 3: Knit to A, repeat **k1f&b** 2x, k to end. (27 sts)
Rnd 4: Knit to A, repeat **k1, p1** 2x, k to end.
Rnd 5: Knit to A, k1f&b, k1, p1, k1f&b, k to end. (29 sts)
Companion rounds
Rnd 6: Knit to A, repeat **k1, p1** to 1 st before B, k to end.
Rnd 7: Knit to A, k1f&b, repeat **k1, p1** until 2 sts before B, k1f&b, k to end.
Repeat companion rounds 6 and 7 another 2x.

Total sts: 35 (23 instep and 12 sole - see picture ①) Knit to A, repeat **k1, p1** to 1 st before B, k to end of instep and stop.

Heel

Work plain heel (page 122), starting at step 3. A and B are already in place. Use 3 for I, 5 for H, and ignore J.

In step 5, return here for these instructions when you reach "resume knitting in the rnd": (instep) k2, repeat **p1, k1** 5x, k1, (sole) k1, k2tog, k to end of sole. *Instep is starting ndl (in left hand).* (13 instep sts and 12 sole sts)

Foot

Rnd 1: Knit 2, repeat **p1, k1** 5x, k to end.
Rnds 2-3: Knit 1, repeat **p1, k1** 6x, k to end.
Rnds 4-5: Knit 2, repeat **p1, k1, p1, k3** 2x, k to end.
Rnds 6: Knit 3, p1, k5, p1, k to end.
Knit until foot measures 3" (7.5 cm) - about 5 rnds.

Toe and ties

Rnd 1: **Knit 3, k2tog** 5x. (20 sts) Rnds 2 and 4: Knit. Rnd 3: **Knit 2, k2tog** 5x. (15 sts) Rnd 5: **Knit 1, k2tog** 5x. (10 sts) Rnd 6: **Knit 2tog** 5x. (5 sts) Cut tail. Use tapestry needle to weave end through remaining sts, pull tight. Weave in all ends. Ties: Use double strand of yarn and crochet hook to chain for 11" (28 cm). Thread through back as shown.

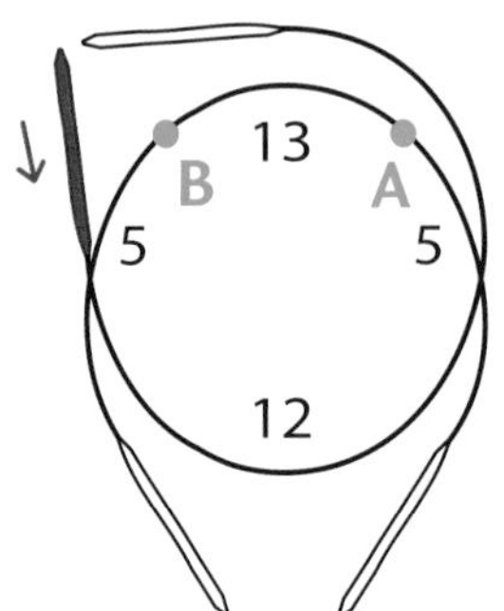

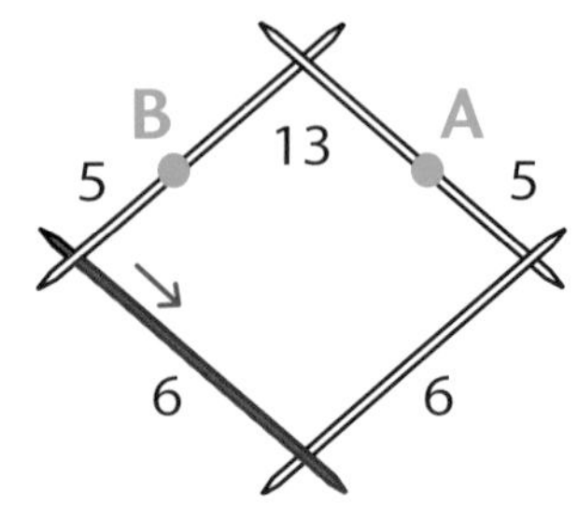

① Stitches at end of arch expansion. Starting needle is now sole. If using dpn's, before beginning heel, put all sole sts on 1 dpn.

Bartholomew's Tantalizing Socks

These socks are tantalizing to knit because of how the linen stitch plays with hand-painted yarns, and the architectural lines are captivating to watch as they emerge.

Yarn: Blue Moon Fiber Arts®, Inc. Socks That Rock® medium-weight (100% wool, 5.5 oz/ 380 yds), 1 skein Metamorphic (see next page) or Jail House Rock (shown on this page)
Needles: 1 (2.5 mm), or size you need to get gauge, plus 1 size larger for working cuff
Gauge: (on smaller size needle) 8 sts = 1" (2.5 cm)
Size: midfoot 5.5 (6.5, 7.5, 8.5, 9.5)" or 14 (16, 19, 21, 24) cm
Markers: A, B, C, and D

Cuff

With larger ndls, cast on 44 (52, 60, 68, 76) sts.
Companion rows:
Row 1: Knit 1, repeat **sl1 wyif, k1** until 1 st rem, k1.
Rows 2 and 4: Purl.
Row 3: Knit 1, repeat **k1, sl1 wyif** until 1 st rem, k1.
Repeat companion rows 1-4 until 1.5" (4 cm) high, ending with a row 1. Divide sts evenly on 2 circs or 4 dpn's. Join by pulling yarn from one end to the other and k 1 rnd.

Leg - picture ①

Companion rounds:
Rnd 1: Repeat **sl1 wyif, k1** to end.
Rnds 2 and 4: Knit.
Rnd 3: Repeat **k1, sl1 wyif** to end.
Repeat companion rnds 1-4 another 1 (1, 2, 3, 3) times, then rnds 1-3 once more. Next rnd: Repeat **k2tog** 2x, k until 4 sts rem, repeat **k2tog** 2x. Total sts: 40 (48, 56, 64, 72) Repeat rnd 1 once more.

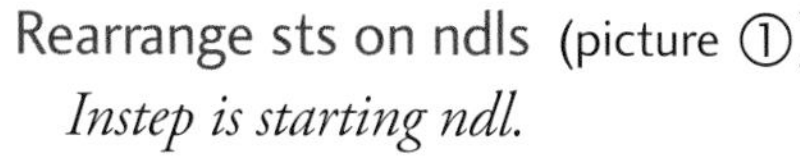

Rearrange sts on ndls (picture ①)
Instep is starting ndl.
Two circs: Knit 10 (12, 14, 16, 18). With smaller circ, k next 20 (24, 28, 32, 36) sts. These sts are now the *instep*. With 2nd smaller circ, k next 20 (24, 28, 32, 36) sts, which are now the *sole*. Dpn's: Knit 10 (12, 14, 16, 18). Using a smaller dpn's, k next 4 groups of 10 (12, 14, 16, 18) sts. Dpn's 1 and 2 together hold 20 (24, 28, 32, 36) sts and are now the *instep*; dpn's 3 and 4 together hold 20 (24, 28, 32, 36) sts and are now the *sole*. Next rnd - both circs and dpn's: Knit 6 (8, 10, 12, 14), k2tog, repeat **k1, sl1 wyif** 2x, k to end of instep, k to end. Total sts: 39 (47, 55, 63, 71)

Companion Rounds:
Rnd 19: Knit 1 rnd.
Rnd 20: Knit 7 (9, 11, 13, 15), repeat **sl1 wyif, k1** 3x, k to end.
Rnd 21: Knit 1 rnd.
Rnd 22: Knit 7 (9, 11, 13, 15), repeat **k1, sl1wyif** 2x, k to end.
Repeat companion rnds 19-22 another 2 (4, 6, 8, 10) times, or until leg is desired height above ankle bone.

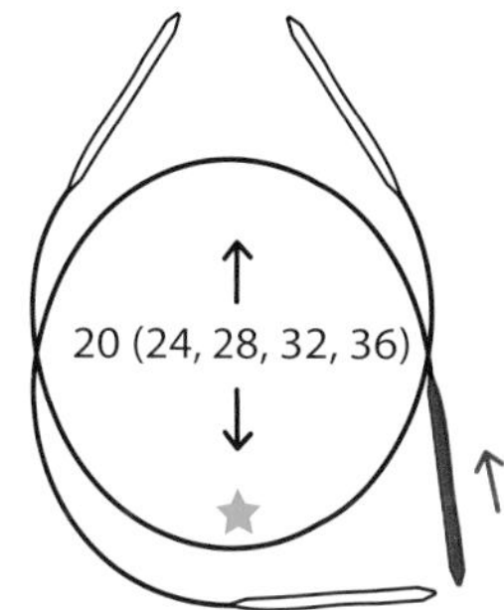

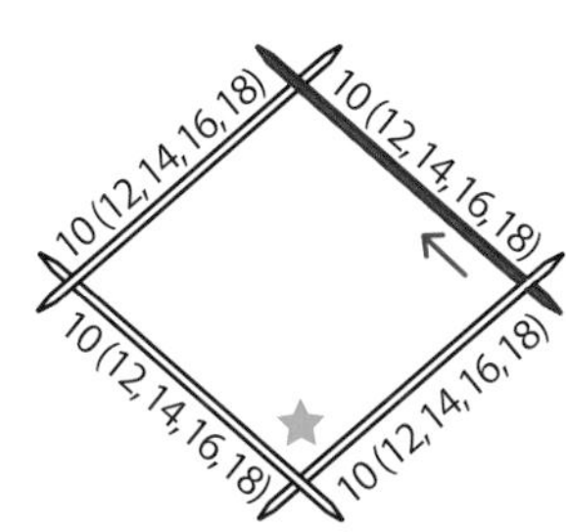

① Stitches rearranged as instep and sole. The blue star indicates location of the cuff's center back, centered on sole ndl(s). Instep is starting ndl.

Arch expansion - chart 1 and picture ②

Rnd 1: Knit 6 (8, 10, 12, 14), place **A**, k7, place **B**, k 6 (8, 10, 12, 14), establish ribbing on sole: Repeat **p1, k2** (1st and 4th sizes) until 5 sts before end, p1, k2, p2tog, (2nd and 5th sizes) until 3 sts before end, p1, k1, k1f&b, (3rd size) until 1 st before end, p1. Total sts: 38 (48, 55, 62, 72)

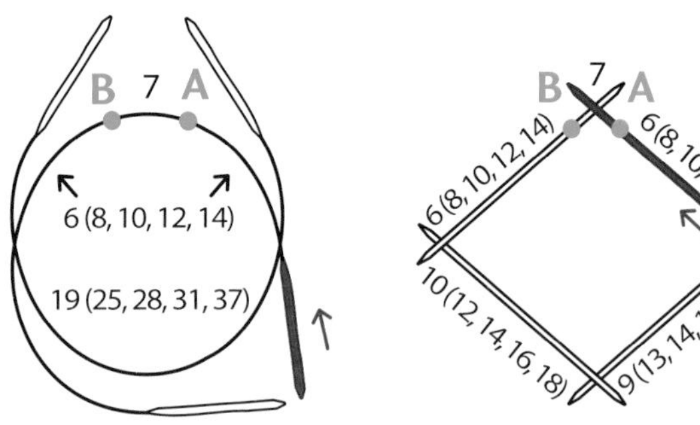

② Stitch arrangement after arch expansion rnd 1.

Rnd 2: Knit to **A**, k1, LLinc, repeat **sl1 wyif, k1** 2x, sl1wyif, LRinc, k to end of instep, work ribbing on sole. Total sts: 40 (50, 57, 64, 74)

Rnd 3: Knit to end of instep, work ribbing on sole.

Rnd 4: Knit to **A**, repeat **k1, sl1 wyif** until 1 st before **B**, k to end of instep, work ribbing on sole.

Rnd 5: Knit to **A**, k1, LLinc, k until 1 st before **B**, LRinc, k to end of instep, work ribbing on sole. Total sts: 42 (52, 59, 66, 76)

Companion Rounds:

Rnds 6 and 16: Knit to **A**, repeat **k1, sl1 wyif** until 1 st before **B**, k to end of instep, work ribbing on sole.

Rnds 7, 9,13 and 15: Knit to end of instep, work ribbing on sole.

Rnd 8: Knit to **A**, k1, LLinc, repeat **k1, sl1 wyif** until 2 sts before **B**, k1, LRinc, k to end of instep, work ribbing on sole.

Rnds 10 and 12: Knit to **A**, repeat **sl1 wyif, k1** until 1 st before **B**, sl1 wyif, k to end of instep, work ribbing on sole.

Rnds 11 and 17: Knit to **A**, k1, LLinc, k until 1 st before **B**, LRinc, k to end of instep, work ribbing on sole.

Rnd 14: Knit to **A**, k1, LLinc, repeat **sl1 wyif, k1** until 2 sts before **B**, sl1 wyif, LRinc, k to end of instep, work ribbing on sole.

Repeat rnds 6-17 until total st count is 58 (72, 83, 94, 108), stopping after a completed rnd 17 (11, 17, 11, 17).

Heel

Setting up: Knit to **A**, remove **A**, k4, place **A** here.

(2nd and 4th sizes) Repeat **sl1 wyif, k1** until 5 sts before **B**, sl1 wyif, move **B** here, k to end of instep and stop.

(1st, 3rd, and 5th sizes) Repeat **k1, sl1 wyif** until 5 sts before **B**, k1, move **B** here, k to end of instep and stop.

Work reinforced heel (page 124), starting at step 3. **A** and **B** are already in place. Use 10 (12, 14, 16, 18) for **H**, 6 (7, 8, 10, 11) for **I** and ignore **J**. Total sts after heel is finished: 38 (48, 56, 62, 72)

Foot (instep is starting ndl)

Set-up for 1st, 3rd, and 5th sizes only: Repeat **sl1 wyif, k1** until 1 instep st remains, k to end of rnd. Knit 1 rnd.

Companion rounds:

Rnd 1: Repeat **k1, sl1 wyif** until 1 instep st remains, k to end.

Rnds 2 and 4: Knit.

Rnd 3: Repeat **sl1 wyif, k1** until 1 instep st remains, sl1 wyif, k to end.

Repeat companion rounds 1-4 until foot is about 3" (7.5 cm) shorter than desired. *(If you'd like to taper the stitch pattern on the foot, see chart 2. Start taper several inches before reaching toe.)* To determine length toe will add, measure rnds-per-inch (RPI) in a stockinette section of sock, and divide RPI into 12 (16, 18, 20, 24). The answer is the length toe will add. Continue repeating companion rnds 1-4 until only this length remains to be added, then begin toe.

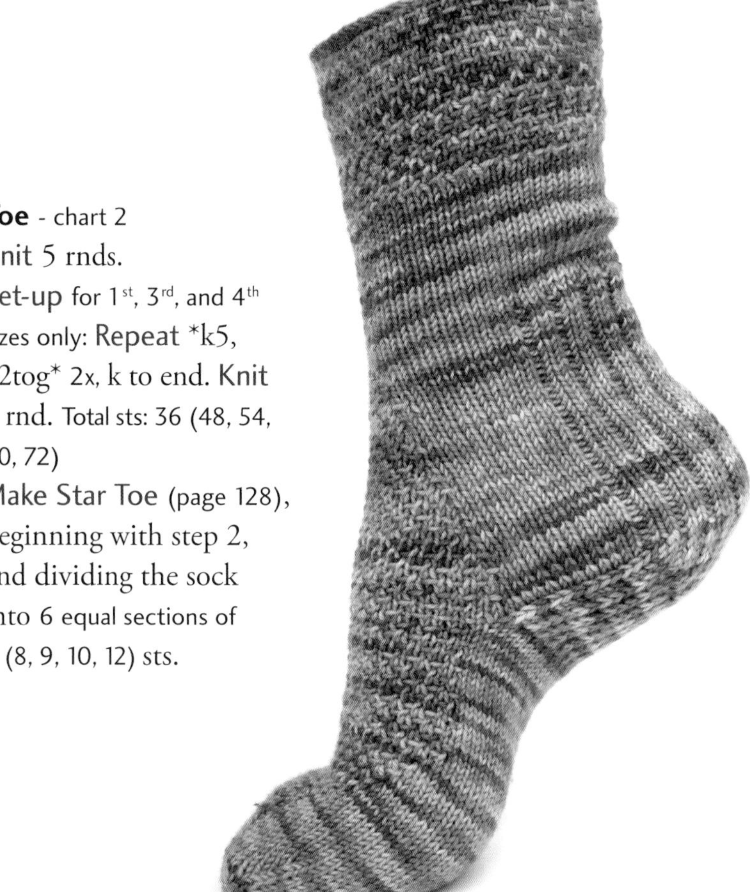

Toe - chart 2

Knit 5 rnds.

Set-up for 1st, 3rd, and 4th sizes only: Repeat *k5, k2tog* 2x, k to end. Knit 1 rnd. Total sts: 36 (48, 54, 60, 72)

Make Star Toe (page 128), beginning with step 2, and dividing the sock into 6 equal sections of 6 (8, 9, 10, 12) sts.

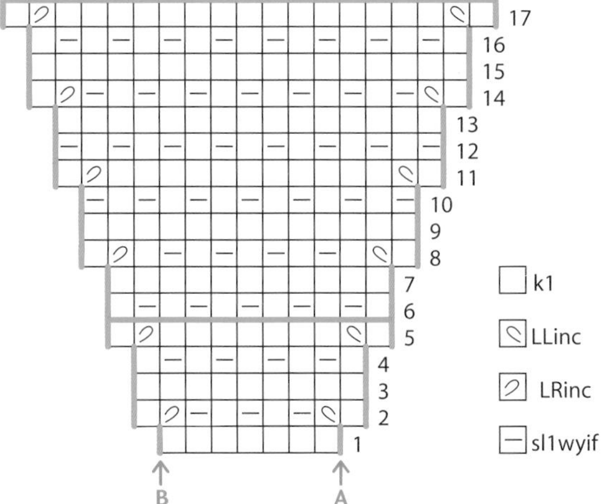

Chart 1 - Arch Expansion

The chart shows sts between A and B only. Green lines indicate marker path and blue lines indicate repeating companion rnds 6-17. As arch expands, number of sts expands beyond what is shown, but pattern between A and B remains consistent (refer to written instructions as needed).

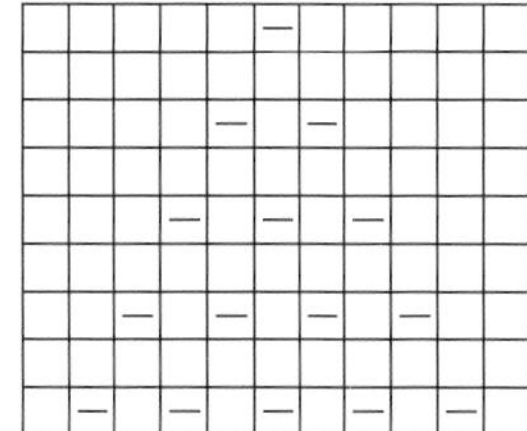

Chart 2 - Tapering design on foot

To taper sides of stitch pattern as it approaches toe, refer to this chart. You could taper to a point as shown, or just taper the sides partway and then switch to stockinette for a more rounded end.

Robin Hood's Fireside Boots

The two-layer cuff of this sock is single-stranded. The rest of the sock is worked double-stranded, and the fabric is one layer. This all evens out to make a boot-like sock ideal for keeping your feet toasty in the winter, in the house or, if you have roomy shoes, outside as well.

Yarn: Blue Moon Fiber Arts®, Inc. Twisted (100% merino, 8 oz/ 560 yds), 2 skeins Rolling Stone
Needles: size 7 (4.5 mm), or size you need to get gauge; cuff requires 2 circs or 1 long circ
Gauge: (single strand) 5 sts = 1" (2.5 cm) (double strand) 4 sts = 1" (2.5 cm)
Markers: A, B, C and D
Size: midfoot 6 (7, 8, 9, 10)" or 15 (18, 20, 23, 25) cm

Cuff

Start Pebble-Edge Cuff (page 133), casting on 42 (48, 54, 60, 66) sts (D) to each parallel ndl, returning here for instructions after knitting 1st rnd. Knit rnds for 1 (1.5, 1.5, 1.5, 2)" or 3 (4, 4, 4, 5) cm. Repeat **k1, LRinc, k19 (22, 25, 28, 31), LLinc, k1** 2x. Knit for 1" (2.5 cm). Repeat increase rnd. Knit for 1" (2.5cm). Total sts: 92 (104, 116, 128, 140)

Remainder of sock is knit double-stranded.

Hold the 2 sets of 46 (52, 58, 64, 70) sts parallel with wrong sides together. Add 2nd strand, leaving tail to weave in later. Use a free ndl to k tog 1 st from each ndl until only 46 (52, 58, 64, 70) sts remain, on 1 ndl. *(Purl ridge from completed row identifies inside of sock.)*

Join cuff - picture ①

Place first 4 sts *from end without working yarn* on holder. Move 21 (24, 27, 30, 33) sts *from end with working yarn* to 2nd circ or to dpn's 1 and 2. (If using dpn's, move remaining 21 (24, 27, 30, 33) sts to dpn's 3 and 4.) With purl ridge to inside, pull working yarn *to end with holder* and begin knitting right after the 4 held sts, evenly distributing 6 (8, 8, 10, 10) k2tog's between here and the 4 held sts. Move 4 held sts from holder to spare ndl, hold *behind* unworked sts (for a mirrored pair, hold in *front* for 2nd sock), and k tog 1 st from each ndl so the 2 sets of 4 sts are joined to make 1 set of 4, and sock is joined in the round. Total sts: 36 (40, 46, 50, 56) Arrange sts as sole and instep (see picture ①): Knit 7 (8, 10, 12, 14), k18 (20, 23, 25, 28) with next circ or next 2 dpn's, k18 (20, 23, 25, 28) with next circ or next 2 dpn's. *Instep is starting ndl (ndl in left hand).*

Leg

Knit 1 (1.5, 1.5, 1.5, 2)" or 3 (4, 4, 4, 5) cm.

Repeat **k7 (8, 9, 10, 12), k2tog, k7 (8, 10, 11, 12), k2tog** 2x.

Total sts: 32 (36, 42, 46, 52)

Knit 1 (1.5, 1.5, 1.5, 2)" or 3 (4, 4, 4, 5) cm.

Repeat **k6 (7, 8, 9, 11), k2tog, k6 (7, 9, 10, 11), k2tog** 2x.

Total sts: 28 (32, 38, 42, 48)

Knit 1 (1.5, 1.5, 1.5, 2)" or 3 (4, 4, 4, 5) cm.

1st and 2nd sizes only: Knit 2 tog at start of instep and sole.

3rd and 4th sizes only: Repeat **k5 (6, 7, 8, 10), k2tog, k5 (6, 8, 9, 10), k2tog** 2x.

5th size only: Repeat **k6, k2tog** to end.

Total sts: 26 (30, 34, 38, 42) Knit 3 rnds.

Arch expansion - picture ② (on next page)

Rnd 1: Knit 6 (7, 8, 9, 10), place **A**, k1 in each strand of next st, place **B**, k to end. Total sts: 27 (31, 35, 39, 43)

Rnds 2-3: Knit.

Rnd 4: Knit to **A**, k1 in each strand of next 2 sts, k to end of rnd.

Total sts: 29 (33, 37, 41, 45)

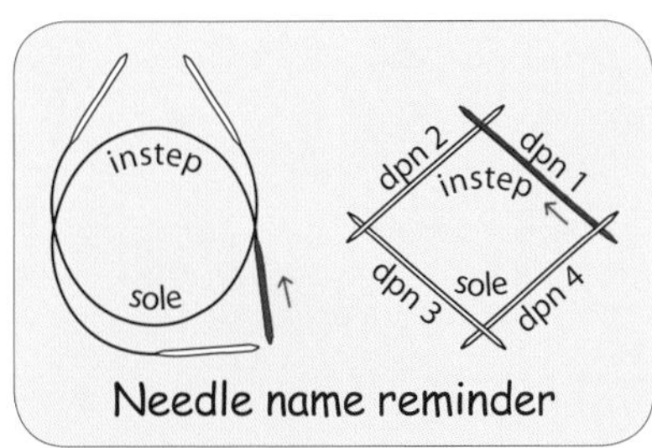

Needle name reminder

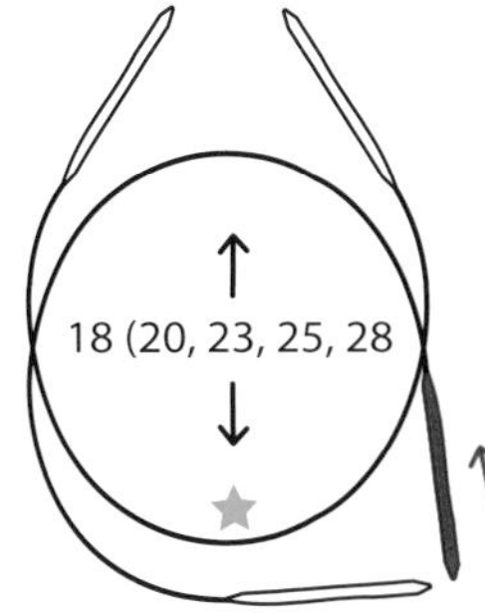

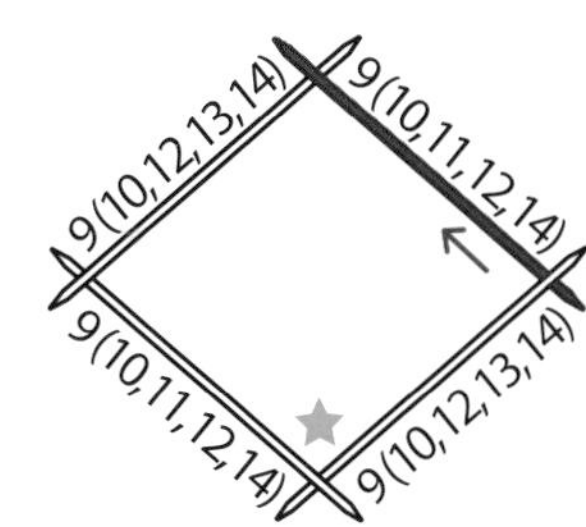

① Cuff is joined and stitches are rearranged as instep and sole. The blue star indicates location of cuff's center back, centered on sole ndl(s). *Instep is starting ndl (ndl in left hand).*

Abbreviations and a list of technique lessons can be found on pages 134-136.

Companion rounds

Rnds 5-6: Knit.

Rnd 7: Knit to A, k1 in each strand of next st, k to 1 st before B, k1 in each strand of next st, k to end. (2 sts added)

Repeat companion rnds 5-7 another 3 (4, 5, 6, 7) times.

Total sts = 37 (43, 49, 55, 61) Knit 1 rnd. Knit to end of instep and stop. See picture ②

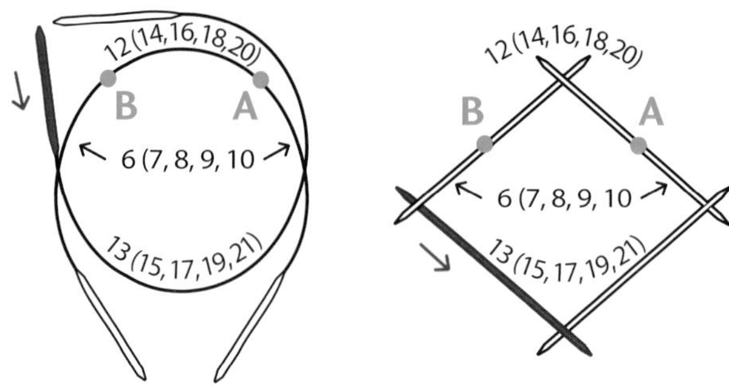

② Stitch and marker arrangement after arch expansion.

Heel

Work plain heel (page 122), starting at step 3. A and B are already in place. Use 6 (7, 8, 9, 10) for Ⓗ and 3 (4, 5, 6, 7) for Ⓘ and ignore Ⓙ. Total sts after heel is finished: 25 (29, 33, 37, 41) – 12 (14, 16, 18, 20) instep and 13 (15, 17, 19, 21) sole

Foot and toe

To determine the length the toe will add, first measure rnds-per-inch (RPI) *in a double-stranded section*. Divide RPI into 10 (12, 14, 14, 16). The answer is the length toe will add. Knit all rnds until only this length remains to be added. Set-up for 2nd size only: LRinc, k to end. Set-up for 3rd size only: Lrinc at start of instep and sole, k all other sts. Set-up for 4th size only: K2tog at start of instep and sole, k all other sts. Set-up for 5th size only: Knit 2tog, k to end. Total sts: 25 (30, 35, 35, 40) All sizes: Knit 1 rnd. Make Star Toe (page 128), beginning with step 2, and dividing the sock into 5 sections of 5 (6, 7, 7, 8) sts.

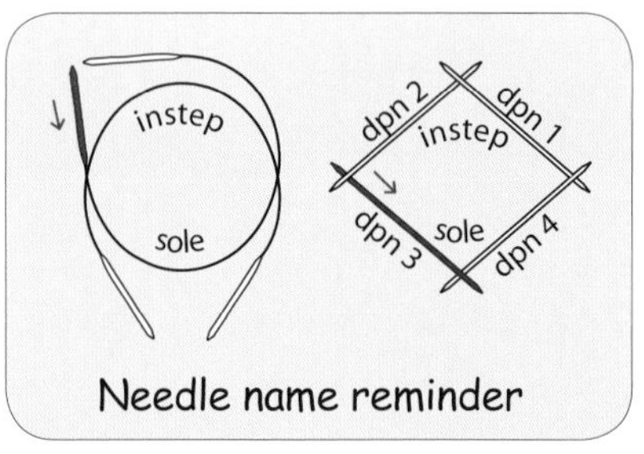

An elf toe variation

When foot needs just 0.5" (1 cm) additional length, work a plain heel turn on the sole sts only (page 122, step 3 only), concealing all k wraps - and work a cw instead of a cw/ssk at the end, then k final sole st, turn and sl 1, p to 1st wrapped p st, conceal all the wraps (working cw instead of cw/p2tog on final wrapped st), p1, turn, slip 1, k back and resume knitting in the rnd, stopping at end of instep. Follow Star Toe directions as above until only 10 sts rem, k 1 rnd, repeat **k2tog** 5x. (5 sts) Knit until the narrow tube is long enough to curl over the toe as shown. Cut tail and use tapestry needle to weave end through all sts, pull tight, and sew tip to toe in a curl. Weave in all ends.

Mountain Colors Bearfoot (60% superwash wool, 25% mohair, 15% nylon, 100 g/ 350 yds), color Juniper

Sky Master Pattern

Find your Master numbers on pages 109-119.

Markers: A, B, C and D
Instep is starting ndl (ndl in left hand).

Complete any cuff (page 132), then knit to top of ankle bone.

Sky arch expansion - picture ①

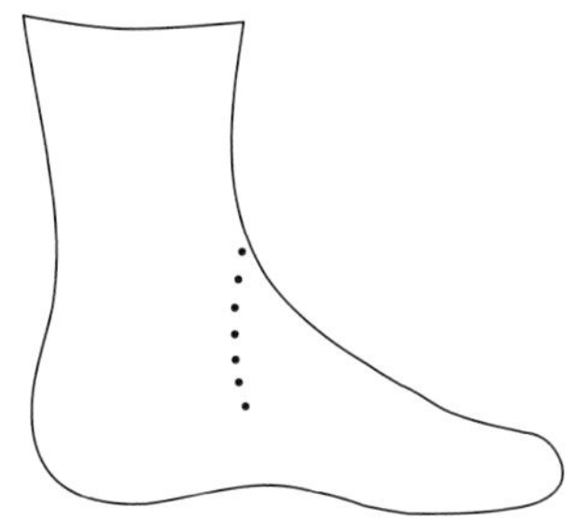

If G is even

Locate 2 center sts on instep. Place A before the 2 center sts. Knit to A, k1f&b, k1, place B, k to end. Knit 1 rnd. Your instep G will have 1 extra st when you work the heel.

If G is odd

Locate center st on instep. Knit until 1 st remains before center st, place A, k3, place B, k to end. Knit 2 rnds.

Arch expansion companion rounds

Rnd 1: K to A, k1, LLinc, k until 1 st before B, LRinc, k to end.

Rnds 2 and 3: Knit.

Repeat companion rnds 1-3, stopping at end of instep after a partial rnd 1, when total stitch count reaches F.

Remove A and B.

Complete heel (page 120), foot, and toe (page 128).

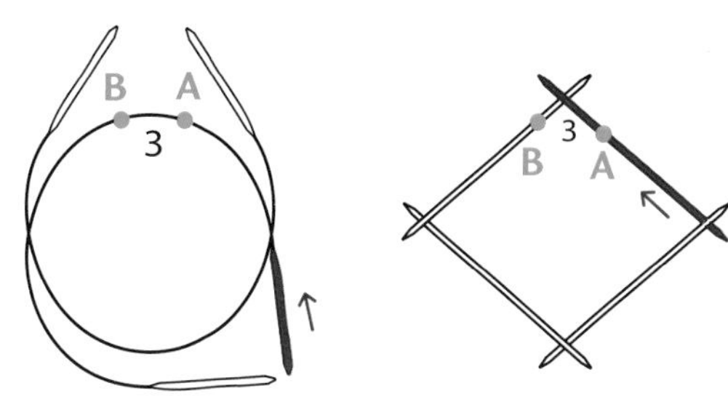

① When companion rounds are ready to begin, there are 3 sts between A and B.

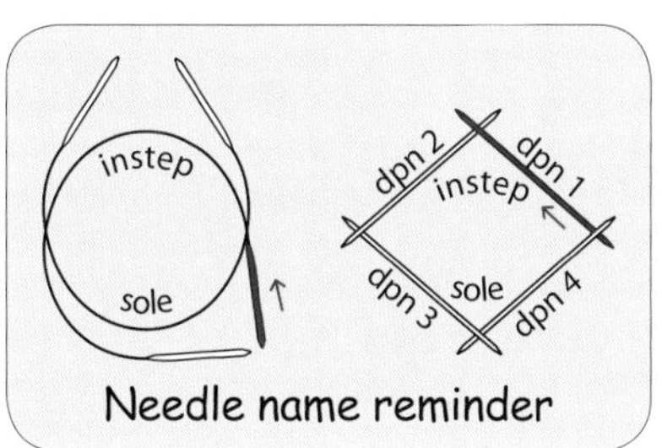

Needle name reminder

Abbreviations and a list of technique lessons can be found on pages 134-136.

Chapter 3 - Cedar Architecture

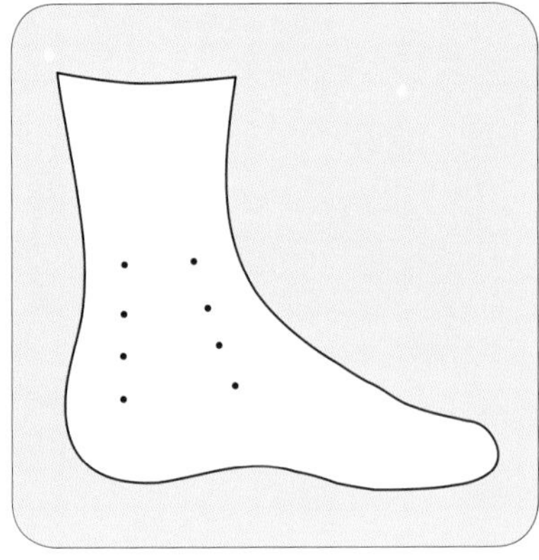

This sock starts at the cuff, traveling down the leg to spread around the ankle and instep like the base of the Cedar trees that grow abundantly in the Pacific Northwest where I live. Like its Foxglove relative, which travels upward from the toe to spread around the instep, Cedar architecture invites you to put the increases *anywhere*. The Cedar Sock illustration to the left shows just one option - evenly spaced lines of increases. In the example here, you can also see how heel stitch (a reinforced heel) runs from the edge of the heel partway down the foot, which is both comfortable and durable. The back of the heel has been left in stockinette to preserve the design, but you could work heel stitch there as well if you choose.

How might you, as a designer, play with this architecture? Imagine cables emerging from a ribbed cuff, growing wider as they approach the base of the foot. You could work increases within the cable itself. For example, start with a 4-stitch cable, grow it to 5 stitches (crossing 3 over 2 or 2 over 3), then grow it to a 6-stitch cable . . . and so on. You need not confine your design to a regular 2 increases every 3 rounds, as long as the increases average out to this proportion. Thus you could use 4 cables and increase them by 1 stitch every 6 rounds.

The Joys of Cedar Architecture

- Increases may be distributed in so many ways: in lines, randomly, or concentrated in chosen areas
- Place designs wherever you like - just cluster all increases in the area without designs
- Learn this pathway and you're ready for Foxglove architecture (Cedar's toe-up relative)

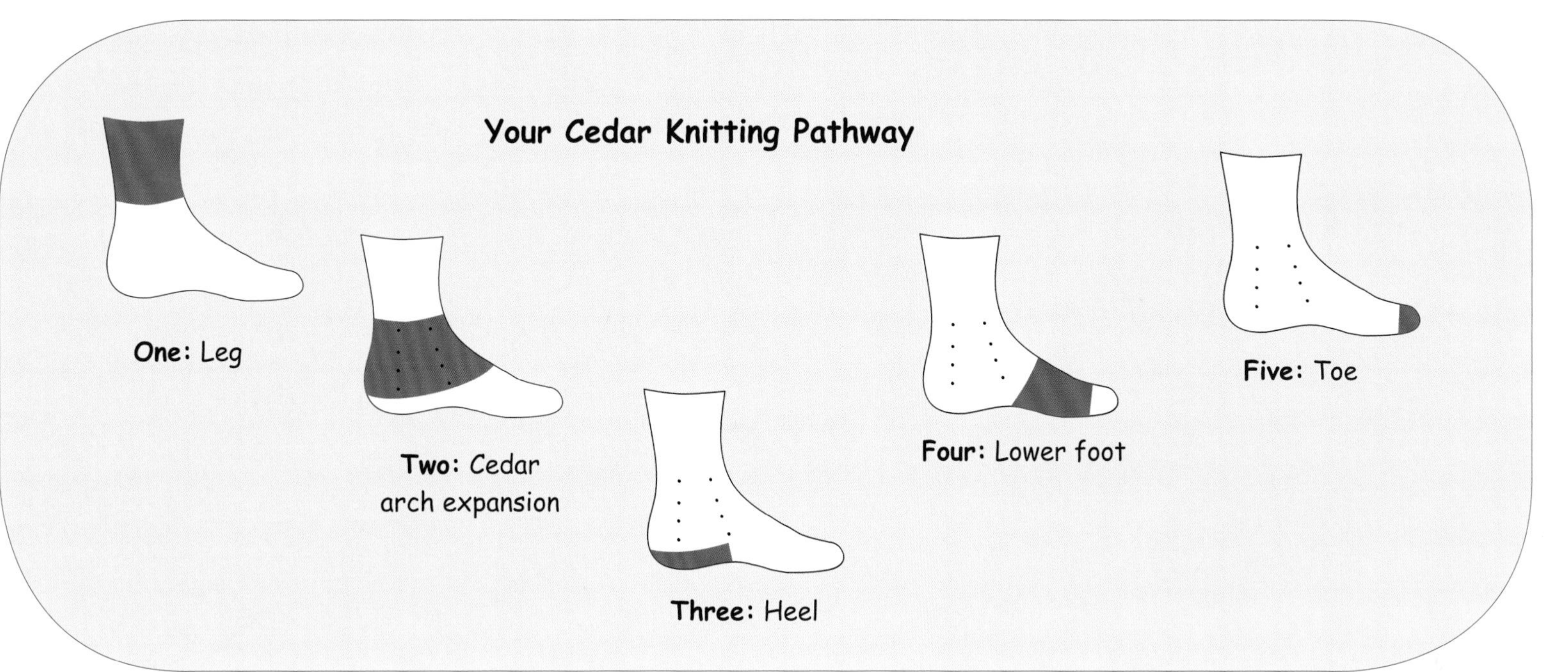

In general, Cedar sockitecture requires slightly fewer increases in the arch expansion area than other architectures. The Cedar Master Pattern at the end of this chapter gives you these adjustments, and the individual patterns have already been adjusted. Sometimes special factors must be considered as well. For instance, in the Veil of Leaves (page 77), the increases are pooled rather closely together (in order to make the leaf design look like leaves), and the number of increases is quite a bit fewer than usual. This lace pattern, with its many yarn-overs, has a great deal of lateral stretch and readily expands around the instep arch. Through a number of revisions, I found that if the normal proportion of increases was used, the arch area was too loose. So keep in mind that you may have to fiddle with a design when introducing stitches which do not follow stockinette proportions.

Max's Springy Ring Socks

Yarn: Nature's Palette Plant-Dyed Merino Fingering™ (100% superwash merino, 50 g / 185 yds), 1 skein each Seafoam, Ice Blue, Autumn Leaf, Lilacs, Mallard, and Coral
Needles: size 2 (3 mm) circular, or size you need to get gauge
Gauge: 8 sts = 1" (2.5 cm)
Markers: **A**, **B**, **C** and **D**
Size: birth to 3 months
Sole is starting ndl (in left hand).

Rings

Ring 1: *(Sea Foam)* Cast on 38 sts and join. Purl 14 rnds. Knit 1 rnd.
Ring 2: *(Ice Blue)* Knit 5 rnds. Purl 11 rnds. Knit 1 rnd.
Ring 3: *(Autumn Leaf)* Knit 5 rnds. Purl 11 rnds. Knit 1 rnd.
Ring 4: *(Lilacs)* Knit 4 rnds. Repeat **k12, LRinc** 3x, k2. Purl 11 rnds. Knit 1 rnd. (41 sts)
Ring 5: *(Mallard)* Knit 4 rnds. Repeat **k10, LRinc** 4x, k1. Purl 11 rnds. Knit 4 rnds. (45 sts)

Ankle - picture ①

(Coral) Knit 2 rnds. Rearrange sts and place markers as shown in picture ①. The first 16 sts stay on sole, and the rest move to the instep, for a total of 29 instep sts.

Heel

Work plain heel (page 122) on sole alone, beginning with step 3. **A** and **B** are already in place. Use 5 for 🅘, and 6 for 🅗.
Total sts after heel is finished: 33.

Foot and toe

Knit until foot measures 3" (7.5 cm) long, ending final rnd with k2tog. (32 sts) Repeat **k2, k2tog** 8x. (24 sts) Knit 1 rnd. Make Star Toe (page 128), beginning with step 2, dividing sock into 4 sections of 8 sts. Weave in all ends.

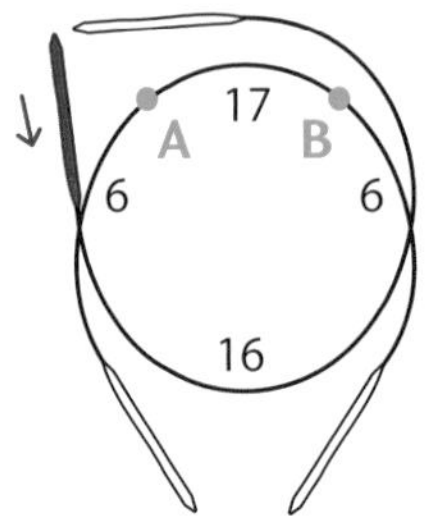

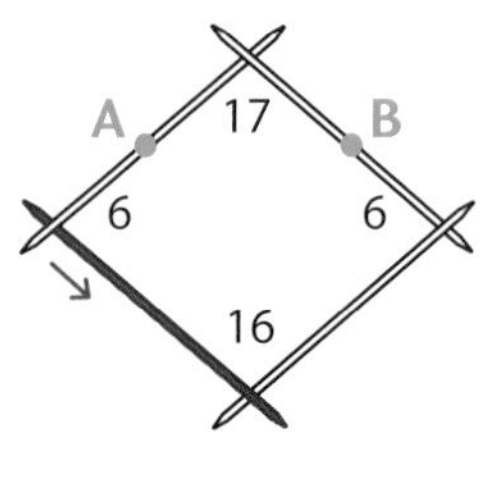

① Ankle stitch and marker distribution.

I've named this sock after my niece's little baby boy, Max - who as I write is practicing standing up, wearing one of the prototypes for the sock you see here. This vegetable-dyed yarn is tender and kind to small feet. Go to page 49 to see how the rings may be scrunched down or pulled up to make over-the-knee socks. Alas, the poofy rings around the lower foot make these unsuitable for shoes, so the style is probably just for babies.

Veil of Leaves

This sock starts out with a 9-stitch leaf lace repeat around the leg. As the lace approaches the swell of the arch area, the leaves grow wider and longer until the repeat is 11 stitches. If you'd like to make the sock larger or smaller, try working in a different gauge.

Yarn: Blue Moon Fiber Arts® Inc. Socks That Rock® Mediumweight (100% wool, 5.5 oz/ 380 yds), 1 skein Coral

Needles: size 1 (2.5 mm), or size you need to get gauge

Gauge: 8 sts = 1" (2.5 cm)

Size: midfoot 8.5" (21 cm)

Markers: A, B, C, and D, also 3 - 5 plain markers

Sole is starting ndl (in left hand).

Cuff - picture ①

Make Cobblestone Cuff (page 132), casting on 72 sts to each parallel ndl, and working 5 rnds before joining. After joining, work this rnd: repeat **k6, k2tog** 9x. (63 sts) Arrange sts and markers as shown in picture ①. There are 36 instep sts and 27 sole sts. Plain markers between the 9-st lace pattern repeats will help you follow the pattern more easily.

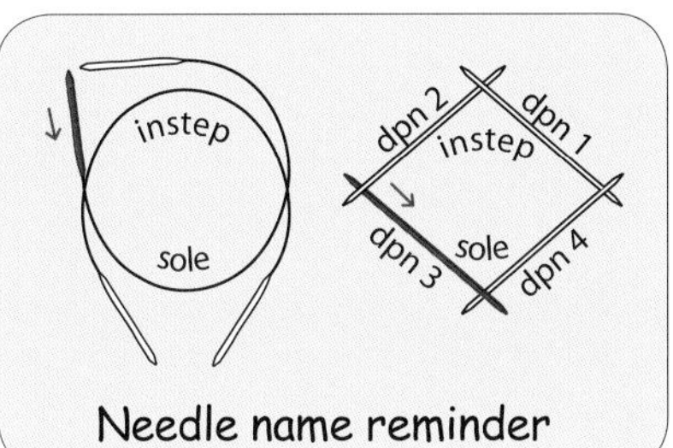

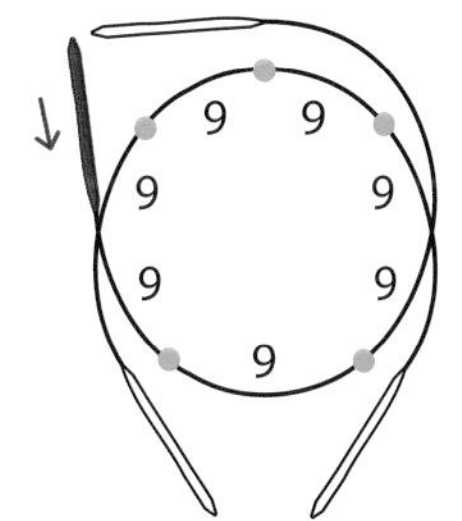

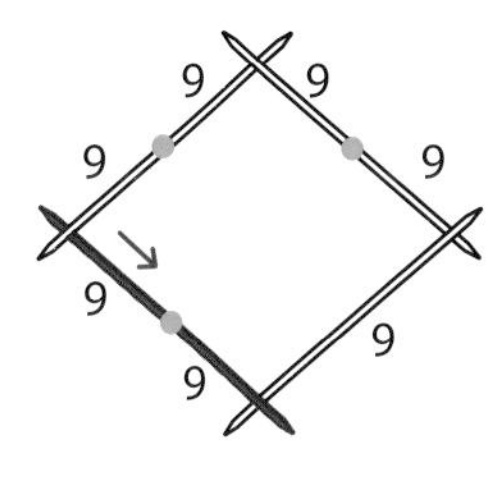

① Stitch and marker distribution.

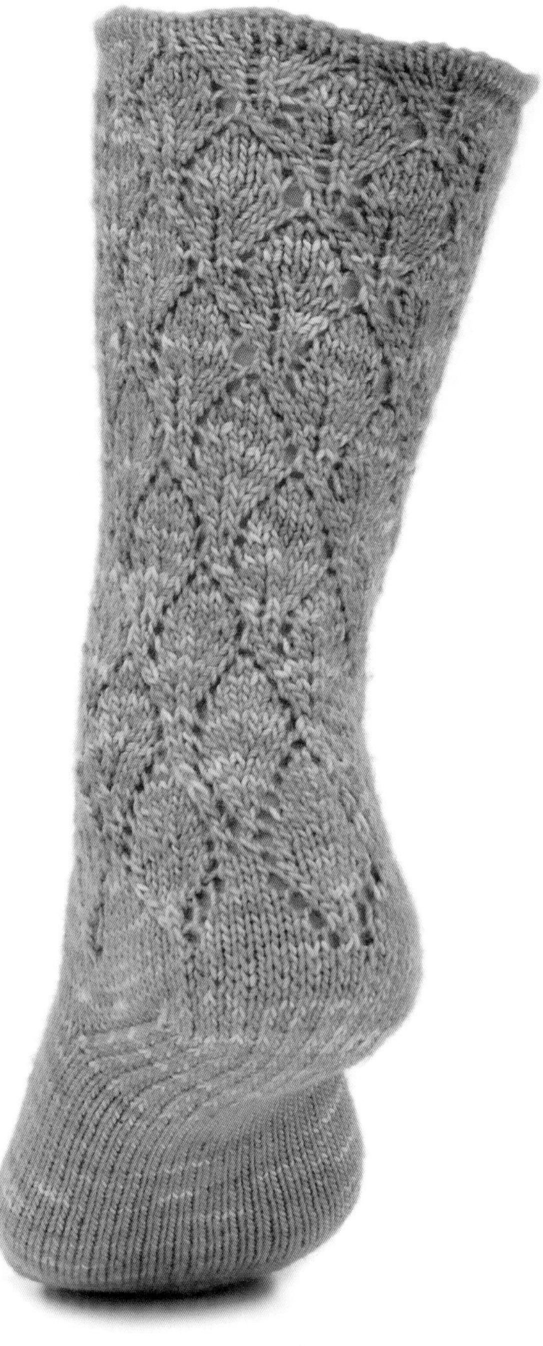

Begin leaf pattern - chart 1

Companion Rounds:

Rnd 1: Repeat **yo, k1, yo, k2, k2tog twice, k2** 7x.

Rnd 2, 4, 6, 8, and 10: Knit.

Rnd 3: Repeat **yo, k3, yo, k1, k2tog twice, k1** 7x.

Rnd 5: Repeat **yo, k5, yo, k2tog twice** 7x.

Rnd 7: Repeat **yo, k2tog, k3, k2tog, yo, k2** 7x.

Rnd 9: Repeat **yo, k3, k2tog, k2, yo, k2tog** 7x.

Repeat companion rnds 1-10 six more times.

Repeat companion rnds 1-6 once more.

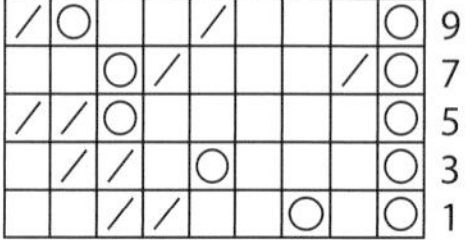

Chart 1
Knit even-numbered rnds.

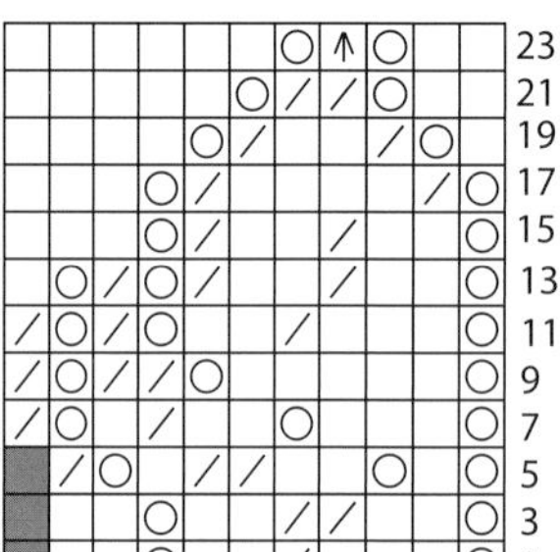

Chart 2
Knit even-numbered rnds.

Key

k   k2tog   cdd   slip   yo   no stitch

Chart 3 (optional - replaces rnds 15-23 of chart 2)
Heel stitch replaces lower half of center rear leaf. Repeat green section 5x. Knit even-numbered rnds.

Arch expansion - picture ② and chart 2

Rnd 1 (chart 2): Repeat **yo, k3, k2tog, k2, yo, k2** 7x. (70 sts)

Rnd 2 and all even rnds: Knit.

Rnd 3: Repeat **yo, k2, k2tog twice, k2, yo, k2** 7x.

Rnd 5: Repeat **yo, k1, yo, k2, k2tog twice, k1, yo, k2tog** 7x.

Rnd 7: Repeat **yo, k3, yo, k2, k2tog, k1, yo, k2tog** 7x. (77 sts)

Rnd 9: Repeat **yo, k5, yo, k2tog twice, yo, k2tog** 7x.

Rnd 11: Repeat **yo, k3, k2tog, k2, yo, k2tog, yo, k2tog** 7x.

Rnd 13: Repeat **yo, k2, k2tog twice, k2, yo, k2tog, yo, k1** 7x.

Rnd 15: Repeat **yo, k2, k2tog, k2, k2tog, yo, k3** 7x.

Rnd 17: Repeat **yo, k2tog, k4, k2tog, yo, k3** 7x.

Rnd 19: Repeat **k1, yo, k2tog, k2, k2tog, yo, k4** 7x.

Rnd 21: Repeat **k2, yo, k2tog twice, yo, k5** 7x.

Rnd 23: Repeat **k2, yo, cdd, yo, k6** 7x. Remove all plain markers in rnd 24.

Rnds 25, 27, and 29: K3, repeat **sl1, k1** 12x, k to end of rnd.

Rnd 30: Knit 29, move next 4 sts to instep before continuing, k1, repeat **LLinc, k2** 4x, place **A**, k until 9 sts rem, place **B**, k1, repeat **LRinc, k2** 4x. Total sts: 85, see picture ②.

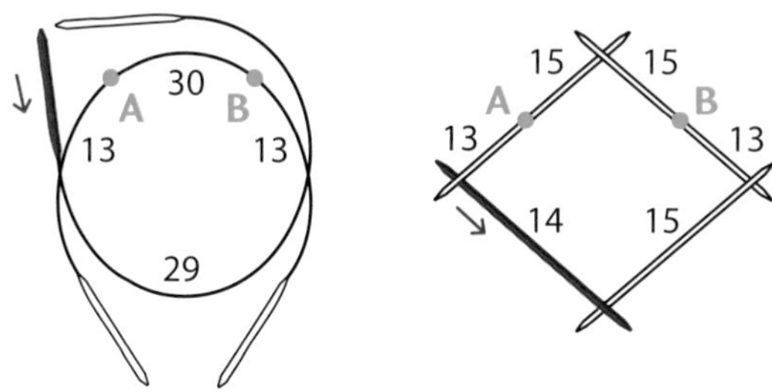

② Stitch and marker distribution after completing rnd 30.

Abbreviations and a list of technique lessons can be found on pages 134-136.

Heel

Work reinforced heel (page 124), starting with step 3. Use 8 for **I** and 13 for **H**. Total sts: 59 Work 1 LRinc mid-sole after about 1" (2.5 cm). Total sts: 60

Foot and Toe

To determine length toe will add, measure rnds-per-inch (RPI) in a stockinette section, and divide RPI into 18. The answer is the length toe will add. Knit all rnds until until only this length remains to be added, then make Star Toe ((page 128), dividing the sock into 6 equal sections of 10 sts.

Optional version - chart 3 replaces rnds 15-23 of chart 2

This version reinforces the area above the heel turn with 10 rows of heel stitch *(this is not the version in the photos).* Follow chart 3 for rnds 15-23 of arch expansion, then resume standard directions with rnd 24. *(Knit all even rnds.)*

Rnd 15: (chart 3) Remove first 2 plain markers before continuing. Yo, k2, k2tog, k2, k2tog, yo, repeat **k1, sl1** 7x, repeat **yo, k2, k2tog, k2, k2tog, yo, k3** 5x.

Rnd 17: Yo, k2tog, k4, k2tog, yo, repeat **k1, sl1** 7x, repeat **yo, k2tog, k4, k2tog, yo, k3** 5x.

Rnd 19: Knit 1, yo, k2tog, k2, k2tog, yo, k1, repeat **k1, sl1** 7x, repeat **k1, yo, k2tog, k2, k2tog, yo, k4** 5x.

Rnd 21: Knit 2, yo, k2tog twice, yo, k2, repeat **k1, sl1** 7x, repeat **k2, yo, k2tog twice, yo, k5** 5x.

Rnd 23: Knit 2, yo, cdd, yo, k3, repeat **k1, sl1** 7x, repeat **k2, yo, cdd, yo, k6** 5x. Remove all plain markers in rnd 24.

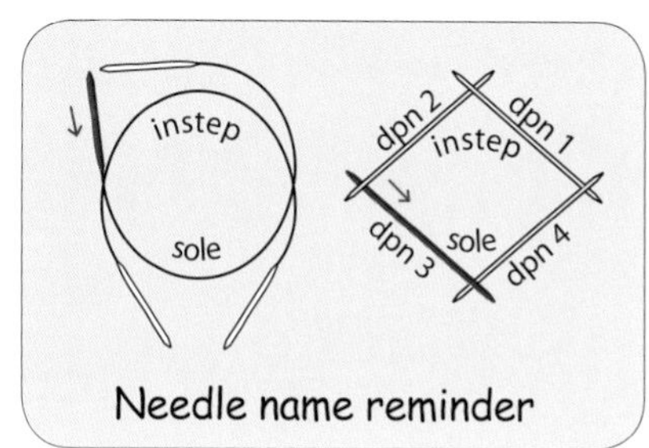

Needle name reminder

Cedar Dancing Socks

This sock reveals its Cedar architecture in the gradual widening of the lace repeats, which you will soon learn by heart. You can also make graduated wrist warmers from this pattern - just work the leg through the end of chart 3, purl 7 rounds, bind off loosely, roll edge to the inside and sew down to match the cobblestone cuff at the other end.

Yarn: Blue Moon Fiber Arts® Inc. Socks That Rock® Mediumweight (100% wool, 5.5 oz/ 380 yds), 1 skein Puck's Mischief

Needles: size 2 (3 mm), or size you need to get gauge

Gauge: 7.5 sts = 1" (2.5 cm) (in stockinette)

Sizes: midfoot 7.5 (8.5)" or 19 (21) cm

Markers: A, B, C and D, also 8 (10) plain markers

Sole is starting ndl (in left hand).

Cuff - picture ①

Make Cobblestone Cuff (page 132), casting on 56 (68) sts to each parallel ndl. After joining, work decrease rnd: (small size) repeat **k5, k2tog** 8x, (large size) repeat **k6, k2tog** 8x, k4. Total sts: 48 (60). Place a plain marker every 6 sts to mark lace pattern repeats. See picture ①. *Plain (knit) rnds are not shown in charts.*

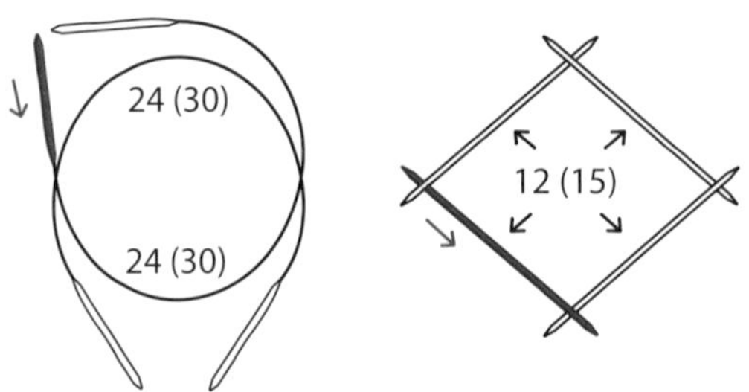

① Stitch distribution after cuff completion. (Plain markers are not shown.)

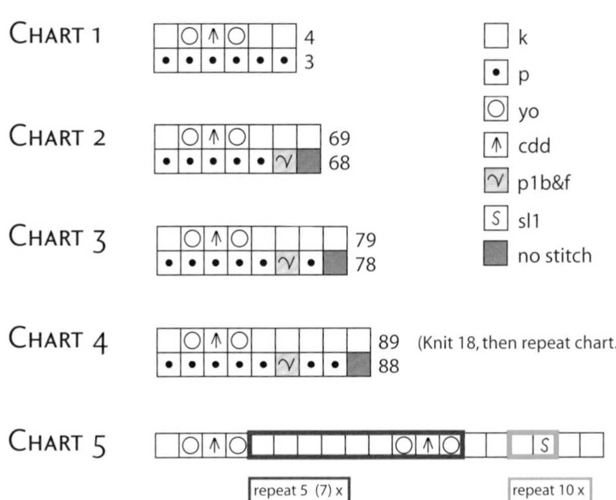

Leg

Rnds 1-2: Knit.

Companion Rounds: (chart 1)

Rnd 3: Purl.

Rnd 4: Repeat **k2, yo, cdd, yo, k1** 8 (10)x.

Rnds 5-7: Knit.

Repeat companion rnds 3-7 another 12x.

Arch expansion - picture ②

Rnd 68 (chart 2): Repeat **p1b&f, p5** 8 (10)x. (56 (70) sts)

Companion Rounds:

Rnd 69: Repeat **k3, yo, cdd, yo, k1** 8 (10)x.

Rnds 70-72: Knit.

Rnd 73: Purl.

Repeat companion rnds 69-72 once more.

Rnd 78 (chart 3): Repeat **p1, p1b&f, p5** 8 (10)x. (64 (80) sts)

Companion Rounds:

Rnd 79: Repeat **k4, yo, cdd, yo, k1** 8 (10)x.

Rnds 80-82: Knit. Rnd 83: Purl.

Repeat rnds 79-82 once more.

Rnd 88 (chart 4): Repeat **p2, p1b&f, p5** 8 (10) x. (72 (90) sts)

Rnd 89: Knit 18, repeat **k5, yo, cdd, yo, k1** 6 (8)x.

Rnds 90-92: Knit.

Rnd 93: P11, p1f&b, p to end. (73 (91) sts)

Rnd 94 (chart 5): Knit 2, repeat **sl1, k1** 10x, k2, repeat **yo, cdd, yo, k6** 5 (7) x, yo, cdd, yo, k1.

Rnd 95: Knit.

Rnd 96: Knit 2, repeat **sl1, k1** 10x, k until 1 st remains unworked at end of rnd. Transfer this st from instep to adjacent end of sole. Transfer 13 (22) sts from other end of sole to adjacent end of instep. Heel turn is worked back and forth on 25 sts remaining on sole. Remove plain markers and place A and B as shown in picture ②.

Heel

Work reinforced heel (page 124) beginning with step 3. A and B are already in place. Use 6 for I, and 12 (16) for H. Total sts after heel is finished: 49 (59) sts total - 24 (34) on instep, 25 on sole.

Foot *(instep is starting ndl)*

Rnd 1: Purl 24 (34), k25.

Companion rows:

Rnd 2: (Small size) repeat **k6, yo, cdd, yo** 2x, k to end, (large size) k2, repeat **yo, cdd, yo, k6** 3x, yo, cdd, yo, k to end.

Rnds 3-5: Knit.

Rnd 6: Purl 24 (34), k25.

Repeat rnds 2-6 until foot measures 1.25"/3.5 cm (1.5"/4 cm) shorter than desired length, stopping after a completed rnd 3, 4, or 5.

Toe

Repeat (small size) **k5, k2tog** 7x. (42 sts) (large size) **k7, k2tog** 5x. (54 sts) Knit 1 rnd. Make Star Toe (page 128), beginning with step 2.

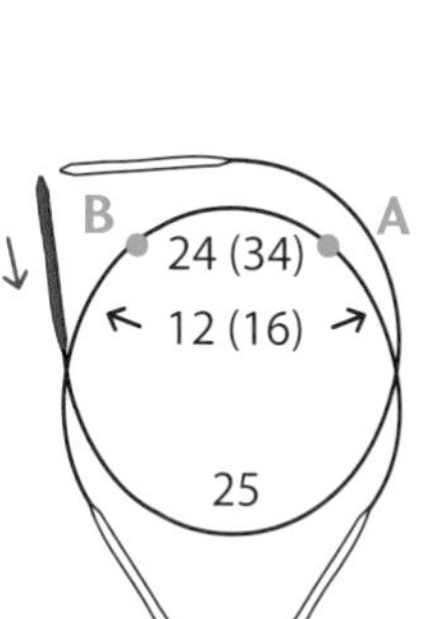

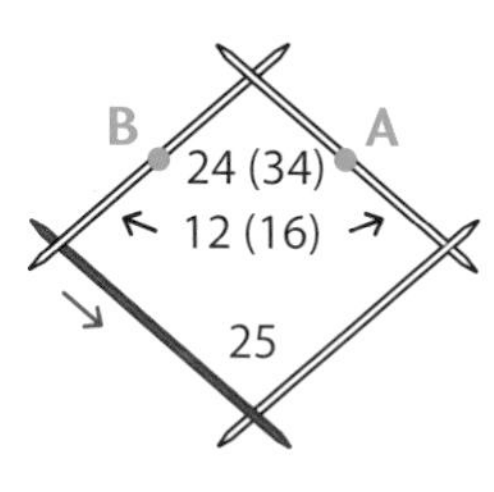

② Arch expansion is complete and heel is ready to begin. Yarn comes from start of sole.

Ocean-Toes

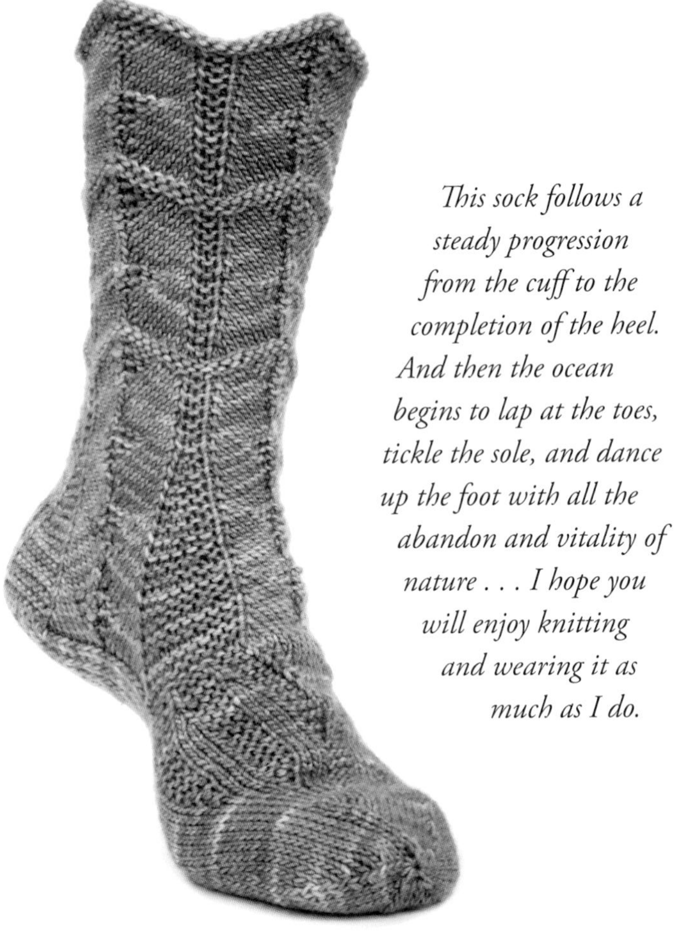

This sock follows a steady progression from the cuff to the completion of the heel. And then the ocean begins to lap at the toes, tickle the sole, and dance up the foot with all the abandon and vitality of nature . . . I hope you will enjoy knitting and wearing it as much as I do.

Yarn: Blue Moon Fiber Arts® Inc. Socks That Rock® Mediumweight (100% wool, 5.5 oz/ 380 yds), 1 skein Stonewash
Needles: size 2 (3 mm), or size you need to get gauge
Gauge: 7 sts = 1" (2.5 cm)
Size: midfoot 8.5" (21 cm)
Markers: A, B, C, D, and E
Sole is starting ndl (in left hand).

Cuff
Make Cobblestone Cuff (page 132), using 64 for D.
After joining, knit 1 rnd.

Leg
For pink sock, follow directions as given. For taller blue sock, repeat **companion rnds 1-12, then companion rnds 1-15** 2x, then repeat **companion rnds 1-12** once more.
Companion rounds: - chart 1
Rnd 1: Repeat **p1, k1, LLinc, k2, p3, cdd, p3, k2, LRinc, k1** 4x.
Rnds 2, 4, 6, and 8: Repeat **k8, p1, k7** 4x.
Rnd 3: Repeat **p1, k1, LLinc, k3, p2, cdd, p2, k3, LRinc, k1** 4x.
Rnd 5: Repeat **p1, k1, LLinc, k4, p1, cdd, p1, k4, LRinc, k1** 4x.
Rnds 7, 9, and 11: Repeat **p1, k1, LLinc, k5, cdd, k5, LRinc, k1** 4x.
Rnds 10, 12, and 15: Knit.
Rnds 13-14: Purl.
Repeat companion rounds 1-15 once more.
Then repeat companion rnds 1-12 once more.

Arch expansion - picture ①, chart 2, and after rnd 12, chart 3
Rnd 1: Repeat **p1b&f, k1, LLinc, k2, p3, cdd, p3, k2, LRinc, k1** 4x.
Rnds 2 and 4: Repeat **k9, p1, k7** 4x.
Rnd 3: Repeat **p2, k1, LLinc, k3, p2, cdd, p2, k3, LRinc, k1** 4x.
Rnd 5: Repeat **p1, p1b&f, k1, LLinc, k4, p1, cdd, p1, k4, LRinc, k1** 4x.
Rnds 6 and 8: Repeat **k10, p1, k7** 4x.
Rnd 7: Repeat **p3, k1, LLinc, k5, cdd, k5, LRinc, k1** 4x.
Rnd 9: Repeat **p1, p1b&f, p1, k1, LLinc, k5, cdd, k5, LRinc, k1** 4x.
Rnd 10: Knit.
Rnd 11: Repeat **p4, k1, LLinc, k5, cdd, k5, LRinc, k1** 4x.
First circular ndl/dpn's 1-2 are sole, 2nd circular/dpn's 3-4 are instep.
Rnd 12: Knit, *placing* A *4 sts and* B *19 sts after start of sole.*
Sole is starting ndl (in left hand). See picture ①.

k | p | ssk | k2tog | LLinc | LRinc | k1f&b | p1b&f | cdd | slip | p2tog | no stitch

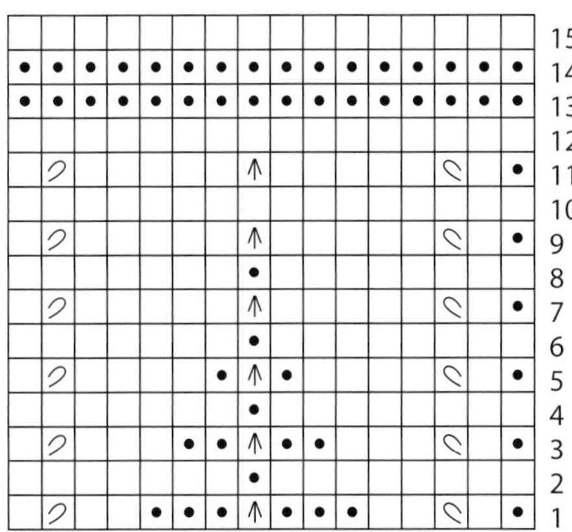

Chart 1 (leg)
After Cobblestone Cuff and 1 rnd of knitting are complete, work rnds 1-15 twice, then rnds 1-12 once more (chart is repeated 4 times around leg).

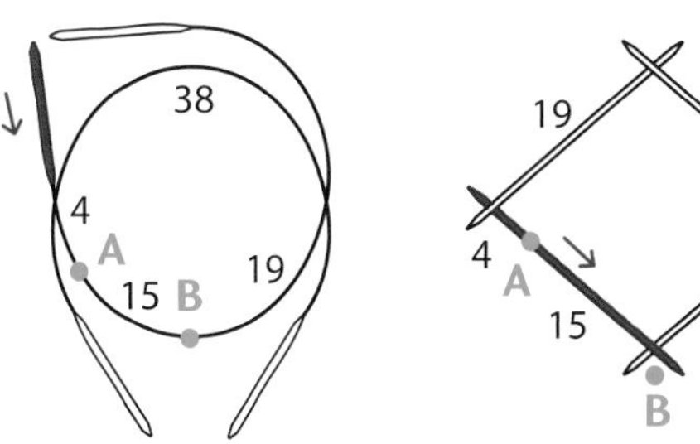

① Stitch and marker distribution after completing arch expansion rnd 12. *Note that sole is starting ndl (in left hand).* For dpn's, B is represented by intersection of sole ndls.

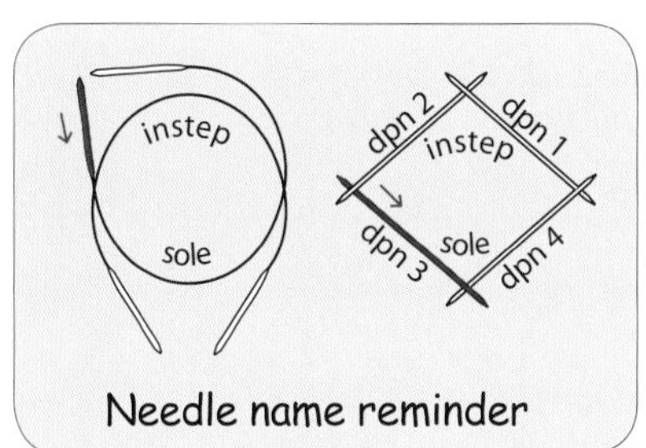

Needle name reminder

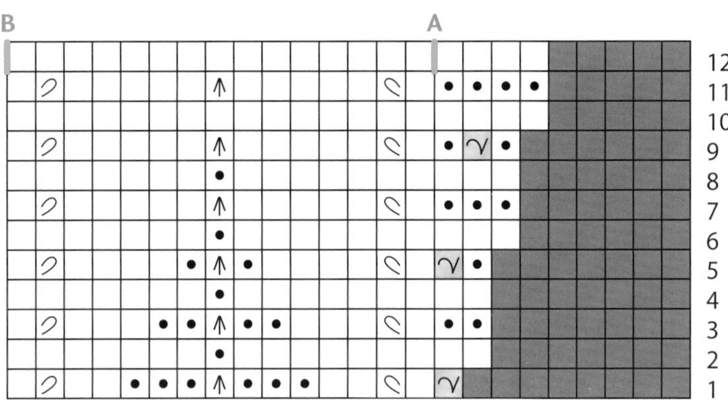

Chart 2 (arch expansion)
Rounds 1 through 12 are worked around the whole foot, with the repeat fitting evenly in 4 equal sections (which grow from 16 to 19 sts). Don't forget to place markers A and B in round 12.

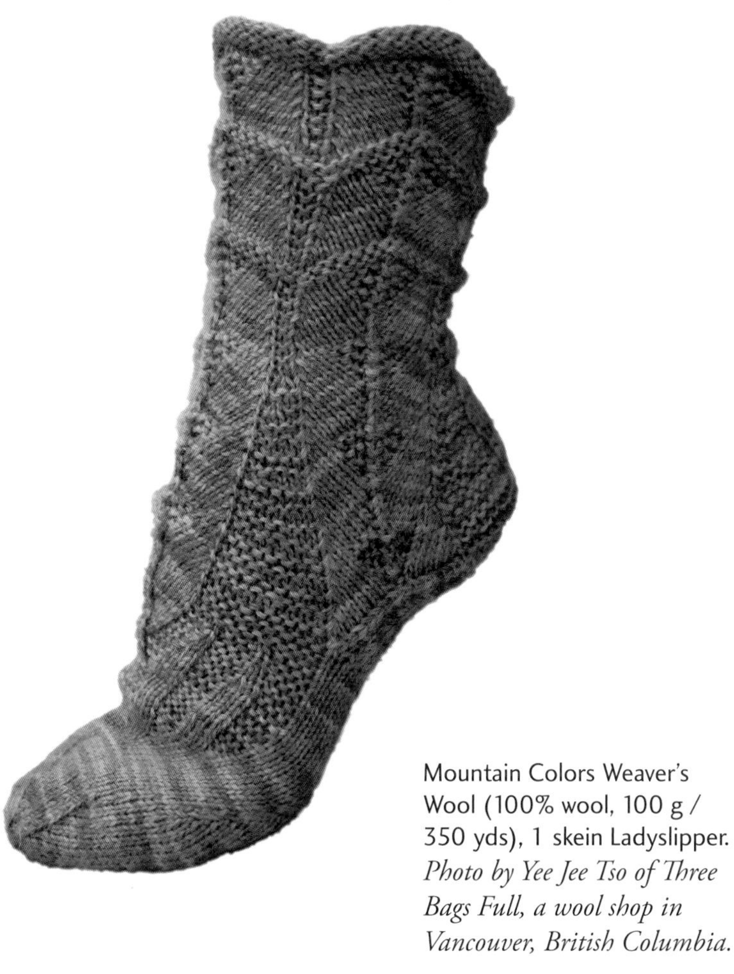

Mountain Colors Weaver's Wool (100% wool, 100 g / 350 yds), 1 skein Ladyslipper. *Photo by Yee Jee Tso of Three Bags Full, a wool shop in Vancouver, British Columbia.*

Rnd 13: (chart 3 begins) Purl 2, p1b&f, p1, (A), repeat *sl1, k1* 7x, sl1, (B), repeat *p2, p1b&f, p1, k1, LLinc, k2, p3, cdd, p3, k2, LRinc, k1* 3x.
Rnds 14 and 16: Knit to B, repeat *k12, p1, k7* 3x.
Rnd 15: Purl 5, (A), repeat *sl1, k1* 7x, sl1, (B), repeat *p5, k1, LLinc, k3, p2, cdd, p2, k3, LRinc, k1* 3x.
Rnd 17: Purl 1, p1b&f, p3, (A), repeat *sl1, k1* 7x, sl1, (B), repeat *p1, p1b&f, p3, k1, LLinc, k4, p1, cdd, p1, k4, LRinc, k1* 3x.
Rnd 18 and 20: Knit to B, repeat *k13, p1, k7* 3x.
Rnd 19: Purl 6, (A), repeat *sl1, k1* 7x, sl1, (B), repeat *p6, k1, LLinc, k5, cdd, k5, LRinc, k1* 3x.
Rnd 21: Purl 3, p1b&f, p2, (A), repeat *sl1, k1* 7x, sl1, (B), repeat *p3, p1b&f, p2, k1, LLinc, k5, cdd, k5, LRinc, k1* 3x.
Rnds 22 and 24: Knit.
Rnd 23: Purl 7, (A), repeat *sl1, k1* 7x, sl1, (B), repeat *p7, k1, LLinc, k 5, cdd, k5, LRinc, k1* 3x.
Rnd 25: P1, p1b&f, p5, (A), repeat *sl1, k1* 7x, sl1, (B), repeat *p1, p1b&f, p5, k1, LLinc, k2, p3, cdd, p3, k2, LRinc, k1* 3x.
Rnds 26 and 28: Knit to B, repeat *k15, p1, k7* 3x.
Rnd 27: Purl 8, (A), repeat *sl1, k1* 7x, sl1, (B), repeat *p8, k1, LLinc, k3, p2, cdd, p2, k3, LLinc, k1* 3x.
Rnd 29: Purl 5, p1b&f, p2, (A), repeat *sl1, k1* 7x, sl1, (B), repeat *p5, p1b&f, p2, k1, LLinc, k4, p1, cdd, p1, k4, LRinc, k1* 3x.
Rnds 30 and 32: Knit to B, repeat *k16, p1, k7* 3x. Remove A and B at the end of rnd 32.
Rnd 31: Purl 9, (A), repeat *sl1, k1* 7x, sl1, (B), repeat *p9, k1, LLinc, k5, cdd, k5, LRinc, k1* 3x.
There are 96 sts total, 48 on sole and 48 on instep.

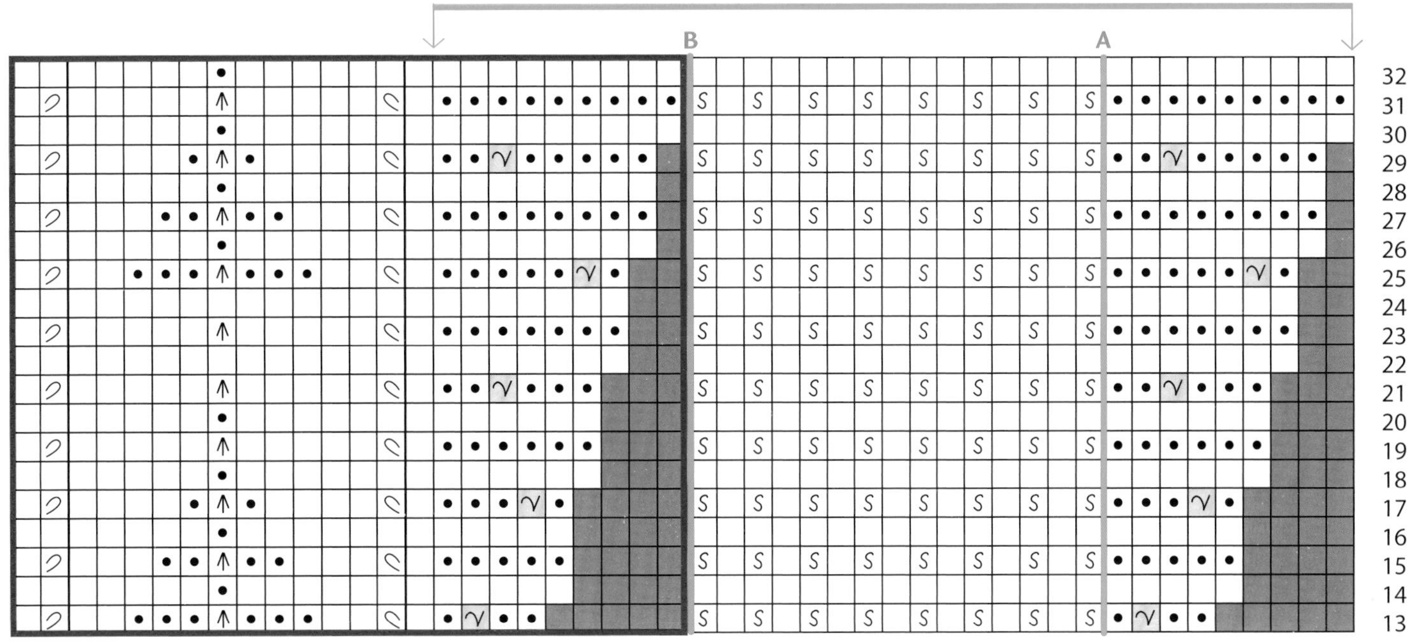

Chart 3 (continuing arch expansion, and heel turn stitches)

Sole ndl(s) follow entire chart, then instep ndl(s) begin with red-boxed section and repeat it twice more. The blue line and arrows indicate the 33 sts remaining on sole after moving 19 sts to instep after rnd 32. The 33 blue-line sts will be used for working the heel turn.

Heel turn

Move last 15 sts on sole (starting ndl) to instep. Heel turn is worked on 33 sole sts remaining (9 garter, 15 heel st, and 9 garter). Instep has 63 sts.

Row 1: Repeat **k1, sl1** 10x, k1, k2tog, k1, turn.

Row 2: Slip 1, p10, ssp, p1, turn.

Row 3: Slip 1, k2, repeat **sl1, k1** 4x, k1, k2tog, k1, turn.

Row 4: Slip 1, p12, ssp, p1, turn.

Row 5: Slip 1, repeat **k1, sl1** 6x, k1, k2tog, k1, turn.

Row 6: Slip 1, p14, ssp, p1, turn.

Row 7: Slip 1, k2, repeat **sl1, k1** 6x, k1, k2tog, k1, turn.

Row 8: Slip 1, p16, ssp, p1, turn.

Row 9: Slip 1, repeat **k1, sl1** 8x, k1, k2tog, k1, turn.

Row 10: Slip 1, p18, ssp,p1, turn.

Row 11: Slip 1, k2, repeat **sl1, k1** 8x, k1, k2tog, turn.

Row 12: Slip 1, p19, ssp, turn. (21 sts on sole, 63 on instep)

Base of sole

Move 15 sts from each end of instep to adjacent end of sole, then shift sts along sole ndl so tips emerge after 15 moved sts. (51 sts on sole, 33 on instep)

Row 1: Pick up a st in intersection and k it, repeat **k1, sl1** 10x, k1, pick up a st in intersection and k it tog with next st, turn.

Companion rows:

Row 2: Slip 1, p21, p2tog, turn.

Row 3: Repeat **sl1, k1** 11x, ssk, turn.

Repeat companion rows 2 and 3 until only 26 sts remain on sole. End next rnd 2 with p3tog instead of p2tog. On rnd 3, do not turn. (56 sts total: 23 on sole, 33 on instep)

Resume knitting in the round as you continue with the foot.

Instep is now starting ndl.

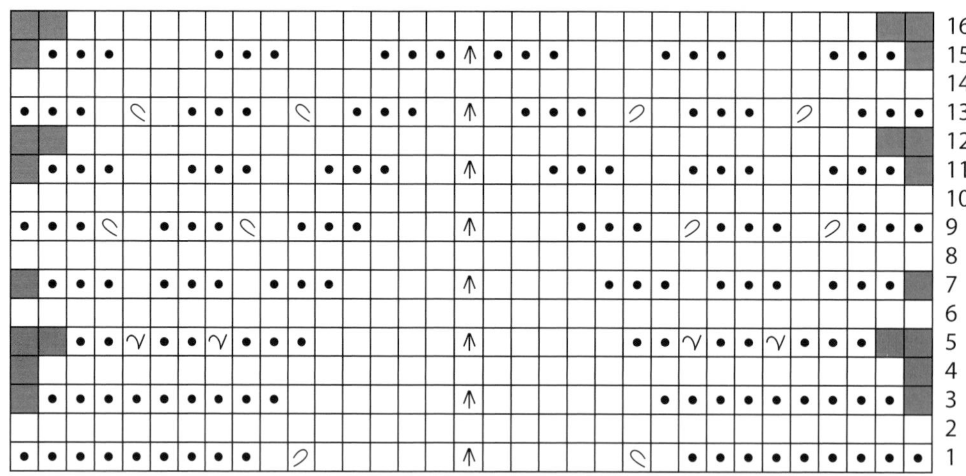

Chart 4 (foot)
Rounds 1-16 of the chart show instep sts only. The remaining 23 sole sts are always knit.

Foot (Chart 4, then chart 5 after rnd 16)

Rnd 1: *Instep is starting ndl (in left hand).* Purl 9, k1, LLinc, k5, cdd, k5, LRinc, k1, p9, (sole) pick up 1 st in intersection and k tog with next st, k22. (56 sts)

Rnd 2 and all even rounds: Knit.

Rnd 3: Purl 9, k6, cdd, k6, p9, k23. (54 sts)

Rnd 5: Purl 3, k1f&b, p2, k1f&b, p2, k5, cdd, k5, p3, k1f&b, p2, k1f&b, p2, k23. (56 sts)

Rnd 7: Repeat **p3, k1** 3x, k3, cdd, k4, **p3, k1** 2x, p3, k23. (54 sts)

Rnd 9: Repeat **p3, LRinc, k1** 2x, p3, k3, cdd, k3, repeat **p3, k1, LLinc** 2x, p3, k23. (56 sts)

Rnd 11: Repeat **p3, k2** 3x, cdd, repeat **k2, p3** 3x, k23. (54 sts)

Rnd 13: Repeat **p3, k1, LRinc, k1** 2x, p3, k1, cdd, k1, repeat **p3, k1, LLinc, k1** 2x, p3, k23. (56 sts)

Rnd 15: Repeat **p3,* k3* 2x, p3, cdd, repeat **p3, k3** 2x, p3, k23. (54 sts)

(chart 5) LRinc's are worked right *after* **A** and LLinc's right *before* **B**.

Rnd 17: Repeat **p3, k3** 2x, p2, cdd, p2, repeat **k3, p3** 2x, k6, place **A**, LRinc, k11, LLinc, place **B**, k6.

Rnd 19: Repeat **p3, k3** 2x, p1, cdd, p1, repeat **k3, p3** 2x, k to **A**, LRinc, k to **B**, LLinc, k6.

Rnd 21: Repeat **p3, k3** 5x, k to **A**, LRinc, k to **B**, LLinc, k6. (56 sts)

Rnd 23: Purl 1, p2tog, repeat **k3, p3** 3x, k3, p2tog, p1, k to **A**, LRinc, k to **B**, LLinc, k6.

Rnd 25: Purl 2tog, repeat **k3, p3** 3x, k3, p2tog, k to **A**, LRinc, k to **B**, LLinc, k6.

Rnd 27: Knit 4, p1, p2tog, k3, p3, k3, p2tog, p1, k to **A**, LRinc, k to **B**, LLinc, k6.

Rnd 29: Knit 4, p2tog, k3, p3, k3, p2tog, k to **A**, LRinc, k to **B**, LLinc, k6.

Rnd 31: Knit 4, p1, k2, ssk, p1, k2tog, k2, p1, k to **A**, LRinc, k to **B**, LLinc, k6.

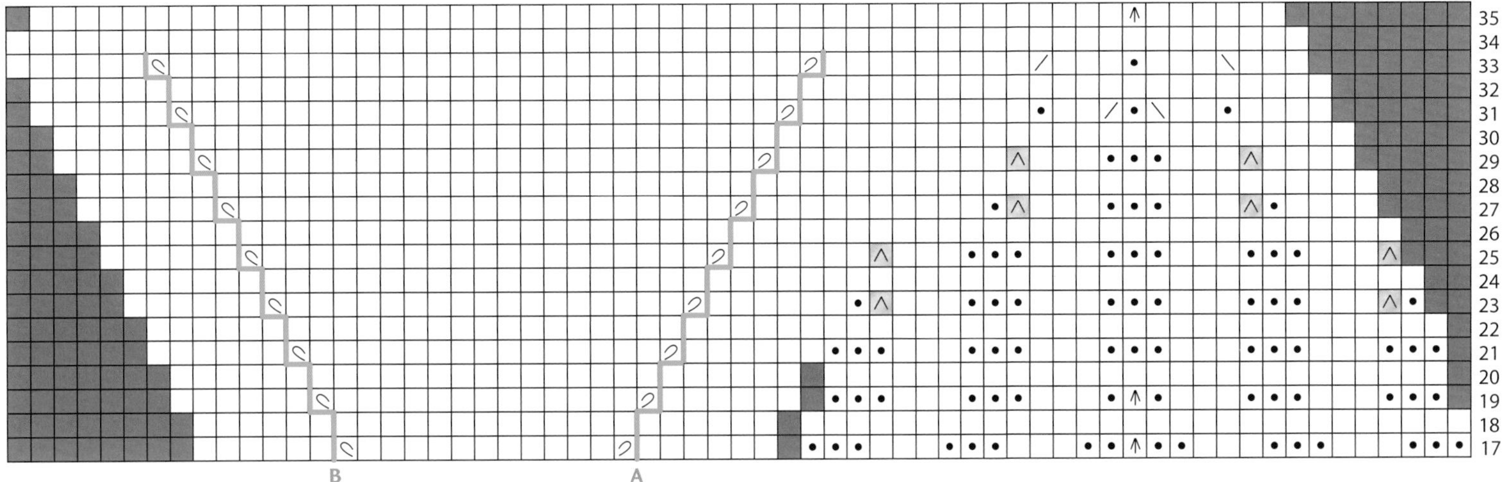

Chart 5 (foot)
Rounds 17-35 show all sts as the foot continues towards the toe. The green stair-step lines mark the slanting path of markers A and B as they are pushed outward by the increases. Remove A and B when you meet them in rnd 34. In rnd 35, place A as instructed.

Rnd 33: Knit 3, ssk, k3, p1, k3, k2tog, k to A, LRinc, k to B, LLinc, k6. Remove A and B in rnd 34.
Rnd 35: Knit 6, cdd, k to end. (54 sts)
Rnd 36: Knit.

Toe

Toe adds another 1.5" (4 cm). *For additional foot length, knit extra rnds before beginning toe.*
Rnd 1: Knit 6, k2tog, place A. Knit 9, k2tog, place B, k9, k2tog, place C, k9, k2tog, place D, k10, place E. E is now end of rnd. (50 sts)
Rnds 2 and 4: Knit.
Rnd 3: Knit to 2 sts before A, k2tog, k to 2 sts before B, k2tog, k to 2 sts before C, k2tog, k to 2 sts before D, k2tog, k to 2 sts before E, k2tog.
Repeat rnds 3 and 4 until after a rnd 3 only 4 sts rem between markers. Repeat rnd 3 twice more. Cut tail, use tapestry needle to weave tail through remaining 10 sts, pull snug, and weave in all ends.

Slipstitch Rings

This two-color sock clearly shows the increasing girth of the cedar arch expansion. It would make a great first 2-color project because only 1 color is worked each round.

Yarn: Fleece Artist Merino 2/6 (100% merino, 115 g/ 325 m), 100 g main color, (MC) 25 g contrast color (CC)
Needles: size 1 (2.5 mm), or size you need to get gauge
Gauge: 8 sts = 1" (2.5 cm)
Sizes: midfoot 6.75 (7.5, 8.5, 9.5, 10.5)" or 17 (19, 21, 24, 26) cm
Markers: A, B, C, and D

Cuff

With MC, make Cobblestone Cuff (page 132), using 48 (54, 60, 66, 72) for D.

Leg

Companion rounds
Rnds 1-2: With CC, knit.
Rnds 3-4: With MC, repeat *k2, sl1* to end.
Repeat companion rnds 1-4 *another* 2x.
Rnds 12-13: With CC, knit.
Rnds 14-25: With MC, knit.
Repeat companion rnds 1-4 and rnds 12-25 *another* 2x.
Repeat companion rnds 1-4 once, then rnds 12-13 once.

Arch expansion

Distribute the LLinc's evenly around the sock.

Companion rounds
Rnds 1-2: (MC) Knit.
Rnds 3 and 8: (MC) Include 3 LLinc's in these rnds.
Rnds 4-7 and 9-12: (MC) Knit.
Rnds 13-14: (CC) Knit.
Rnds 15-16: (MC) Repeat *k2, sl1* to end.
Rnds 18-20: (CC) Knit.
Repeat companion rnds 1-20 another 2 (1, 3, 2, 1) times.
Total sts: 66 (66, 84, 84, 84)

Additional companion rounds
(for 2nd, 4th, and 5th sizes only)
Rnds 21-22: (MC) Knit.
Rnd 23: (MC) Include 5 LLinc's in this rnd.
Rnds 24-28 and 30-32: (MC) Knit.
Rnd 29: (MC) Include 4 LLinc's in this rnd.
Rnds 33-34 and 37-38: (CC) Knit.
Rnds 35-36: (MC) Repeat *k2, sl1* to end.
(5th size only) Repeat companion rnds 21-38 once more.
Total sts: 66 (75, 84, 93, 102)
Knit 1 rnd with MC (for 2nd and 4th sizes only, include 1 LLinc in this rnd).
Total sts: 66 (76, 84, 94, 102)

Heel

Next 24 (27, 30, 33, 36) sts *are heel and remaining sts are instep. Put all sole sts on 1 circ or 1 dpn.* Work reinforced heel (page 120), starting at step 1. Use 24 (27, 30, 33, 36) for G, 9 (11, 12, 14, 15) for H, and 7 (8, 9, 10, 11) for I. Total sts after heel is finished: 49 (54, 61, 66, 73)

Foot and toe

To determine length toe will add, measure rnds-per-inch (RPI) in a stockinette section, and divide RPI into 14 (16, 18, 20, 22). The answer is the length toe will add. Knit all rnds until until only this length remains to be added, then make Star Toe ((page 128), dividing the sock into 6 equal sections of 8 (9, 10, 11, 12) sts.

Cedar Master Pattern

Find your Master numbers on pages 109-119.

Markers: A, B, C and D

Complete any cuff (page 132), then knit to top of ankle bone.

Cedar arch expansion - picture ①
Divide sts on each ndl into approximate ⅓'s. Place A after ⅓ and B after ⅔ of the sts on instep. Repeat on sole, using C and D.

Companion rounds:
- Rnd 1: LRinc at start of instep and sole, k to end.
- Rnds 2-3, 5-6, and 8-9: Knit.
- Rnd 4: LRinc right after A and C, k to end.
- Rnd 7: LRinc right after B and D, k to end.

Repeat companion rnds, stopping after a completed rnd 1, 4, or 7, when total stitch count reaches the following custom instep number (round off result to a whole number):

- For a high instep: use F
- For a medium instep: multiply F by 0.9
- For a low instep: multiply F by 0.8

Remove A, B, C and D when done.

Complete heel (page 120), foot, and toe (page 128).

Abbreviations and a list of technique lessons can be found on pages 134-136.

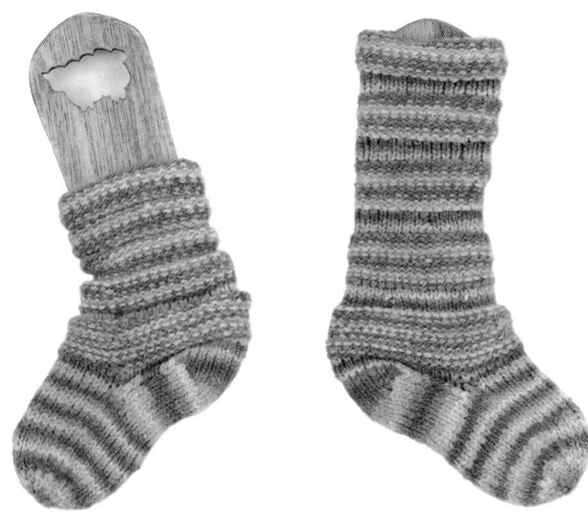

Max's Springy Ring Socks (page 36) may be pulled up to be over-the-knee socks, worked here in Cascade Fixation (98.3% cotton, 1.7% elastic, 50 g/ 186 yds)

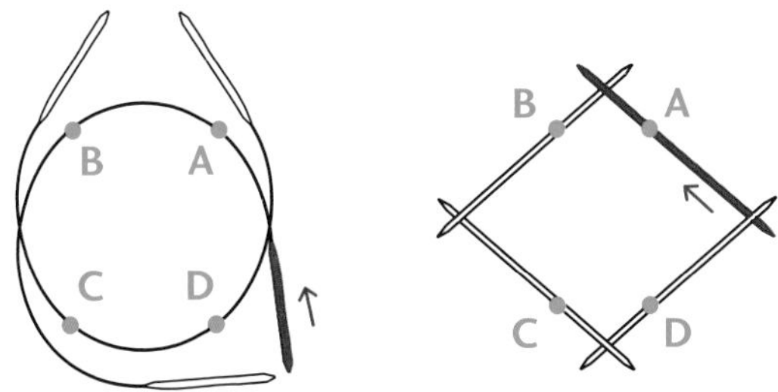

① Instep and sole are divided into thirds. Increases cycle between the start of instep/ sole (rnd 1), A and C (rnd 4), and finally B and D (rnd 7).

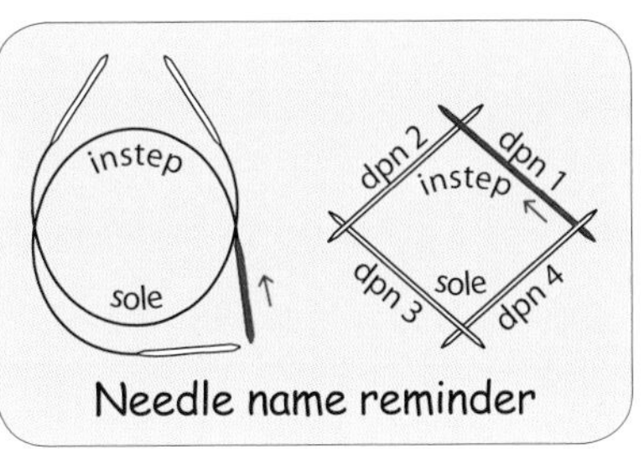

Chapter 4 - Coriolis Architecture

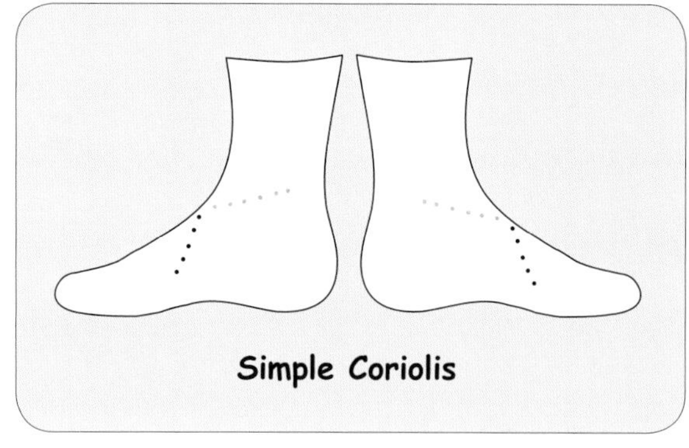
Simple Coriolis

Since childhood I've dreamed of sailing to Australia to see the water swirl down the sink in the opposite direction. And what would happen right on the equator? Would the water go straight down? I'd heard that the Coriolis Force was behind this mystery, but had never investigated it further. Under the spell of my childhood fantasy and Monsieur Gaspard-Gustave Coriolis's lovely surname (a French scientist and mathematician who described this force of nature in 1835), I designed these socks. I pictured an intrepid knitter wearing a pair while crossing the equator. At the moment he reached the imaginary dividing line, he could plant one foot in the northern hemisphere and one in the southern, each Coriolis band swirling in harmony with the forces of nature.

The Joys of Coriolis Architecture

- The basic architecture is so pure that you may not want to add stitch designs
- Hand-painted yarns throw their colors at an angle in the Coriolis band, looking stunning
- The band can spiral up the leg of knee socks

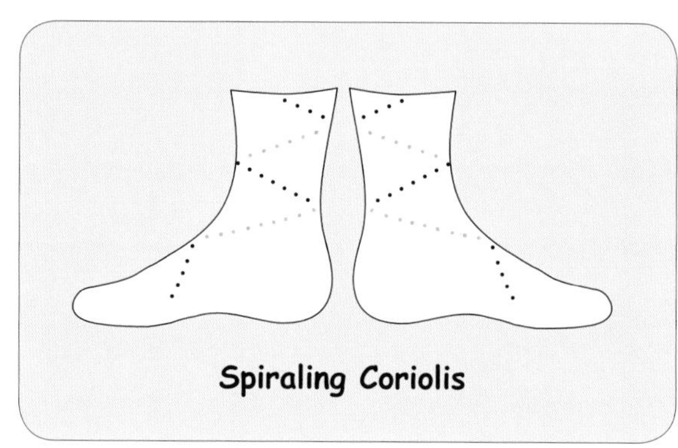
Spiraling Coriolis

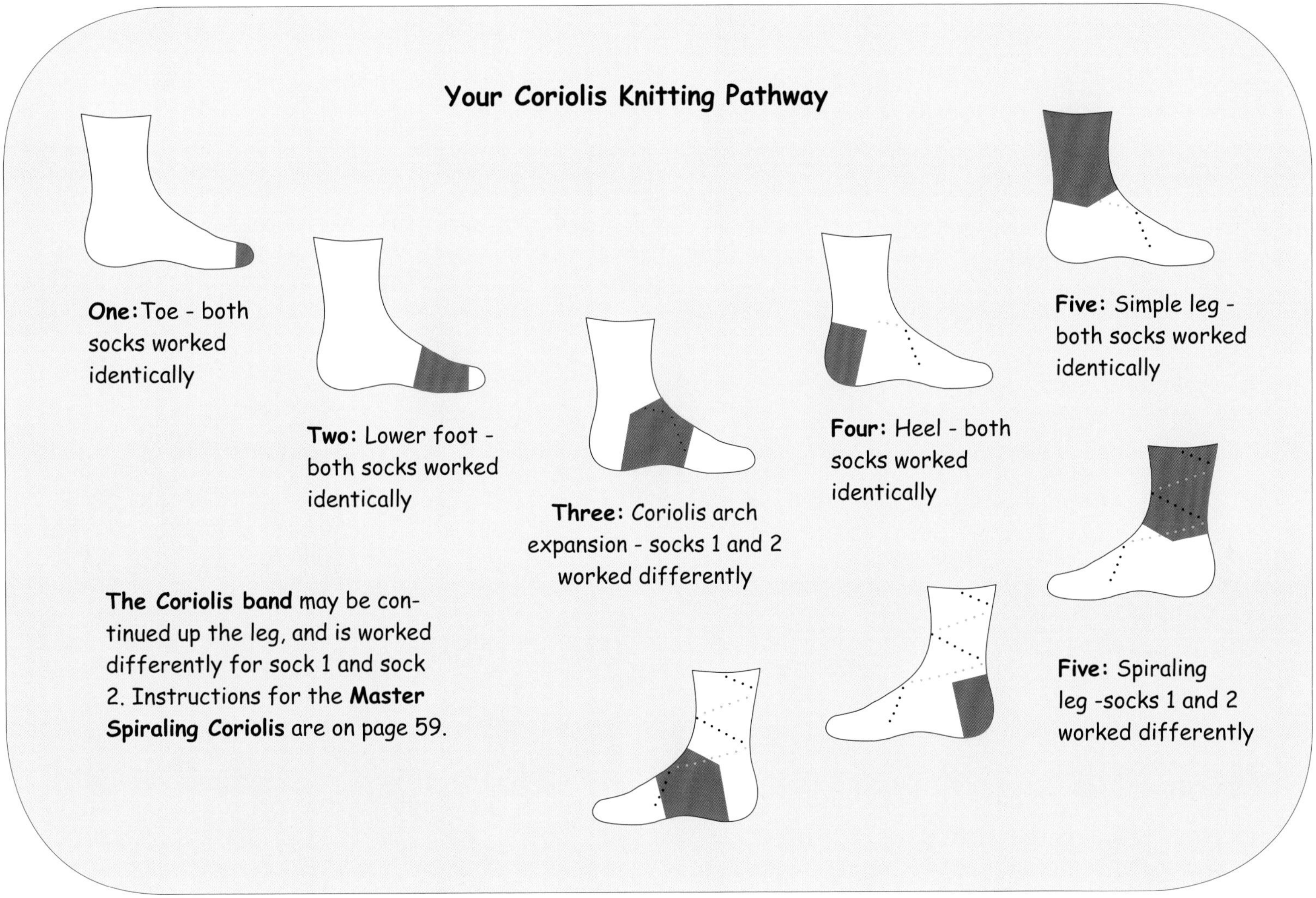

Your Coriolis Knitting Pathway

One: Toe - both socks worked identically

Two: Lower foot - both socks worked identically

Three: Coriolis arch expansion - socks 1 and 2 worked differently

Four: Heel - both socks worked identically

Five: Simple leg - both socks worked identically

Five: Spiraling leg -socks 1 and 2 worked differently

The Coriolis band may be continued up the leg, and is worked differently for sock 1 and sock 2. Instructions for the **Master Spiraling Coriolis** are on page 59.

I have since learned, to my dismay, that water goes down the drain the same way on both sides of the equator. Apparently the Coriolis Force is not strong enough to alter the direction of draining water. Like the weather systems that rotate counter-clockwise in the northern hemisphere and clockwise in the southern (in this case, the Coriolis Force is strong enough to be a real factor), these socks stack their "Coriolis Force" in a band of arch expansion that swirls either to the left or right across the instep, and on up the leg if you desire. Every round you *increase* on one side of the band, and every third round you *decrease* on the other side - resulting in our desired net gain of two increases every three rounds. Depending on which side the increases and decreases are worked, the band spirals to the left or to the right.

In this chapter you'll find several individual Coriolis designs. The variations are minor: a wider band, a unique cuff, and a child's sock spiffed up with dragon tails. Why haven't I gone farther afield? I think you'll discover the answer for yourself: the simple elegance of the basic design is so satisfying that any further adornment seems almost a shame. Still, you might consider these possibilities: a contrasting stitch pattern on the foot and leg above the Coriolis band, or a wider band with a colorful motif decorating its length like Swiss embroidered ribbon, or a criss-crossing of Coriolis bands - combining the mirror reflections in one sock (this would be easiest using the bubble trail method on page 65).

Tall Tibetan Coriolis

This version of the pattern on page 56 is finished with a strong and handsome bound edge, and the sizing is different (and so is the gauge). See page 56 for rest of pattern.

Yarn: Blue Moon Fiber Arts® Inc. Socks That Rock® Mediumweight (100% wool, 5.5 oz/ 380 yds), 1 skein Philosopher's Stone

Needles: size 2 (3 mm), or size you need to get gauge

Gauge: 7 sts = 1" (2.5 cm)

Size: midfoot 5.5 (6.5, 7.5, 8.5, 9.5, 10.5)" or 14 (16, 19, 21, 24, 26) cm

When leg is about 0.5" (1 cm) taller than desired height, bind off using double strand of yarn. Fold over edge to *outside* about 0.25" (.5 cm), and sew down loosely. Weave in all ends.

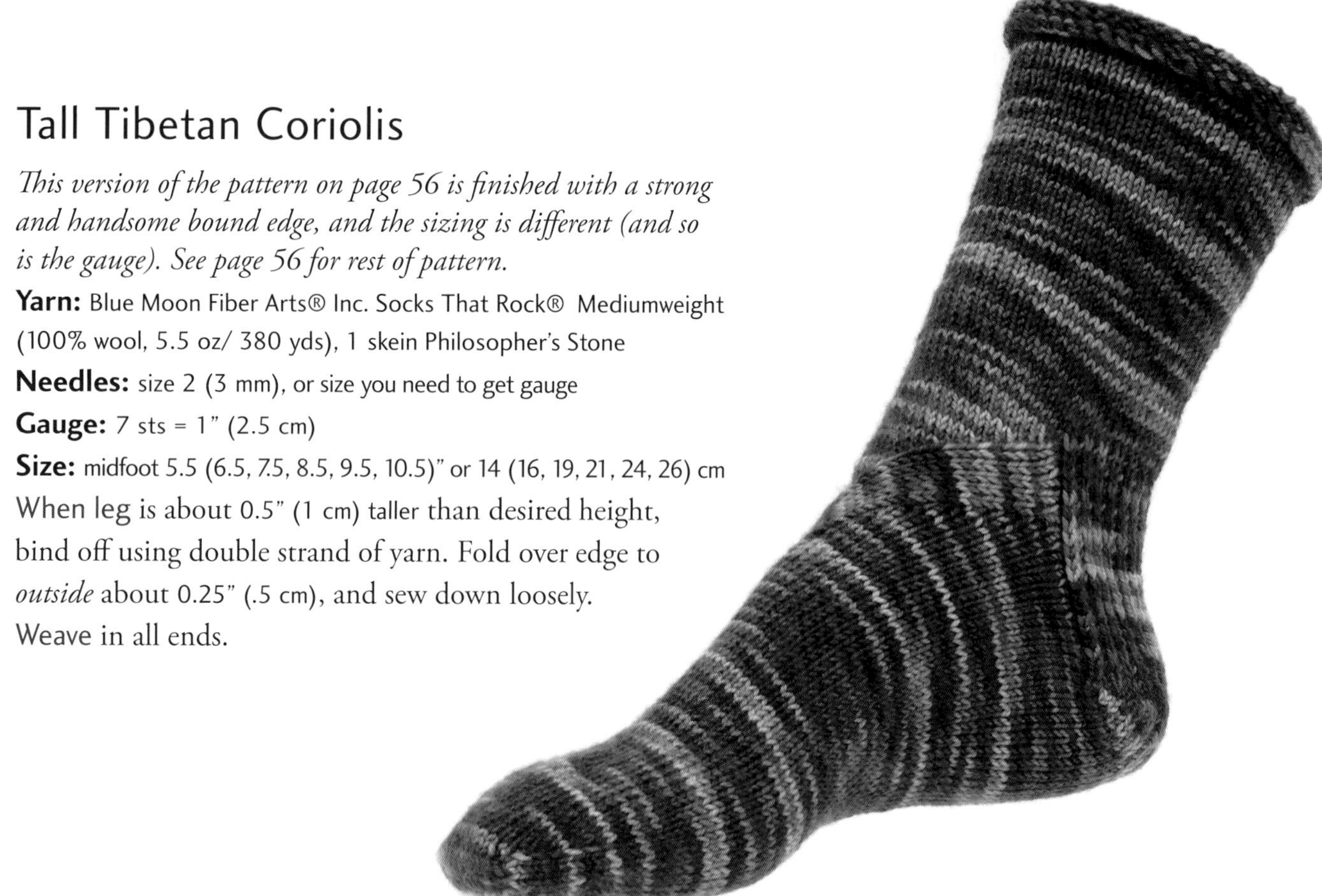

Spiraling Coriolis

I could knit just these socks forever and be perfectly happy.

Yarn: Fleece Artist Merino 2/6 (100% merino, 115 g / 325 m), 1 skein Jester, or Mountain Colors Bearfoot (60% superwash wool, 25% mohair, 15% nylon, 100 g/ 350 yds), 1 skein Juniper

Needles: two size 2 (3 mm), or size you need to get gauge

Gauge: 8.5 sts = 1" (2.5 cm) **Size:** your choice

Follow Spiraling Master Coriolis pattern on page 59.

Fleece Artist version has a purl ridge hem (when sock is tall enough, p 1 rnd, k about .75" or 2 cm, bind off loosely, fold to inside along purl ridge, and gently sew edge to inside.)

For cuff of Mountain Colors version: Rnd 1: Repeat **k1, p1**. Rnd 2: Repeat **p1, k1**. Repeat rnds 1 and 2 another 2x. Bind off with a double strand of yarn.

Fleece Artist Merino 2/6

Mountain Colors Bearfoot

Camel sense: avoid ladders between needles

Many sock knitters struggle with ladders - a loose column of stitches that appears at needle intersections. This problem is easily solved. Work the first stitch on the new needle without worrying about tension. This first stitch has just one hump of yarn, like a Dromedary camel. Even if you concentrate on snugging it up, once you begin the second stitch, the yarn relaxes. Don't worry. It's the second stitch

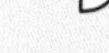

that matters. Work the second stitch, pulling the yarn firmly as you do. These two stitches now form two humps, like a Bactrian camel, and the dual waves work together to hold the tension. So use your camel sense and always give your second stitch a good tug to avoid ladders!

Charlie's Dragon Socks

The dragon tails either sleep peacefully around the leg, secured by a button in the back, or unfurl to fly behind the young dragon-child dashing lickitysplit through your home. If you are an adult longing to be a dragon, follow the Master Simple Coriolis pattern on page 57, add seed stitch cuffs, and make the tails longer by casting on 80 sts, then turning around 8 sts (instead of 5 sts) earlier every 2 rows (start row 3 with knit 72). *Add extra tail spikes, and you're ready to play!*

Yarn: Claudia Hand Painted Yarns Worsted (100% Superwash merino, 100 g/ 225 yds), 1 skein "Midnight," and Sport (100% Superwash merino, 100 g/ 168 yds), 1 skein "Chocolate Cherry"
Needles: size 6 (4 mm), or size you need to get gauge
Gauge: 5 sts = 1" (2.5 cm)
Sizes: midfoot 5 (5.5, 6, 6.5)" or 13 (14, 15, 16) cm
Notions: 2 buttons, size F (1.25 mm) crochet hook
Markers: A, B, C, and D

Toe

Make Whirlpool Toe (page 126), finishing with total st count (D) of 22 (24, 26, 30). When toe is at least 1.5" (3.5 cm) long, use D to determine length of toe section (page 112). Knit toe to this length.

Coriolis arch expansion

Instep is starting ndl (in left hand).
First Sock Companion Rounds
Place A 2 sts before end of instep.
Rnd 1: Knit until 2 sts before A, k2tog, k1f&b, k to end.
Rnds 2 and 3: Knit to A, k1f&b, k to end.
Second Sock Companion Rounds
Place B 2 sts after start of instep.
Rnd 1: Knit to 2 sts before B (*1st time, there are only 2 sts before* B) k1f&b, k1, ssk, k to end of rnd.
Rnds 2 and 3: Knit to 2 sts before B, k1f&b, k to end of rnd.
Both Socks: repeat companion rnds 1-3, stopping when total st count reaches 34 (36, 40, 44), after a completed rnd 3.

Place markers for instep and move wing stitches

First Sock: Move A 3 (2, 3, 1) sts to the *left* and place B 11 (12, 13, 15) sts to the *left* of A.
Second Sock: Move B 3 (2, 3, 1) sts to the *right* and place A 11 (12, 13, 15) sts to the *right* of B.
Both socks: Instep has 6 (6, 7, 7) wing sts before A and after B, with 11 (12, 13, 15) sts between A and B. Sole has 11 (12, 13, 15) sts.

Heel

Work reinforced heel (page 120), beginning with step 1. A and B are already in place. Use 11 (12, 13, 15) for G, 6 (6, 7, 7) for H, 2 (2, 3, 3) for J, and 3 (3, 3, 4) for I. Total sts after heel is finished: 22 (25, 26, 30)

Leg

Knit until leg is 1" (2.5 cm) shorter than desired height.
(2nd size only: Knit 1 rnd, working a k2tog somewhere - 24 sts total.)
Repeat **k1, p1* for 1 rnd, *then p1, k1* for 1 rnd* 5x. Bind off with EZ's sewn bind-off (page 130) and weave in all ends.

Abbreviations and a list of technique lessons can be found on pages 134-136.

Dragon tails (worked separately from sock)

Cast on 45 sts with Midnight. You will work short rows in stockinette, but no wrapping is necessary.
Rows 1: Knit, and 2: Purl.
Rows 3: Knit 40, turn, and 4: Slip 1, p to end.
Rows 5: Knit 35, turn, and 6: Slip 1, p to end.
Rows 7: Knit 30, turn, and 8: Slip 1, p to end.
Rows 9: Knit 25, turn, and 10: Slip 1, p to end.
Rows 11: Knit 20, turn, and 12: Slip 1, p to end.
Rows 13: Knit 15, turn, and 14: Slip 1, p to end.
Rows 15: Knit 10, turn, and 16: Slip 1, p to end.
Row 17: Knit to end. Cut Midnight, leaving 6" (15 cm) end to weave in later. With Chocolate Cherry, *knit* next 3 rows.

Tail Spikes *are worked 1 at a time, starting at wide end of tail and becoming smaller as they approach the narrow end.*
First spike: Knit 9, turn. Knit 2tog, k7, turn. Knit 2tog, k6, turn. Knit 2tog, k5, turn. Knit 2tog, k4, turn. Knit 2tog, k3, turn. Knit 2tog, k2, turn. Knit 2tog, k1, turn. Knit 2tog. Cut 6" (15 cm) end of yarn and weave in end.
Second and third spikes: Same routine as first spike *(k2tog at start of each row until only 1 st remains; cut tail and weave in end)*, but start with 8 sts instead of 9.
Fourth and fifth spikes: Start with 7 sts.
Sixth spike: Start with 6 sts.

Make button loop at tip of tail:
With Midnight and crochet hook, chain a small loop to fit button. Attach loop securely to tip of tail. If you like, knit additional Chocolate Cherry tail spike at very tip of tail, knitting partly onto button loop. Sew wide end of tail to sock (purl side showing), attaching rolled base to end of Coriolis band and sewing edge up to base of first tail spike. Sew button to center back of cuff. Tail should wrap around the leg in same direction as Coriolis band.

Tibetan Socks

This Coriolis sock has a wider band and evokes the strength and spiritual beauty of traditional Tibetan garments. The doubled strand of Trekking - with the colors not lined up - blends the colorway to produce a beautiful hand-painted effect.

Yarn: Zitron Trekking XXL (75% wool, 25% nylon, 100 g / 459 yds), 1 (2 for 3 largest sizes) skein color 108
Needles: size 5 (3.75 mm), or size you need to get gauge
Gauge: (double-stranded) 6 sts = 1" (2.5 cm)
Size: midfoot 6.5 (7.5, 8.5, 9.5, 10.5, 11.5)" or 16 (19, 21, 24, 26, 29) cm
Markers: A, B, C, and D
Instep is starting ndl (in left hand).

Toe

Make Standard Toe (page 126), casting on 7 (8, 10, 11, 12, 13) sts to each parallel ndl, and completing toe with a total st count (D) of 34 (40, 44, 50, 56, 62) sts. When toe is about 2" (5 cm) long, use D to determine length of toe section (page 112). Knit toe to this length.

Coriolis arch expansion

First sock set-up: Place A 5 sts before end of instep.

First sock companion rounds

Rnd 1: Knit until 2 sts before A, k2tog, k 3, k1f&b, k to end.

Rnds 2 and 3: Knit to 3 sts past A, k1f&b, k to end.

Second sock set-up: Place B 5 sts after start of instep.

Second sock companion rounds

Rnd 1: (*1st time, there are only 5 sts before* B) Knit to 5 sts before B, k1f&b, k4, ssk, k to end of rnd.

Rnds 2 and 3: Knit to 5 sts before B, k1f&b, k to end of rnd.

Both socks: Repeat appropriate companion rnds 1-3, stopping when total st count reaches 52 (60, 66, 74, 84, 92), after a completed rnd 3.

Place markers for instep

First sock: Move A 6 (5, 5, 4, 5, 4) sts to the *left*. Place B 17 (20, 22, 25, 28, 31) sts to the *left* of A. Second sock: Move B 6 (5, 5, 4, 5, 4) sts to the *right*. Place A 17 (20, 22, 25, 28, 31) sts to the *right* of B.

Heel

Work reinforced heel (page 120), beginning with step 1. A and B are already in place. Use 17 (20, 22, 25, 28, 31) for G, 9 (10, 11, 12, 14, 15) for H, 3 (4, 4, 5, 5, 6) for J, and 5 (6, 6, 7, 8, 9) for I. Total sts after heel is finished: 34 (41, 45, 50, 57, 62)

Leg and cuff

Knit 4 rnds. If total st count is odd, work 1 LRinc somewhere during 4th rnd. Purl 4 rnds. Repeat **k1, p1** for 2 rnds. Repeat **p1, k1** for 2 rnds. Repeat **k1, p1** for 2 rnds. Knit 6 rnds. Bind off with EZ's sewn bind-off (page 130) and weave in all ends.

Coriolis Master Patterns

Master numbers are on pages 109-119.

Markers: A, B, C and D (add E for Spiraling Coriolis)

The Simple Master Coriolis's *band crosses the instep and ends beside the ankle.* The Spiraling Master Coriolis's *band crosses the instep, passes the heel without a collision, and spirals up the leg. For all Corioli, mirroring versions (first sock and second sock) are given.*

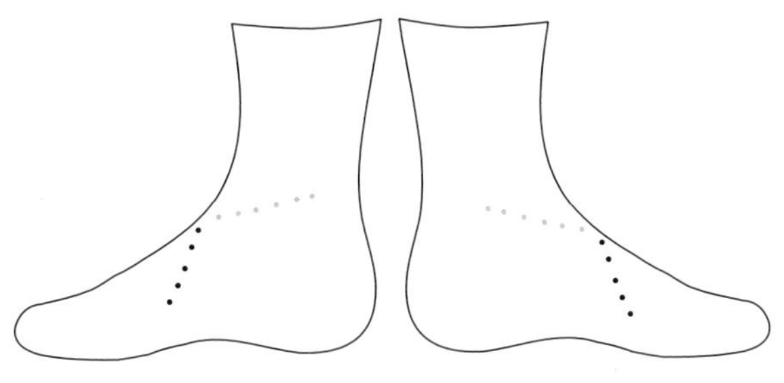

Simple Master Coriolis

Complete any toe (page 126). Knit toe **E** inches long.

Coriolis arch expansion - picture ①
Instep is starting ndl (in left hand).
First Sock Companion Rounds
Place A 2 sts before end of instep.
Rnd 1: Knit until 2 sts before A, k2tog, k1f&b, k to end.
Rnds 2 and 3: Knit to A, k1f&b, k to end.
Second Sock Companion Rounds
Place B 2 sts after start of instep.
Rnd 1: Knit to 2 sts before B *(1st time, there are only 2 sts before* B) k1f&b, k1, ssk, k to end of rnd.
Rnds 2 and 3: Knit to 2 sts before B, k1f&b, k to end of rnd.
Both socks: Repeat appropriate companion rnds 1-3, stopping when total st count reaches **F**, after a completed rnd 3.

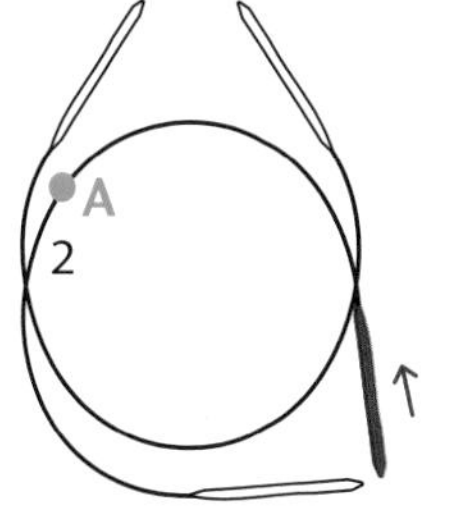

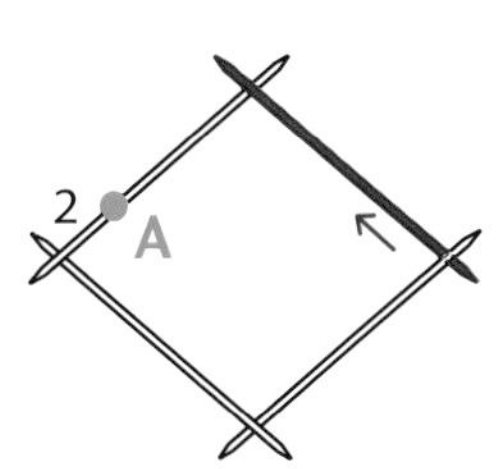

① First sock *(above)*: Place A 2 sts before end of instep.
Second sock *(below)*: Place B 2 sts after start of instep.

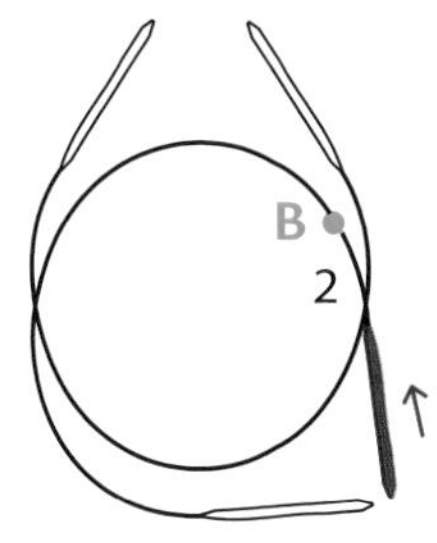

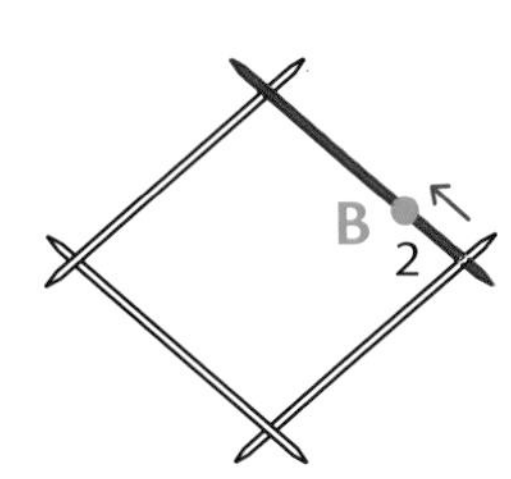

Abbreviations and a list of technique lessons can be found on pages 134-136.

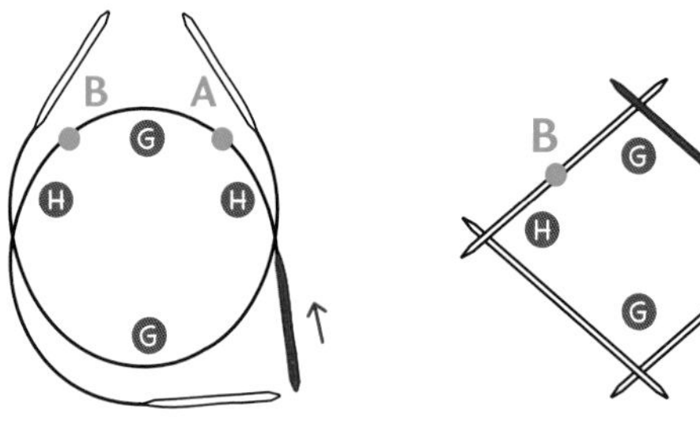

② Instep marker placement for both socks.

Place markers for instep - picture ②

First sock: Move A 4 sts to the *left*. Place B Ⓖ sts to the *left* of A.
Second sock: Move B 4 sts to the *right*. Place A Ⓖ sts to the *right* of B.
Both socks: Shift sts between sole and instep so there are Ⓗ sts before A and Ⓗ sts following B on the instep. (Sole holds remaining Ⓖ sts.) If the yarn is not coming from intersection between start of instep and end of sole, unknit or knit sts so it does come from this intersection.

Begin heel with step 1 (page 120). A and B are already in place.

Knit leg, then finish with cuff (page 130) of your choice.

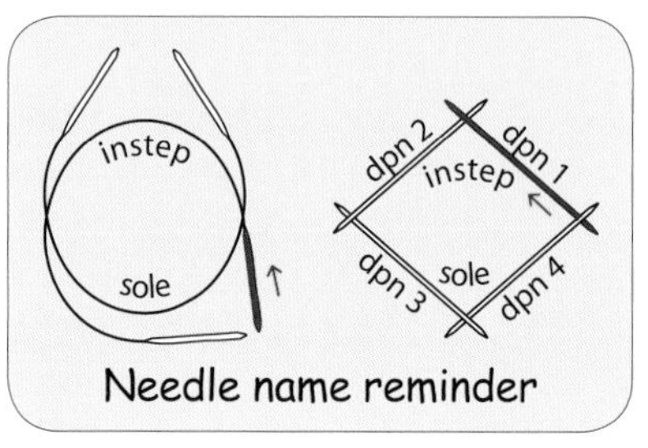

Widening a simple Coriolis band

You can widen the Simple Master Coriolis band from the basic 2 stitch width to as much as about 20% of the midfoot stitch count (Ⓓ). For the first sock, add stitches immediately after A. For the second sock, add stitches immediately before B.

Before placing markers for the instep and moving A or B, add the number of extra stitches to 4 (the number of stitches each marker is normally moved). Thus, if you added 5 stitches, then 4 + 5 = 9, so you would move A or B 9 stitches instead of 4.

Spiraling Master Coriolis, Fleece Artist Merino 2/6, see page 59.

Spiraling Master Coriolis

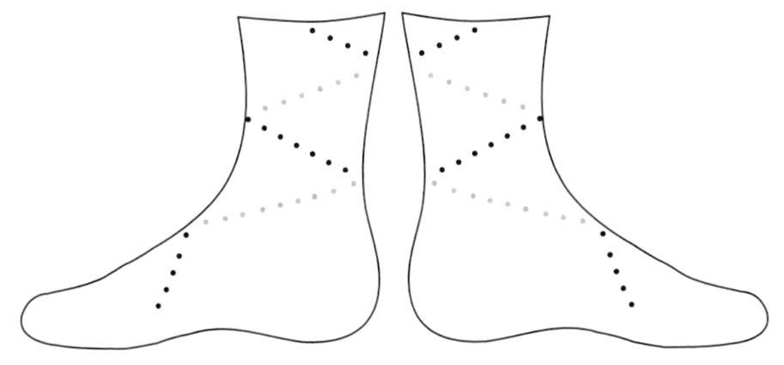

Make a Whirlpool Toe (page 126), ending with **D** sts. *(This toe can be rotated freely, allowing the Coriolis band to pass above the heel.)*
Knit until toe measures **E** inches long.

Coriolis arch expansion
Instep is starting ndl (in left hand).
Follow instructions for Simple Coriolis Master Pattern. On final arch expansion rnd, replace A with E *(first sock)* or B with E *(second sock).*

Place markers for instep - picture ③
First sock: Place A 3 sts to the *right* of E. Move B **G** sts to the *left* of A.
Second sock: Place B 3 sts to the *left* of E. Move A **G** sts to the *right* of B.
Both socks: Shift sts between sole and instep so there are **H** sts before A and **H** sts following B on the instep. (Sole holds remaining **G** sts.) Now the yarn is temporarily inaccessible - not at the intersection between start of instep and end of sole - so unknit or knit sts until it is at this intersection.

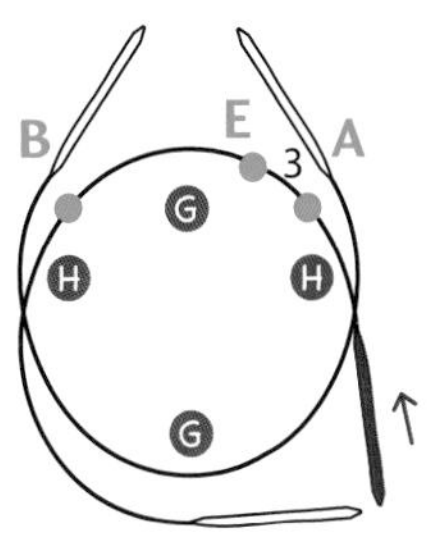

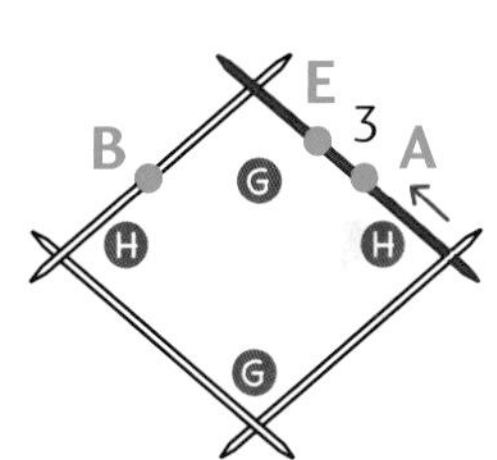

③ First sock *(above)*: Place A 3 sts to the right of E.
Second sock *(below)*: Place B 3 sts to the left of E.

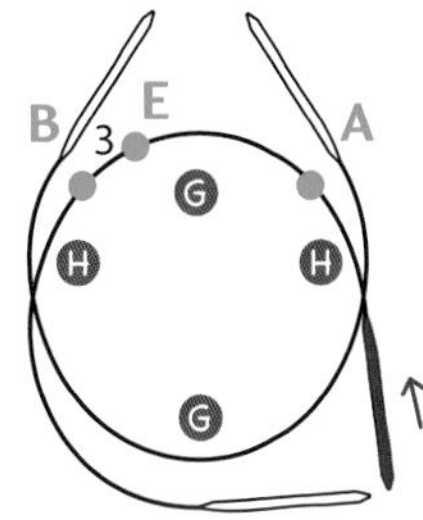

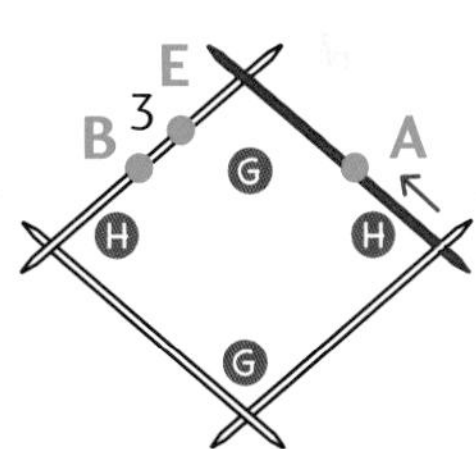

Heel
Begin heel with step 1 (page 120). A and B are already in place.
From now on until leg is done, each time you find yourself 2 sts before E, *(first sock)* k2tog, k1f&b, and continue knitting, or *(second sock)* k1f&b, k1, ssk, and continue knitting.

Leg
As knitting progresses, shift sts from ndl to ndl as necessary so you have easy access to the sts needed to work the band.
Optional: To widen the leg as it grows upward, occasionally *skip a decrease* (the ssk or k2tog). Each time you do so, you add 1 st. Just think - you could make knee socks, even tights!

Finish with cuff of your choice (page 130).

Abbreviations and a list of technique lessons can be found on pages 134-136.

Chapter 5 - Foxglove Sock Architecture

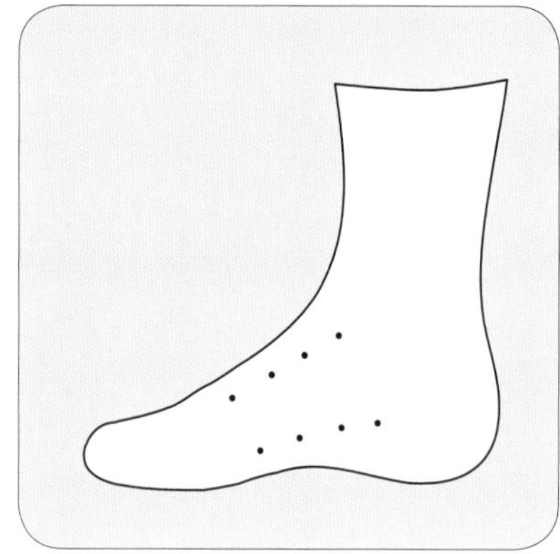

The Foxglove is a very relaxing style of sock architecture to knit. The other styles organize your increases for you (except for Cedar, which is a relative of Foxglove), but this one leaves it all up to you. You're free to be as random or methodical as you like. In a nutshell, you may distribute your increases anywhere you like within the arch increase section, as long as they average two every three rounds. Anywhere really does mean *anywhere*. The increases could follow one another in a line, be distributed methodically – or – added as the whim strikes you. You may confine them to the instep, to the sole, or spread them all around. You are free.

The Joys of Foxglove Architecture

- The increases may be distributed in any way: randomly, in lines, or concentrated in chosen areas
- This is the ideal architecture if you want freedom to place designs on a toe-up sock. Reserve the design space, and work all increases in the remaining area
- Learn this pathway and you're ready for Cedar architecture (a top-down relative of Foxglove)

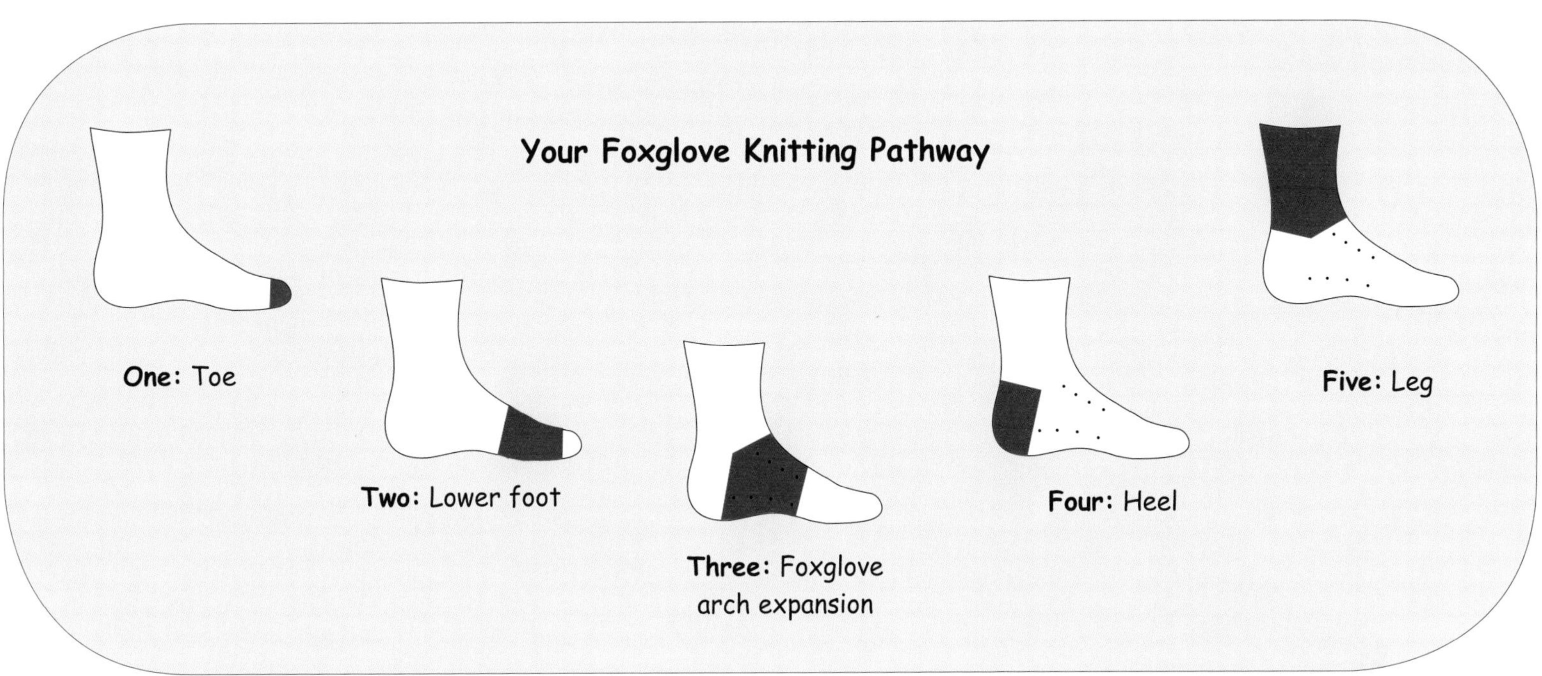

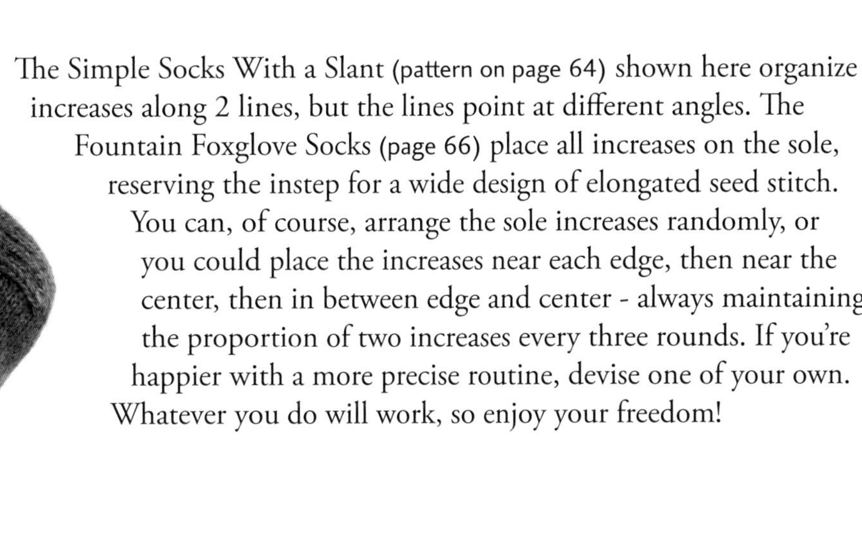

The Simple Socks With a Slant (pattern on page 64) shown here organize increases along 2 lines, but the lines point at different angles. The Fountain Foxglove Socks (page 66) place all increases on the sole, reserving the instep for a wide design of elongated seed stitch. You can, of course, arrange the sole increases randomly, or you could place the increases near each edge, then near the center, then in between edge and center - always maintaining the proportion of two increases every three rounds. If you're happier with a more precise routine, devise one of your own. Whatever you do will work, so enjoy your freedom!

Marcelo's Seven-League Boots

This dashing pair of socks was designed for a dear young man, Marcelo Loring Jones. His doting grandmother, Susan Druding, is the matriarch of a fiber Shangri-la, one of the oldest fiber businesses in North America - Crystal Palace Yarn, formerly Straw Into Gold, in California. Marcelo was the first "yarn baby" to come to my attention when I began designing baby socks for this book. Marcelo's Seven-League Boots are knit with Grandma Susan's excellent Panda Wool, and the swashbuckling style makes them a fine choice for rainy day pirating in a boat fashioned of blankets, skeins of yarn (sailing cordage) and overturned chairs.

Yarn: Crystal Palace Panda Wool (46% bamboo, 43% wool, 11% nylon, 50 g / 170 yds), 2 balls Vine Green

Needles: (with double strand - sock is knit double-stranded) 5 (3.75 mm), or size you need to get gauge

Gauge: 6 sts = 1" (2.5 cm)

Finished size: midfoot 4 (5, 6, 7)" or 10 (13, 15, 18) cm

Markers: A, B, C, and D

Garter Stitch Toe

Make Garter Stitch Toe (page 127), casting on 6 (7, 8, 9) sts to each parallel ndl, and finishing with total st count (D) of 24 (28, 32, 36). Knit all rnds for 1" (2.5 cm). Use D to determine length of toe section (page 112). Knit toe to this length.

Next circ or next 2 dpn's are instep.

Arch expansion - picture ①

Place A after 4 (4, 5, 6) sts and B 4 (6, 6, 6) sts after A on *instep*. Repeat on *sole* with C and D.

Companion Rounds:

Increases are worked at start of instep and sole, or right after markers.

Rnd 1: LRinc, k to end of *instep*, LRinc, k to end.

Rnds 2-3, 5-6, and 8-9: Knit.

Rnd 4: Knit to A, LRinc, k to C, LRinc, k to end.

Rnd 7: Knit to B, LRinc, k to D, LRinc, k to end.

Repeat companion rnds 1-9, stopping after a completed rnd 1, 4, or 7, when total stitch count reaches 36 (42, 48, 54). Remove A, B, C, and D. Knit 6 (7, 8, 9), place A, k 12 (14, 16, 18), place B, k 6 (7, 8, 9) sts from sole onto instep, and stop. Total instep sts: 24 (28, 32, 36) and sole sts: 12 (14, 16, 18). See picture ①.

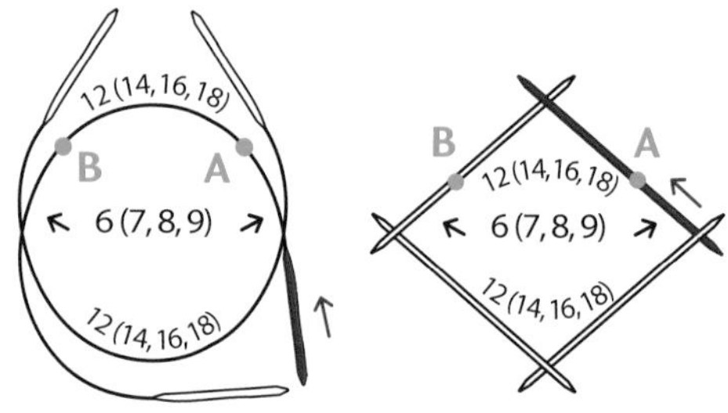

① Stitch distribution at end of arch expansion.

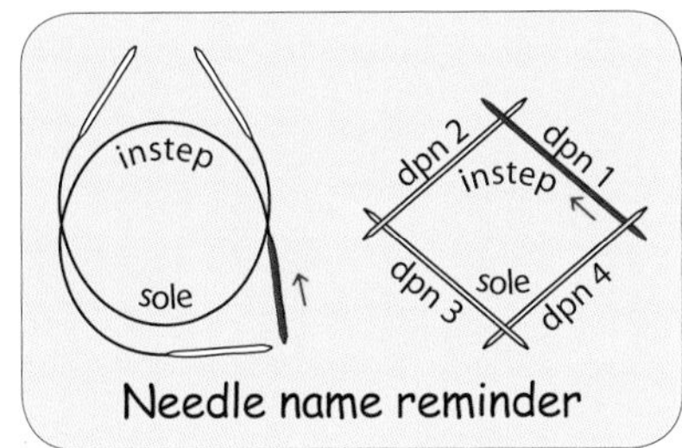

Heel

If using dpn's, put all sole sts on 1 ndl.

Work plain heel (page 122), beginning with step 3 (A and B are already in place), use 3 (4, 4, 5) for Ⓘ, ignore Ⓙ, and 6 (7, 8, 9) for Ⓗ. Continue through step 4 only.

Return here for Step 5:

Row 1: (RS) Slip 1, k until 1 st before C, p2tog, removing C, turn.

Row 2: (WS) Slip 1, k until 1 st before gap, k2tog, turn.

Heel companion rows:

Row 3: (RS) Slip 1, k until 1 st before gap, p2tog, turn.

Row 4: (WS) Slip 1, k until 1 st before gap, k2tog, turn.

Repeat companion rows 3-4 until only 2 sts rem on outer sides of gaps. (RS) Slip 1, k until 1 st before gap, p2tog, k1. *Resume knitting in the round.* (instep) Knit to end of instep. (sole) Knit 1, k2tog, p until 1 st rem on sole, k1. *Instep is now starting needle.* Total sts after heel is finished: 24 (28, 32, 36)

Leg and cuff

Knit for 1" (2.5 cm).

Rnd 1: (instep) Knit 5 (6, 7, 8), k1f&b, k to end of instep, LLinc, (sole) k5 (6, 7, 8), k1f&b, k to end, LLinc.

Rnds 2, 4, 6, and 8: Knit.

Rnd 3: Knit 5 (6, 7, 8), k1f&b, place A, k1f&b, k to end.

Rnds 5 and 7: Knit to 1 st before A, k1f&b, (A), k1f&b, k to end. Total sts: 34 (38, 42, 46)

Leg Shaping Companion Rounds:

Rnd 9: Knit 2tog, k to 1 st before A, k1f&b, (A), k1f&b, k until 2 *instep* sts rem, ssk, k to end.

Rnd 10: Knit.

Repeat companion rnds 9-10 another 3 (3, 4, 4) times.

Next rnd: Purl to 1 st before A, p1b&f, (A), p1b&f, p to end. Total sts: 36 (40, 44, 48) Remove A. Repeat **k 1 rnd, p 1 rnd** 2x. Bind off loosely and weave in all ends.

Abbreviations and a list of technique lessons can be found on pages 134-136.

Simple Socks with a Slant

This mirrored pair of asymmetric socks are quick and easy to make. See the acorn panel on page 65 for an invitation to trace any sock architecture with "bubble trails." The yarn is used double-stranded, with color changes not lined up, which results in a unique and vibrant blend of the beautiful colorways.

Abbreviations and a list of technique lessons can be found on pages 134-136.

Yarn: Trekking XXL (75% wool, 25% nylon, 100 g / 420 m), 1 ball color 110 *(or 2 balls for 2 largest sizes)*

Needles: 6 (4 mm), or size you need to get gauge

Gauge: (using double strand of yarn) 6 sts = 1" (2.5 cm)

Sizes: midfoot 6 (7, 8, 9, 10)" or 15 (18, 20, 23, 25) cm

Markers: A, B, C and D

Toe

Make Standard Toe (page 126), casting on 6 (7, 9, 10, 13) sts to each parallel ndl, and finishing with total st count (Ⓓ) of 32 (38, 42, 48, 54). When toe is about 2" (5 cm) long, use Ⓓ to determine length of toe section (page 112). Knit toe to this length. Place A 5 (6, 7, 8, 9) sts after start of instep and B 5 (6, 7, 8, 9) sts after A.

Instep is starting ndl - ndl in left hand.

Arch expansion

Companion Rounds:

Rnd 1: Knit to A, yo before passing A, k to B, yo before passing B, k to end. *(Rnd 1 for second sock: Knit to A, yo after A, k to B, yo after B, k to end.)*

Rnds 2-3: Knit.

Repeat companion rnds 1-3, stopping after a completed rnd 3 when total stitch count reaches 48 (56, 62, 72, 80).

Total instep sts: 32 (37, 41, 48, 53) and sole sts: 16 (19, 21, 24, 27). Remove A and B, then place A 8 (9, 10, 12, 13) sts *after start of instep* and B 8 (9, 10, 12, 13) sts *before end of instep.*

Heel

Work reinforced heel (page 120), starting at step 1. A and B are already in place. Use 16 (19, 21, 24, 27) for Ⓖ, 8 (9, 10, 12, 13) for Ⓗ, 3 (4, 4, 5, 5) for Ⓙ, and 4 (5, 6, 7, 8) for Ⓘ. Total sts after heel is finished: 33 (38, 42, 49, 54)

Leg and cuff

Knit rnds until leg needs only 2.5" (6 cm) more length to suit you, working 0 (1, 0, 2, 0) evenly distributed LRinc's during these rnds. Total sts: 33 (39, 42, 51, 54). Work k2, p1 ribbing for 2" (5 cm). Next rnd: Repeat *k1f&b, k1, p1* to end. Repeat this rnd twice more. Bind off loosely and weave in all ends.

Yarn-over "Bubble Trails"

Like a trail of bubbles, yarn-over (yo) eyelets lead the eye along two different angles in the Simple Socks with a Slant design to the left. The second sock in the pair is made to mirror the first - a matched and unique asymmetrical pair. Bubble trails may be used in any styles of sock architecture (although Riverbed seems inadvisable - eyelet holes on the sole don't make much sense).

For all Master Patterns except the Coriolis, just replace each LRinc or LLinc with a yarn-over. For Coriolis architecture, replace each k1f&b with a yarn-over.

If you'd like to explore what happens with yarn-overs, here are some elements to play around with:

If you work all yarn-overs in front of a marker, the expansion will spread to the right of the marker and the bubble trail will lean to the left. The marker keeps your line very clean without any need to count. Conversely, if you work all yarn-overs after the marker, the expansion will spread to the left and the trail leans to the right. The only "rule" is to make 2 increases every 3 rounds. You can combine different directions of spread, or change course partway - you're the designer!

To form a trail of expanding yarn-over's without the line leaning in either direction, and growth spreading on both sides, try working a yarn-over to the right of the marker on the first increase round, then to the left on the next one, and so on. The yarn-over bubble trail will dance slightly side to side, and your marker will keep you on track - no need to count.

The Eyelet Anklet to the right has yarn-overs worked before A and after B, with a non-increasing trail of dancing bubbles in between (each yarn-over is paired with a decrease, first an ssk, then next time, a k2tog).

Unsure? Swatch these ideas to see for yourself how bubble trails move, then try them in a sock.

Upstream Master Pattern (page 79), worked "bubble-style" in Trekking XXL, color 77

Home & Hearth Eyelet Anklet (see page 93 for pattern), Ridgeline architecture

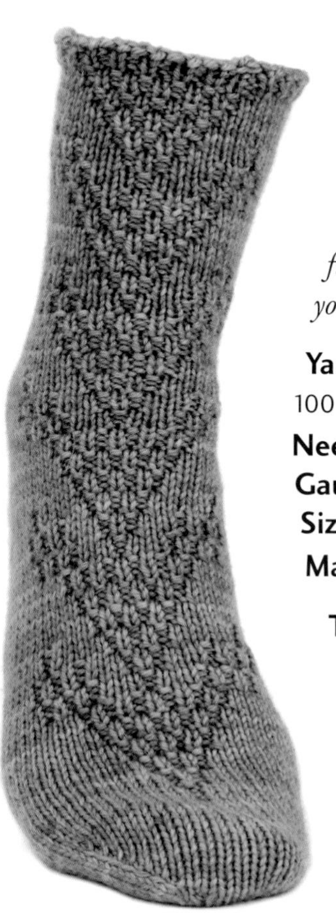

Fountain Foxgloves

These easy socks display a knit and purl design from toe to cuff, with the increases worked anywhere you'd like to put them on the sides and sole.

Yarn: Mountain Colors 4/8's Wool (100% wool, 100 g / 250 yds), 1 skein Northwind

Needles: 3 (3.25 mm), or size you need to get gauge

Gauge: 6.5 sts = 1" (2.5 cm)

Sizes: midfoot 7.5 (8.75, 10)" or 19 (22, 25) cm

Markers: A, B, C and D

Toe

Make Standard Toe (page 126), casting on 7 (7, 9) sts to each parallel ndl, and finishing with total st count (D) of 42 (50, 58). Begin 19-st Fountain Panel, centering it on instep and continuing up leg. When toe is about 2" (5 cm) long, use D to determine length of toe section (page 112). Knit toe to this length.

Arch expansion

Instep is starting ndl (ndl in left hand).

Companion Rounds:

Rnd 1: Work panel on instep as established and k all other sts, including 2 LRinc's *anywhere* (really - it works!) on sole.

Rnds 2-3: Knit.

Each line of the chart represents 3 rounds. After completing rnds 1-27, repeat blue-boxed rnds only.

	•						•		•		•						•		25-27
•		•		•				•		•				•		•		•	22-24
	•		•		•				•				•		•		•		19-21
				•		•		•		•		•		•					16-18
					•		•		•		•		•						13-15
						•		•		•		•							10-12
							•		•		•								7-9
								•		•									4-6
									•										1-3

□ k

• p

Repeat companion rnds 1-3, stopping after a completed rnd 1 when total stitch count reaches 64 (76, 88). Knit to end of instep, k11 (13, 15) *from sole onto instep*, then k until 11 (13, 15) sts remain on sole. Transfer these 11 (13, 15) unworked sts to adjacent end of instep. Total instep sts: 43 (51, 59) and sole sts: 21 (25, 29).

Heel

Work reinforced heel (page 120), beginning with step 1, using 21 (25, 29) for G, 11 (13, 15) for H, 4 (5, 6) for J, and 6 (7, 8) for I. Total sts after heel is finished: 42 (50, 58).

Leg and cuff

Continue fountain panel on instep. When leg is nearly desired length after a completed panel rnd 12, 15, 18, 21, 24, or 27, k to 1 st before next p, place A to mark new start of rnd, repeat **p1, k1** to end. Repeat last rnd twice more. Bind off loosely and weave in all ends.

Foxglove Master Pattern

Master numbers are on pages 109-119.

Markers: A, B, C and D

The Foxglove arch expansion directions below organize your increases for you, but you may distribute the 2 increases per 3 rounds anywhere you like around the foot within the arch expansion area.

Complete any toe (page 126). Knit toe E inches long.

Foxglove arch expansion - picture ①
Instep is starting ndl (ndl in left hand).
Divide instep sts into approximate thirds. Place A after one third and B after two thirds of instep sts. Repeat on sole, using C and D.

Companion Rounds:
Increases are worked at start of instep and sole, or right after markers.

Rnd 1: LRinc at start of instep and sole, k to end.
Rnds 2-3, 5-6, and 8-9: Knit.
Rnd 4: LRinc right after A and C, k to end.
Rnd 7: LRinc right after B and D, k to end.

Repeat companion rnds, stopping after a completed rnd 1, 4, or 7, when total stitch count reaches F. Remove markers.

Complete heel (page 120), leg, and cuff (page 130).

Abbreviations and a list of technique lessons can be found on pages 134-136.

Foxglove Master Pattern, Fleece Artist Sea Wool (115 g/ 350 m, 70% merino, 30% Seacell®), 1 skein "Seashore," with short sections of ribbing on the leg and several rounds of purl before binding off.

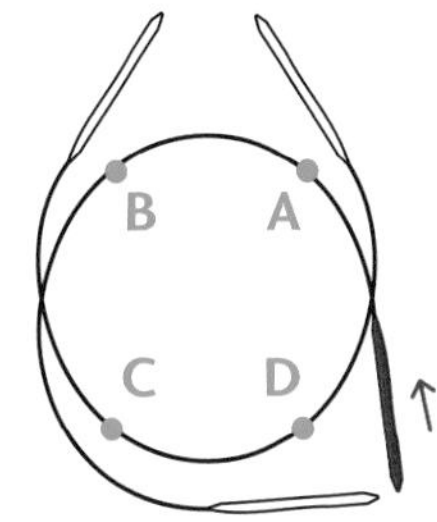

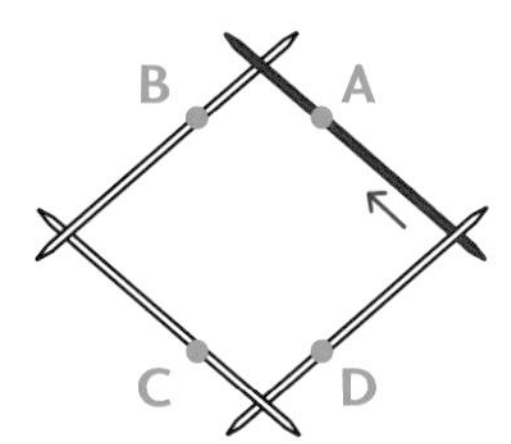

① Instep and sole are divided into thirds. Increases cycle between the start of instep and sole (rnd 1), A and C (rnd 4), and finally B and D (rnd 7).

Chapter 6 - Upstream Sock Architecture

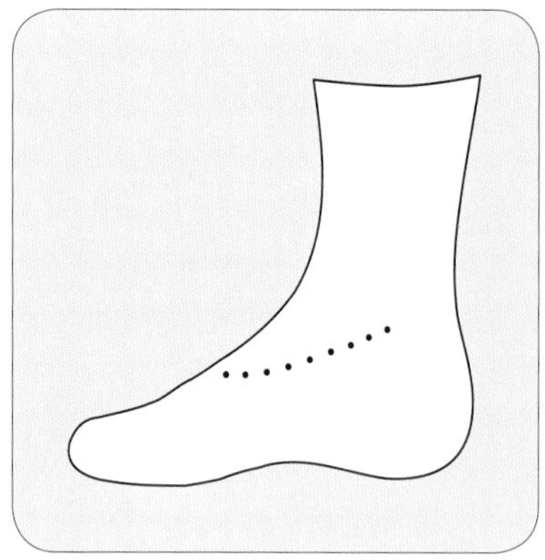

The Upstream architecture was the first new approach to occur to me, over six years ago, and is the acorn that slowly grew into this oak tree of a book (which, in your clever hands, may branch out into still more architectures). My original thought was, why not slide the traditional triangular gussets from the sides of the ankle up to meet one another as a larger triangle on the top of the instep? I fiddled around and came up with a stitch pattern that expanded at exactly the rate I thought was needed. To my surprise, not only did the sock fit perfectly, but the stitch pattern I'd devised turned out to be reversible - that is, both sides looked distinctive yet beautiful. That sock, the "Forerunner," will appear in Anne Claxon's *Inside Outside - You Decide*, to be published by School House Press, a reversible stitch dictionary (hurrah! - I've always wished for one) which will also include a collection of reversible knitting designs.

The Joys of Upstream Sockitecture

- The increases truly reflect your foot's shape
- It welcomes expanding stitch patterns
- Sides of foot remain free for designs
- Learn this pathway and you're ready for Riverbed, Sidestream, and Ridgeline architectures

Upstream Master Pattern (page 79), Lana Grossa Meilenweit Multieffekt, (100 g/ 420 m, 80% wool, 20% nylon) color 3010. The cuff is a k1, p1 rib, with several knit rnds at the top, which rolls to the outside.

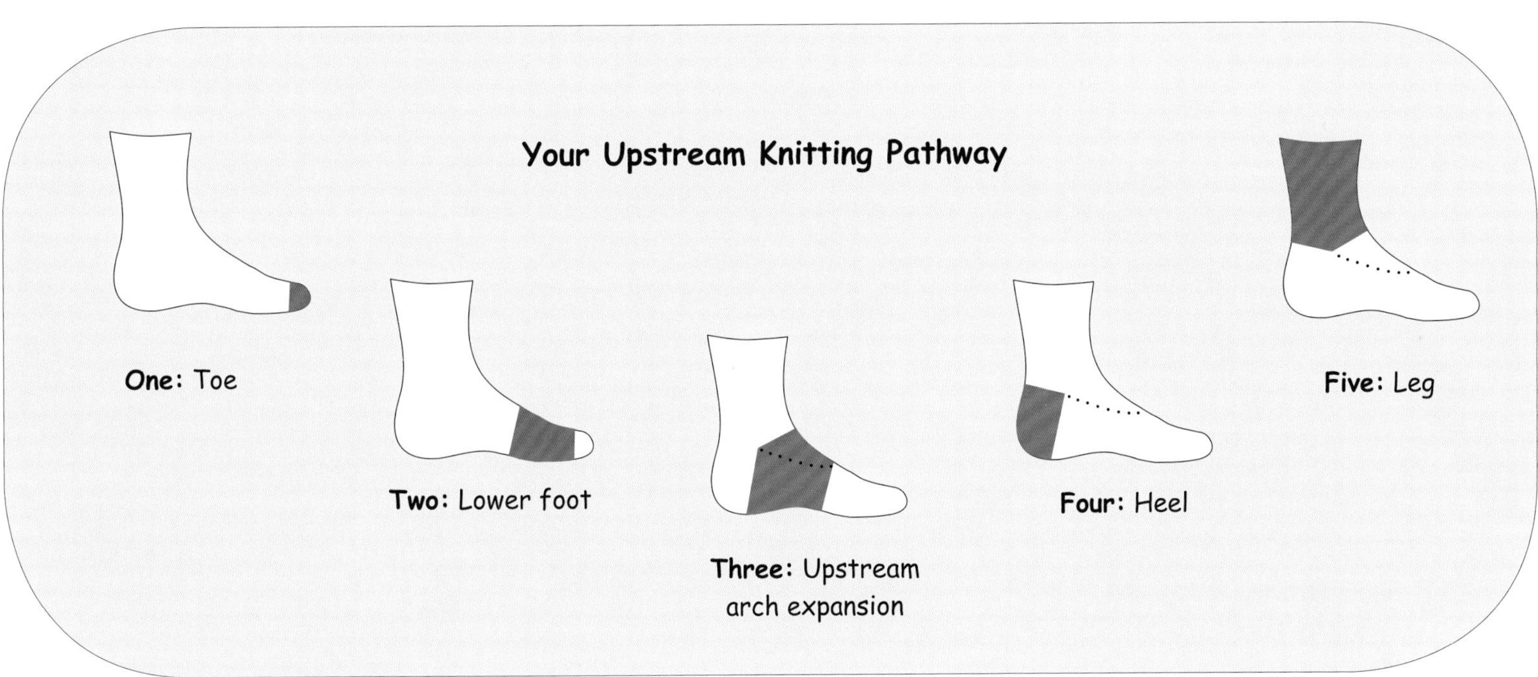

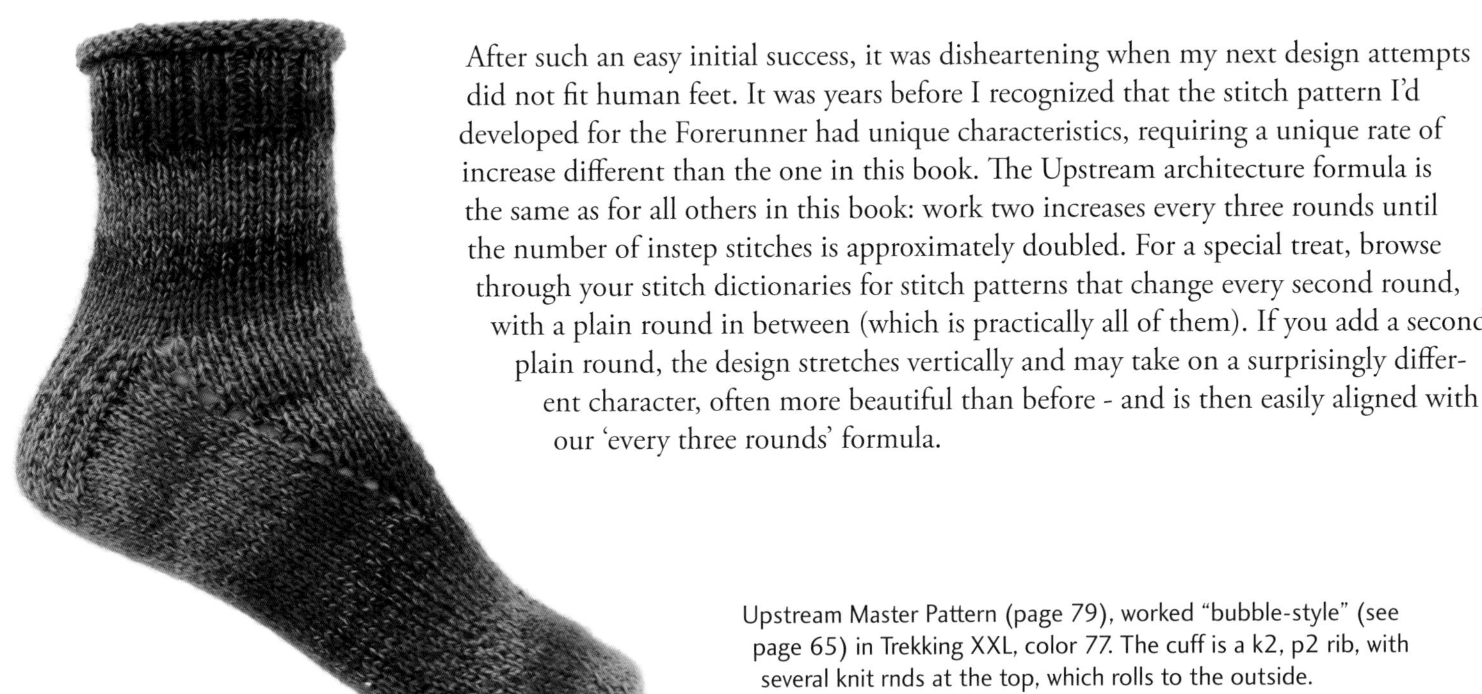

After such an easy initial success, it was disheartening when my next design attempts did not fit human feet. It was years before I recognized that the stitch pattern I'd developed for the Forerunner had unique characteristics, requiring a unique rate of increase different than the one in this book. The Upstream architecture formula is the same as for all others in this book: work two increases every three rounds until the number of instep stitches is approximately doubled. For a special treat, browse through your stitch dictionaries for stitch patterns that change every second round, with a plain round in between (which is practically all of them). If you add a second plain round, the design stretches vertically and may take on a surprisingly different character, often more beautiful than before - and is then easily aligned with our 'every three rounds' formula.

Upstream Master Pattern (page 79), worked "bubble-style" (see page 65) in Trekking XXL, color 77. The cuff is a k2, p2 rib, with several knit rnds at the top, which rolls to the outside.

Etta Mae's Baby Bootikins

This sweet bootikin was designed for Jana Dempsey's (Handmaiden Fine Yarn, Vancouver, British Columbia) baby daughter, Etta Mae. Little Etta Mae has already spent the first year of her life wearing sumptuously dyed hand-knit luxury fibers - and is known as the mini-maiden. This pink cashmere is knit together with the main yarn, with short ends cut after each round. This makes the knitting simple, and caresses a baby's foot with cashmere whispers, as they deserve.

Yarn: Fleece Artist Kid Aran (50% Kid Mohair, 50% Wool, 250 g/ 400 m), 1 skein "Natural", and Handmaiden Cashmere 4-ply (100% cashmere, 50 g/ 170 m), 1 skein "Lily Pond"

Needles: 2 size 6 (4 mm), or size you need to get gauge

Gauge: (with Kid Aran) 5 sts = 1" (2.5 cm)

Size: 6-9 mos (midfoot 5" or 13 cm, foot length also 5" or 13 cm)

Markers: A, B, C, and D

Toe

Make Whirlpool Toe (page 126), finishing with a total st count of 24 . Knit until toe measures 1" (2.5 cm) long.

Arch expansion - picture ①

Instep is starting ndl (ndl in left hand).

Work all sts between A and B *with both yarns held together,* cutting short tails of cashmere after each rnd. The ends stay inside, spreading their softness.

Rnd 1: Knit 5, place A, k1f&b, k1, place B, k to end.

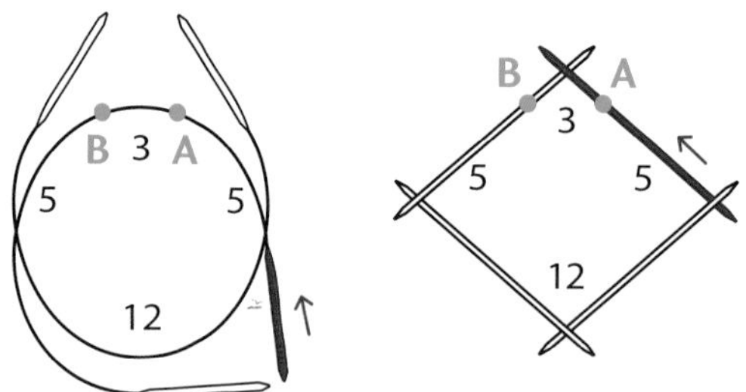

① Stitch distribution after rnd 1 of arch expansion. Sts between A and B are worked with Cashmere and Kid Aran held together.

Companion rounds

Rnds 2-3: Knit.

Rnd 4: K to A, k1, LLinc, k until 1 st before B, LRinc, k to end.

Repeat companion rnds 1-3, stopping after a completed rnd 4 when total stitch count reaches 41. Move A 1 st to the left and B 1 st to the right (17 sts between A and B).

Heel

Continue with Kid Aran alone. Knit to end of instep. Work plain heel (page 120), beginning with step 3. A and B are already in place. Use 6 for H, 3 for I, and ignore J. Total sts after heel is finished: 29

Make a Button-Bobble

First make a tiny felted ball. Cut a 15" length of Kid Aran (a felting yarn), pull the plies apart, and tear them into short pieces. Wet the fiber and roll and mash it between your palms, coaxing it into a firmly felted ball. Knit the bobble: LRinc, (k1, p1, k1, p1), all in the same st, LLinc. Turn, sl1, p5. Turn, sl1, k5. Turn, sl1, p5. Turn, sl1, k3, k2tog. Turn, sl1, p2, p2tog. Turn, sl2, k2tog, pass 2 slipped sts over the k2tog st. Stuff the felted ball inside the bobble. Wind the yarn tightly around the base of the button-bobble twice before continuing.

Leg and cuff

Knit 3 rnds. Knit 8. Make button-bobble *(see yellow panel)* in 9th st (center instep st), k to end. Knit 2 rnds. Repeat **LRinc, k3** until only 2 sts rem, LRinc, k to end. Total sts: 39 Knit until leg measures 2" (5 cm) above bobble. Bind off loosely and weave in all ends.

Tie

With cashmere alone, make 4-st I-cord: cast on 4 sts to smaller ndls, k4. Repeat **return 4 sts to left ndl, k4** until I-cord is 9" (22 cm) long. I-cord eyelet opening: Return 4 sts to left ndl, yo, k2tog, yo, k2tog. Resume I-cord: Repeat **return 4 sts to left ndl, k4** until I-cord is 18" (44 cm) long. Cut a short tail and use a tapestry needle to weave it through end sts, pull tight, then secure tail inside I-cord. Conceal other tail. Press eyelet opening (line up the 2 holes) over button-bobble, pull ends around ankle, then wrap and tie around button-bobble.

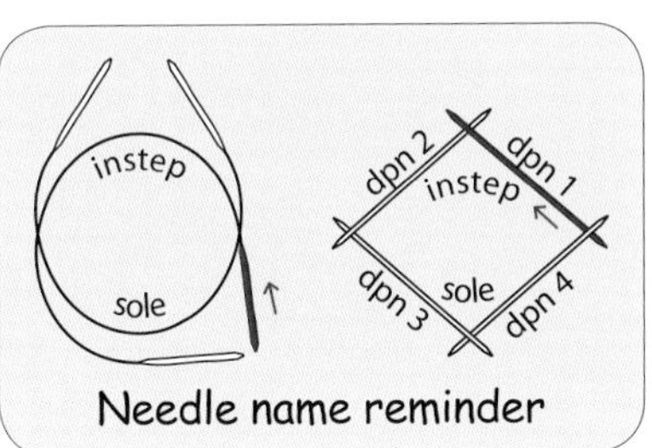

Needle name reminder

Philosopher's House Socks

I designed this house sock in between morel-hunting expeditions and visiting barn cats in the hayloft at Anne and Eugene Bourgeois' idyllic farm in Inverhuron, Ontario, where they sell their beautiful Philosopher's Wool kits.

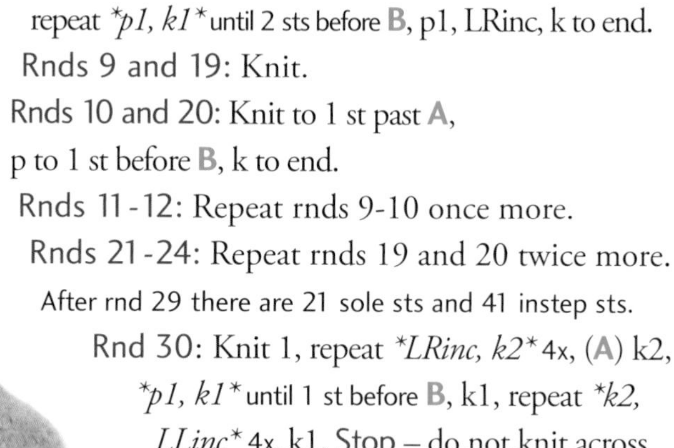

Yarn: Philosopher's Wool (100% wool, 120 g / 210 yds), 1 skein Spring Green
Needles: size 5 (3.5 mm), or size you need to get gauge
Gauge: 5 sts = 1" (2.5 cm)
Sizes: midfoot 8.5" (21 cm)
Markers: A, B, C, and D

Toe

Make Standard Toe (page 126), casting on 9 sts to each parallel ndl, and finishing with total st count (D) of 42. When toe is about 2" (5 cm) long, use D to determine length of toe section (page 112). Knit toe to this length.

Arch expansion - picture ①

Instep is starting ndl (ndl in left hand).

Rnd 1: Knit 9, place A, k1, LLinc, p1, LRinc, k1, place B, k to end.
Rnd 2: Knit to 2 sts past A, p1, k to end.
Rnd 3: Knit to 1 st past A, LLinc, p1, k1, p1, LRinc, k to end.
Rnds 4, 6, 8, 14, 16, 18, 26, and 28: Knit to 1 st past A, repeat *k1, p1* until 2 sts before B, k to end.
Rnds 5, 7, 13, 15, 17, 25, 27, and 29: Knit to 1 past A, LLinc, repeat *p1, k1* until 2 sts before B, p1, LRinc, k to end.
Rnds 9 and 19: Knit.
Rnds 10 and 20: Knit to 1 st past A, p to 1 st before B, k to end.
Rnds 11-12: Repeat rnds 9-10 once more.
Rnds 21-24: Repeat rnds 19 and 20 twice more.
After rnd 29 there are 21 sole sts and 41 instep sts.
Rnd 30: Knit 1, repeat *LRinc, k2* 4x, (A) k2, *p1, k1* until 1 st before B, k1, repeat *k2, LLinc* 4x, k1. Stop – do not knit across sole. (49 sts on instep, 21 on sole)

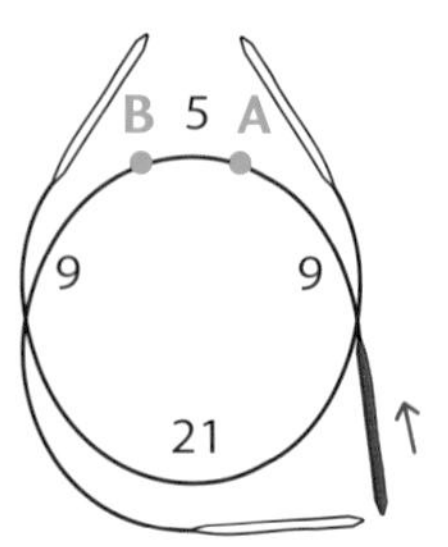

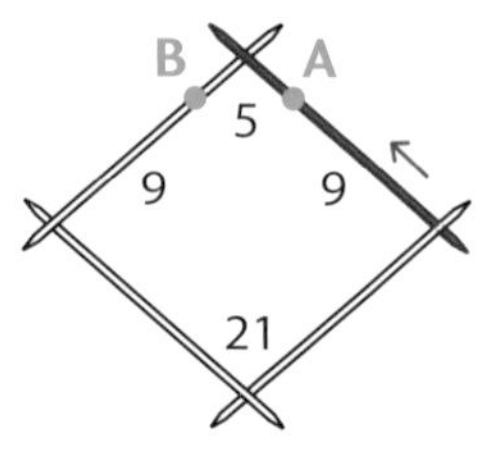

① Stitch distribution after rnd 1 of arch expansion.

Heel

Work plain heel turn (page 122, steps 3-4) and reinforced back of heel (page 125, step 5). A and B are already in place. Use 13 for H, 6 for I, and ignore J. Total sts after heel is finished: 44

Leg and cuff

Repeat *p 1 rnd, k 1 rnd* 3x. Work 2 rnds of *k1, p1*, 2 rnds of *p1, k1*, and 2 rnds of *k1, p1*. Repeat *k 1 rnd, p 1 rnd* 5x. Bind off with EZ's sewn bind-off (page 130), and weave in all ends.

Dove Socks

The upstream arch expansion is outlined with purl lines every third round, then the purl outline is worked in reverse (but without increases) to form a large diamond shape.

Yarn: Claudia Hand Painted Yarns (100% merino, 100 g/ 225 yds), 2 skeins Honey
Needles: size 3 (3.25 mm), or size you need to get gauge
Gauge: 7 sts = 1" (2.5 cm)
Size: midfoot 6 (7, 8, 9)" or 15 (18, 20, 23 cm)
Markers: A, B, C, and D

Toe

Make Whirlpool Toe (page 126), finishing with total st count (D) of 38 (44, 50, 56). When toe is about 2" (5 cm) long, use D to determine length of toe section (page 112). Knit toe to this length For 2nd and 4th sizes, move 1 st from sole to instep. Instep has 19 (23, 25, 29) sts and sole has 19 (21, 25, 27).

Arch expansion - picture ①

Instep is starting ndl (ndl in left hand).

Rnd 1: Knit 8 (10, 11, 13), place A, k1, p1, k1, place B, k to end.

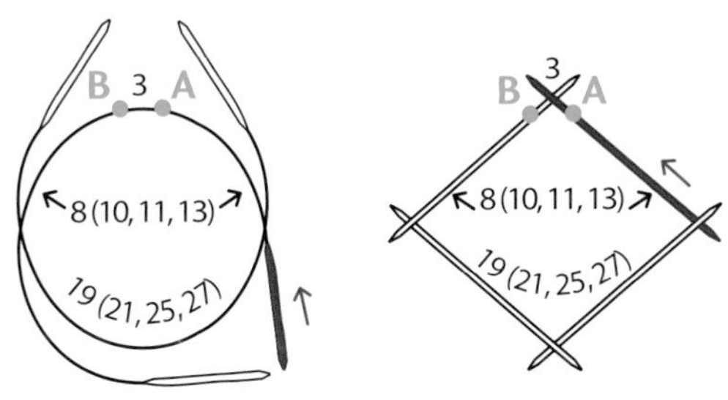

① Stitch distribution after rnd 1 of arch expansion.

Companion Rounds:

Rnd 2: Knit to A, k1, LLinc, k to 1 st before B, LRinc, k to end.
Rnd 3: Knit.
Rnd 4: Knit to A, k1, p to 1 st before B, k to end.

Repeat companion rnds 2-4 another 2x, then rnds 2-3 once more.

Rnd 13: Knit to A, k1, p4, k1, p4, k to end.

Companion rounds:

Rnd 14: Knit to A, k1, LLinc, k to 1 st before B, LRinc, k to end.
Rnd 15: Knit.
Rnd 16: Knit to A, k1, p4, k until 5 sts before B, p4, k to end.

Repeat companion rnds 14-16, stopping after a completed rnd 16 when total sts is 58 (66, 76, 84). Put away A and B.

Heel

Work reinforced heel (page 120), beginning with step 1, using 19 (23, 25, 29) for *instep* G, 19 (21, 25, 27) for *sole* G, 10 (11, 13, 14) for H, 4 (5, 5, 6) for J, and 5 (6, 7, 8) for I. Total sts after heel is finished: 38 (44, 50, 56)

Leg and cuff

In each pattern rnd the groups of 4 p sts move closer together. Work 2 knit rnds in between pattern rnds. Instep is starting ndl.

Rnd 1: Purl 4, k until 4 instep sts remain, p4, k to end.
Rnd 4: Knit 1, p4, k until 5 instep sts remain, p4, k to end.
Rnd 7: Knit 2, p4, k until 6 instep sts remain, p4, k to end.
Rnd 10: Knit 3, p4, k until 7 instep sts remain, p4, k to end.

Continue as above until 9 center instep sts are: p4, k1, p4. Place A before the 9 center instep sts. Knit 2 rnds after this rnd.

Knit to 1 st past A, p7, k to end. Knit 2 rnds. Knit to 2 sts past A, p5, k to end. Knit 2 rnds. Knit to 3 sts past A, p3, k to end. Knit 2 rnds. Knit to 4 sts past A, p1, k to end. Knit 2 rnds.

Cuff

Set-up rnd: LRinc, k to end. Total sts: 39 (45, 51, 57)
Repeat **k2, p1** for 1" (2.5 cm).
Bind off with double strand and weave in all ends.

Milkmaid's Stockings

Fortissima Socka

I picture these socks, with a few bits of straw stuck to the wool, warming the feet of a woman high in the Swiss Alps as she perches on a battered wooden stool, quietly milking the family cow at dawn. I offer you both single and two-color versions.

Yarn: Fortissima Socka 6-fach (75% wool, 25% nylon, 50 g/ 125 m), 3 balls 2248 Cream and 1 ball 2231 denim

Needles: two size 2 (3 mm), or size you need to get gauge

Gauge: 7.5 sts = 1" (2.5 cm)

Sizes: midfoot 8.5" (21 cm)

Markers: A, B, C, and D

Instep is starting ndl (ndl in left hand).

Toe

Make Standard Toe (page 126), casting on 11 sts to each parallel ndl, and finishing with total st count of 58 (D). When toe is about 2" (5 cm) long, use D to determine length of toe section (page 112). Knit toe to this length.

Arch expansion - pictures ① and ②, chart 1

St counts are given for instep only (sole remains 29 sts).

Rnd 1: Knit 14, place A, p1, place B, k to end of rnd. See picture ①. For dpn's, B cannot be placed until after rnd 2, as it would be between dpn's. In rnd 2, work 2nd yo at start of dpn 2, then place B .

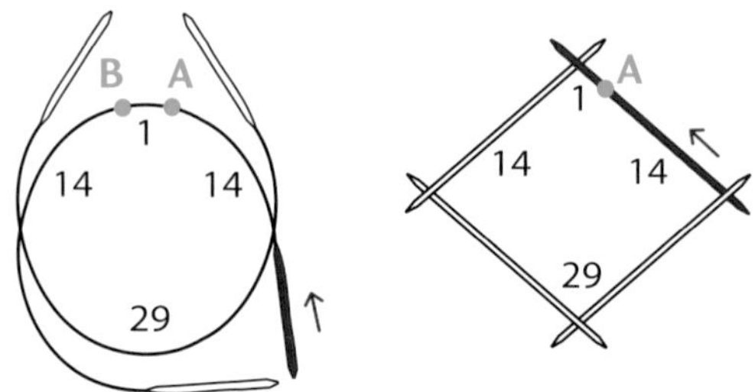

① Stitch distribution after rnd 1 of arch expansion.

Rnd 2: Knit to A, yo, p1, yo, k to end of rnd. (31 sts)
Rnds 3-4: Knit to A, k1, p1, k to end of rnd.
Rnd 5: Knit to A, k1, yo, p1, yo, k to end of rnd. (33 sts)
Rnds 6-7: Knit to A, k2, p1, k to end of rnd.
Rnd 8: Knit to A, k2, yo, p1, yo, k to end of rnd. (35 sts)
Rnds 9-10: Knit to A, k2, p3, k to end.
Rnd 11: Knit to A, k2, yo, p3, yo, k to end. (37 sts)
Rnds 12-13: Knit to A, k2, p5, k to end.
Rnd 14: Knit to A, k2, yo, p5, yo, k to end. (39 sts)
Rnds 15-16: Knit to A, k2, p7, k to end.
Rnd 17: Knit to A, k2, yo, p7, yo, k to end. (41 sts)
Rnds 18-19: Knit to A, k2, p9, k to end.
Rnd 20: Knit to A, yo, k2tog, yo, p9, yo, ssk, yo, k to end. (43 st)
Rnds 21-22: Knit to A, k3, p9, k to end.

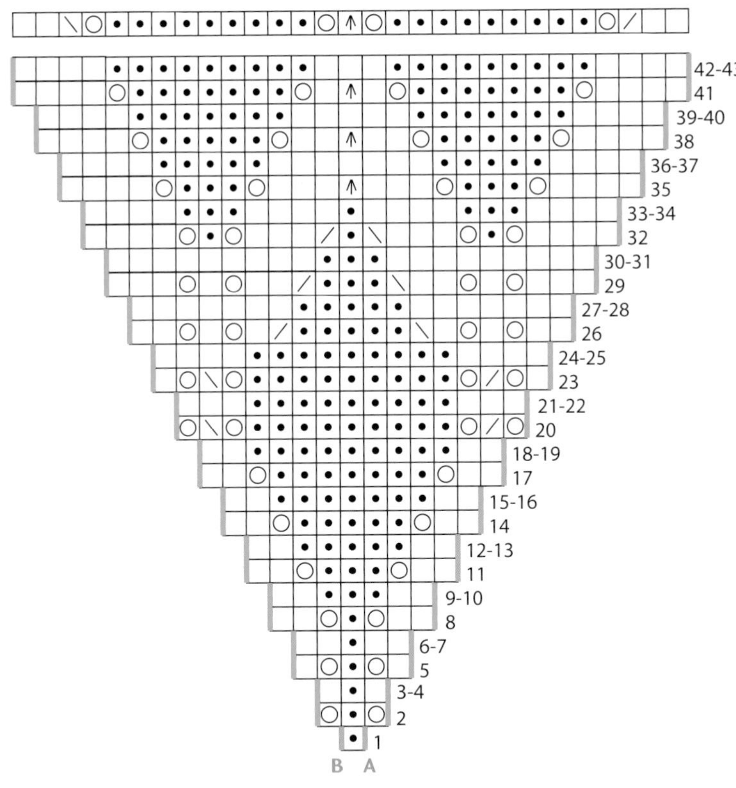

Chart 1

This chart shows the instep only between A and B. All stitches before A and after B are knit. The chart line floating above rnd 34 is worked at the end of the heel when knitting in the rnd resumes (see heading, "Heel").

☐ k ⊡ p ⧅ ssk ⧄ k2tog ▨ p2tog ⧅ k1, LLinc ◯ yo ⍏ cdd ■ no stitch

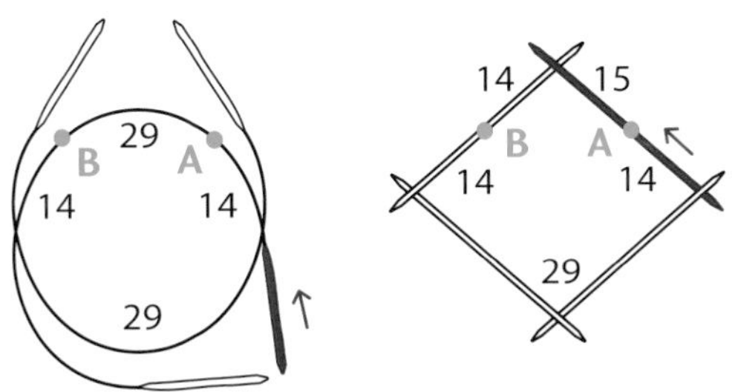

② Stitch distribution after rnd 43 of arch expansion.

Rnd 23: Knit to A, k1, yo, k2tog, yo, p9, yo, ssk, yo, k to end. (45 sts)

Rnds 24-25: Knit to A, k4, p9, k to end.

Rnd 26: Knit to A, k2, repeat **yo, k1** 2x, ssk, p5, k2tog, repeat **k1, yo** 2x, k to end. (47 sts)

Rnds 27-28: Knit to A, k7, p5, k to end.

Rnd 29: Knit to A, k3, yo, k1, yo, k2, ssk, p3, k2tog, k2, yo, k1, yo, k to end. (49 sts)

Rnds 30-31: Knit to A, k9, p3, k to end.

Rnd 32: Knit to A, k4, yo, p1, yo, k3, ssk, p1, k2tog, k3, yo, p1, yo, k to end. (51 sts)

Rnds 33-34: Knit to A, k4, p3, k4, p1, k4, p3, k to end.

Rnd 35: Knit to A, k4, yo, p3, yo, k3, cdd, k3, yo, p3, yo, k to end. (53 sts)

Rnds 36-37: Knit to A, k4, p5, k7, p5, k to end.

Rnd 38: Knit to A, k4, yo, p5, yo, k2, cdd, k2, yo, p5, yo, k to end. (55 sts)

Rnds 39-40: Knit to A, k4, p7, k5, p7, k to end.

Rnd 41: Knit to A, k4, yo, p7, yo, k1, cdd, k1, yo, p7, yo, k to end. (57 sts)

Rnd 42: Knit to A, k4, p9, k3, p9, k to end.

Rnd 43: Knit to A, k4, p9, k3, p9, k18 *(stop at end of instep)*. See picture ②.

Total sts: 57 instep and 29 sole

Blue Moon Fiber Arts® Inc. Socks That Rock® Medium-weight, (100% wool, 5.5 oz/ 380 yds), 1 skein Falcon Eye

Blue Sky Alpaca & Silk (50% alpaca, 50% silk, 50 g/ 133 m), 4 skeins "Oyster", 1 skein "Ginger"

Heel - top rnd of chart 1

Work reinforced heel (page 124), beginning with step 3. A and B are already in place. Use 9 for **I**, 14 for **H**, and ignore **J**. In step 5, repeat back of heel companion rows until only 29 sole sts rem after a completed row 4. Work a row 3, but do not turn after the ssk. Instead, pick up and k 1 st in intersection. Resume working in the rnd (see top line of chart 1): (instep) K2, k2tog, yo, p9, yo, cdd, yo, p9, yo, ssk, k2. (sole) Pick up and k 1 in intersection, k2tog, k to end of sole. (58 sts total - 29 instep and 29 sole)

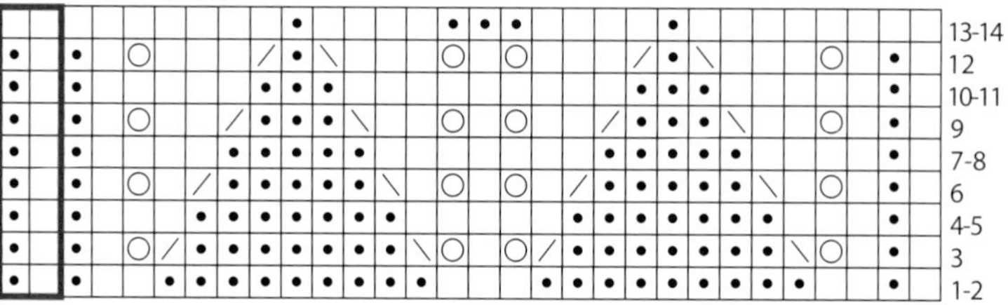

Chart 2 (leg rnds 1-14)
Work the first section, then repeat red-boxed section 15 times.

Leg *Instep is starting ndl (ndl in left hand).*

Rnds 1-2 (chart 2 begins): Knit 1, p1, k2, p9, k3, p9, k2, p1, repeat **k1, p1** 15x.

Rnd 3: Knit 1, p1, k1, yo, ssk, p7, k2tog, yo, k1, yo, ssk, p7, k2tog, yo, k1, p1, repeat **k1, p1** 15x.

Rnds 4-5: Knit 1, p1, k3, p7, k5, p7, k3, p1, repeat **k1, p1** 15x.

Rnd 6: Knit 1, p1, k1, yo, k1, ssk, p5, k2tog, k1, yo, k1, yo, k1, ssk, p5, k2tog, k1, yo, k1, p1, repeat **k1, p1** 15x.

Rnds 7-8: Knit 1, p1, k4, p5, k7, p5, k4, p1, repeat **k1, p1** 15x.

Rnd 9: Knit 1, p1, k1, yo, k2, ssk, p3, k2tog, k2, yo, k1, yo, k2, ssk, p3, k2tog, k2, yo, k1, p1, repeat **k1, p1** 15x.

Rnds 10-11: Knit 1, p1, k5, p3, k9, p3, k5, p1, repeat **k1, p1** 15x.

Rnd 12: Knit 1, p1, k1, yo, k3, ssk, p1, k2tog, k3, yo, k1, yo, k3, ssk, p1, k2tog, k3, yo, k1, p1, repeat **k1, p1** 15x.

Rnd 13: Knit 8, p1, k4, p3, k4, p1, k to end, working 3 LRinc's evenly distributed on sole. (61 sts)

Rnd 14: Knit 8, p1, k4, p3, k4, p1, k to end. (chart 2 ends)

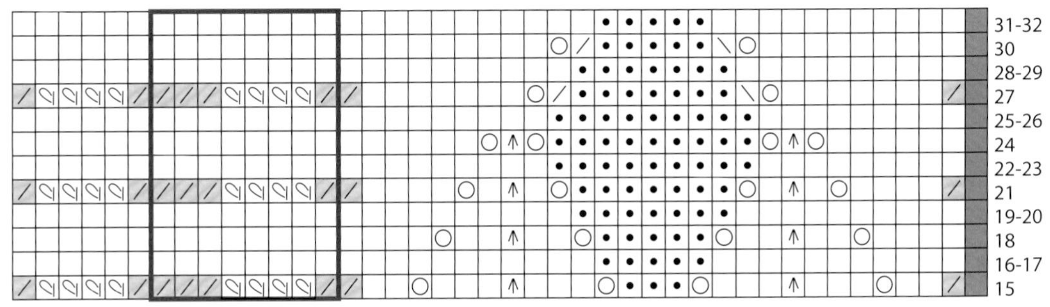

The symbol for LLinc in the Milkmaid's Stockings represents *both* the LLinc *and* the st which donates the leg for the LLinc. Read the chart symbol as k1, LLinc.

Chart 3 (leg rnds 15-32) Work the first section, repeat red-boxed section twice, then work final section.

Rnd 15: (Chart 3 begins.) Purl 2tog, k2, yo, k3, cdd, k3, yo, p3, yo, k3, cdd, k3, yo, k2, p2tog, repeat **p2tog, (k1, LLinc)* 4x, *(p2tog)* 3x* 2x, p2tog, repeat **k1, LLinc** 4x, p2tog.

Rnds 16-17: Knit 11, p5, k to end.

Rnd 18: Knit 4, yo, k2, cdd, k2, yo, p5, yo, k2, cdd, k2, yo, k to end.

At end of rnds 20, 26, and 32, do not k final sole st. Instead, transfer it to adjacent end of instep. Move final instep st to adjacent end of sole.

Rnds 19-20: Knit 10, p7, k to end.

Rnd 21: Purl 2tog, k4, yo, k1, cdd, k1, yo, p7, yo, k1, cdd, k1, yo, k4, p2tog, repeat **p2tog, (k1, LLinc)* 4x, *(p2tog)* 3x* 2x, p2tog, repeat **k1, LLinc** 4x, p2tog.

Rnds 22-23 and 25-26: Knit 9, p9, k to end.

Rnd 24: Knit 6, yo, cdd, yo, p9, yo, cdd, yo, k to end.

Rnd 27: Purl 2tog, k7, yo, ssk, p7, k2tog, yo, k7, p2tog, repeat **p2tog, (k1, LLinc)* 4x, *(p2tog)* 3x* 2x, p2tog, repeat **k1, LLinc** 4x, p2tog.

Rnds 28-29: Knit 10, p7, k to end.

Rnd 30: Knit 9, yo, ssk, p5, k2tog, yo, k to end.

Rnds 31-32: Knit 11, p5, k to end. (chart 3 ends)

Abbreviations and a list of technique lessons can be found on pages 134-136.

k · p · ssk · k2tog · p2tog · k1, LLinc · yo · cdd · no stitch

Rnd 33: (Chart 4 begins.) Repeat **p2tog** 4x, repeat **k1, LLinc** 2x, k3, yo, ssk, p3, k2tog, yo, k3, repeat **k1, LLinc** 2x, repeat (**p2tog** 4x, **k1, LLinc** 4x) 3x.
Rnds 34-35: Knit 13, p3, k to end.
Rnd 36: Knit 12, yo, ssk, p1, k2tog, yo, k to end.
Rnds 37-38: Knit 14, p1, k to end. *Transfer 2 sts from ends of sole to adjacent ends of instep before beginning rnds 39, 45, 51, 54, and 57.*
Rnd 39: Repeat **p2tog** 4x, **k1, LLinc** 2x, k5, yo, cdd, yo, k5, repeat **k1, LLinc** 2x, repeat (**p2tog** 4x, **k1, LLinc** 4x) 3x.
Two-color version: Work rnds 40, 46, 52, 55 and 58 in blue.
Rnds 40-41, 43-44, 46-47, 49-50, 52-53, and 55-56: Knit.
Rnd 42: Knit 14, yo, k1, yo, k to end of rnd. (63 sts)
Rnd 45: Repeat **p2tog** 4x, **k1, LLinc** 4x, **p2tog** 2x, **k1, yo** 2x, k1, **p2tog** 2x, **k1, LLinc** 4x, repeat (**p2tog** 4x, **k1, LLinc** 4x) 3x. (65 sts)
Rnd 48: Knit 16, yo, k1, yo, k to end of rnd. (67 sts)
Rnd 51: Repeat **p2tog** 4x, **k1, LLinc** 4x, **p2tog** 2x, k3, yo, k1, yo, k3, repeat (**p2tog** 2x, **k1, LLinc** 4x, repeat (**p2tog** 4x, **k1, LLinc** 4x) 3x. (69 sts)
Rnd 54: Repeat **p2tog** 4x, **k1, LLinc** 4x, **p2tog** 3x, **k1, LLinc** 5x, **p2tog** 3x, **k1, LLinc** 4x, repeat (**p2tog** 4x, **k1, LLinc** 4x) 3x. (Chart 4 ends.) (72 sts)
Rnd 57: (Chart 5) Repeat (**p2tog** 4x, **k1, LLinc** 4x) 6x.
Rnds 58-60: Knit.
Repeat rnds 57-60 twice more *(55 and 58 are blue)*. Knit 1 rnd. Purl 3 rnds. Bind off with EZ's sewn bind-off (page 130) and weave in all ends.

Chart 4
(leg rnds 33-54)
Work first section, then repeat red-boxed section 3 times. All rnds not shown are knit.

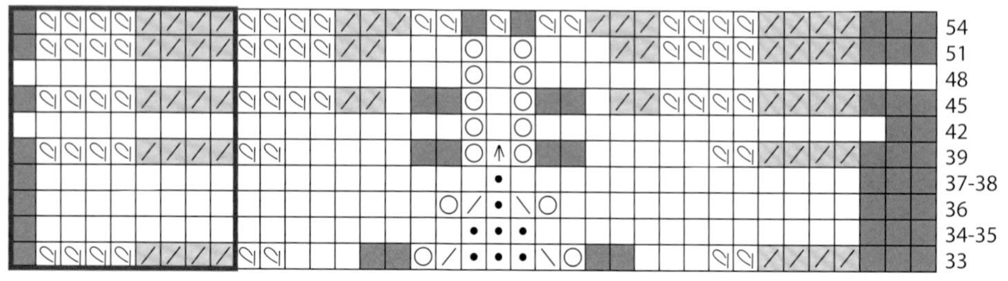

57

Chart 5 (leg rnd 57)
Repeat 6 times.

Upstream Master Pattern

Find your Master numbers on pages 109-119.

Markers: A, B, C, and D

Instep is starting ndl (ndl in left hand).

Complete any toe (page 126). Knit toe Ⓔ inches long.

Marker placement if Ⓖ is an even number - picture ①

Locate 4 center instep sts. Place A before and B after 4 center sts.

Marker placement if Ⓖ is an odd number - picture ②

Locate 3 center sts on instep. Place A before and B after 3 center sts.

Upstream arch expansion

Arch expansion companion rounds

Rnd 1: K to A, k1, LLinc, k until 1 st before B, LRinc, k to end.

Rnds 2 and 3: Knit.

Repeat companion rnds 1-3, stopping after a completed rnd 1 when total stitch count reaches Ⓕ. Remove markers.

Complete heel (page 120), leg, and cuff (page 130).

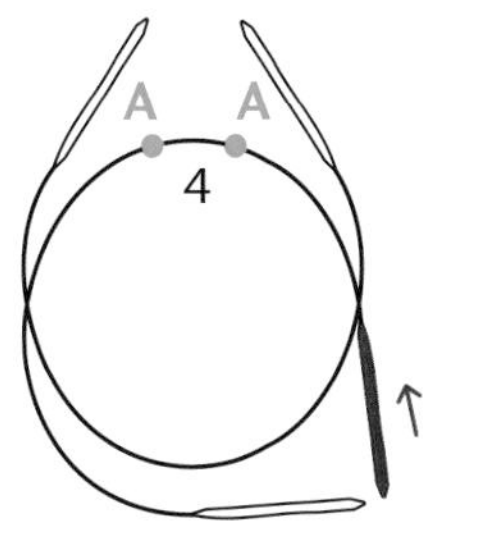

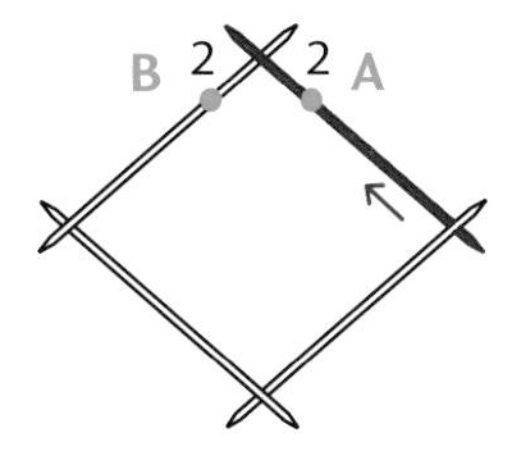

① If Ⓖ is even, place A before and B after the 4 center sts, for a total of 4 sts between A and B.

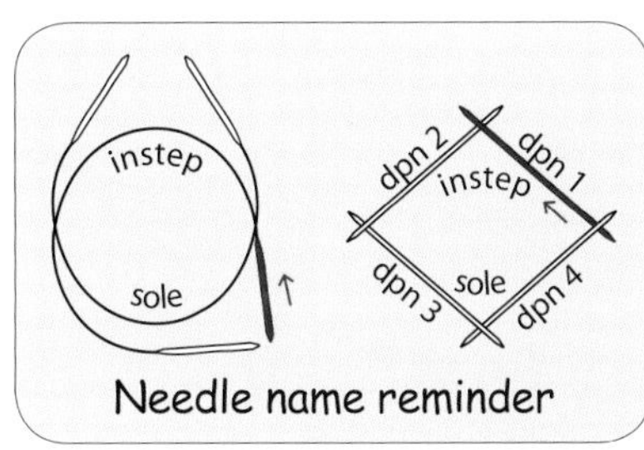

Needle name reminder

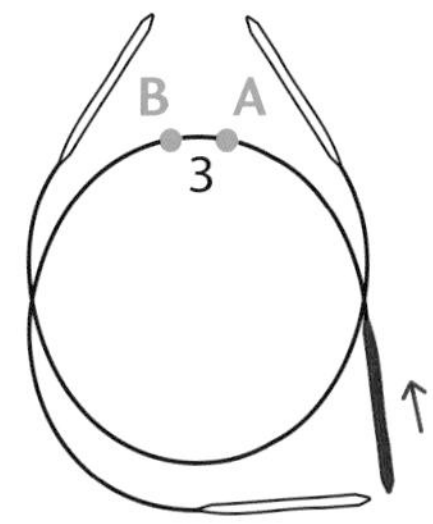

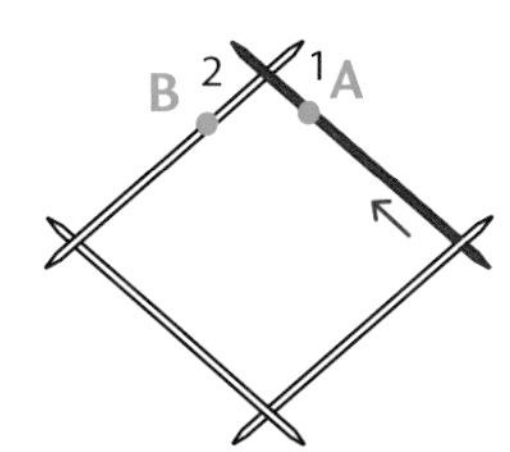

② If Ⓖ is odd, place A before and B after the 3 center sts, for a total of 3 sts between A and B.

Abbreviations and a list of technique lessons can be found on pages 134-136.

Chapter 7 - Riverbed Architecture

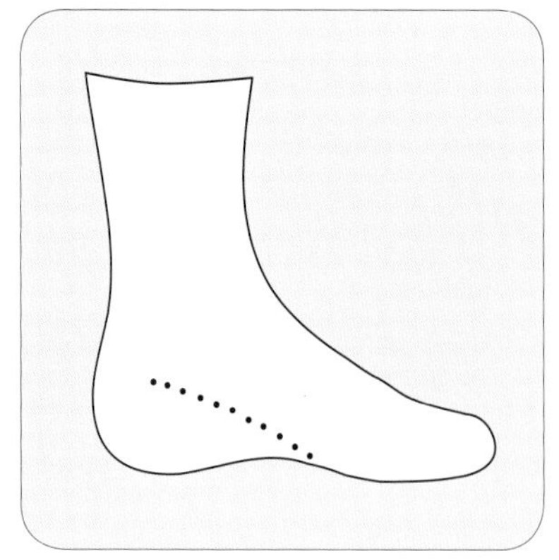

In Riverbed architecture, the arch expansion runs beneath the sole. The elegant result allows you to spread a favorite stitch pattern over the foot's visible surface without maneuvering around a single increase. Because the arch expansion is worked on the sole, all Riverbed patterns start with the sole needle rather than the instep needle. When you are ready to work the heel, you can either move the wing stitches to the instep to get them out of the way, or keep them on the sole so they'll be in place after the heel turn is complete.

Riverbed architecture seems to fit many people exceptionally well, perhaps because it hugs the contours of the foot so naturally, reaching up towards the instep from the hollows of the under-arch. Best of all, the entire sock, except for the sole, is available for a favorite small stitch pattern, like the one shown here. Even the back of the heel can be worked in a design.

The Joys of Riverbed Architecture

- Increases hug your sole
- The entire surface is free for designs
- Learn this pathway, and you're ready for Upstream, Sidestream, and Ridgeline architectures

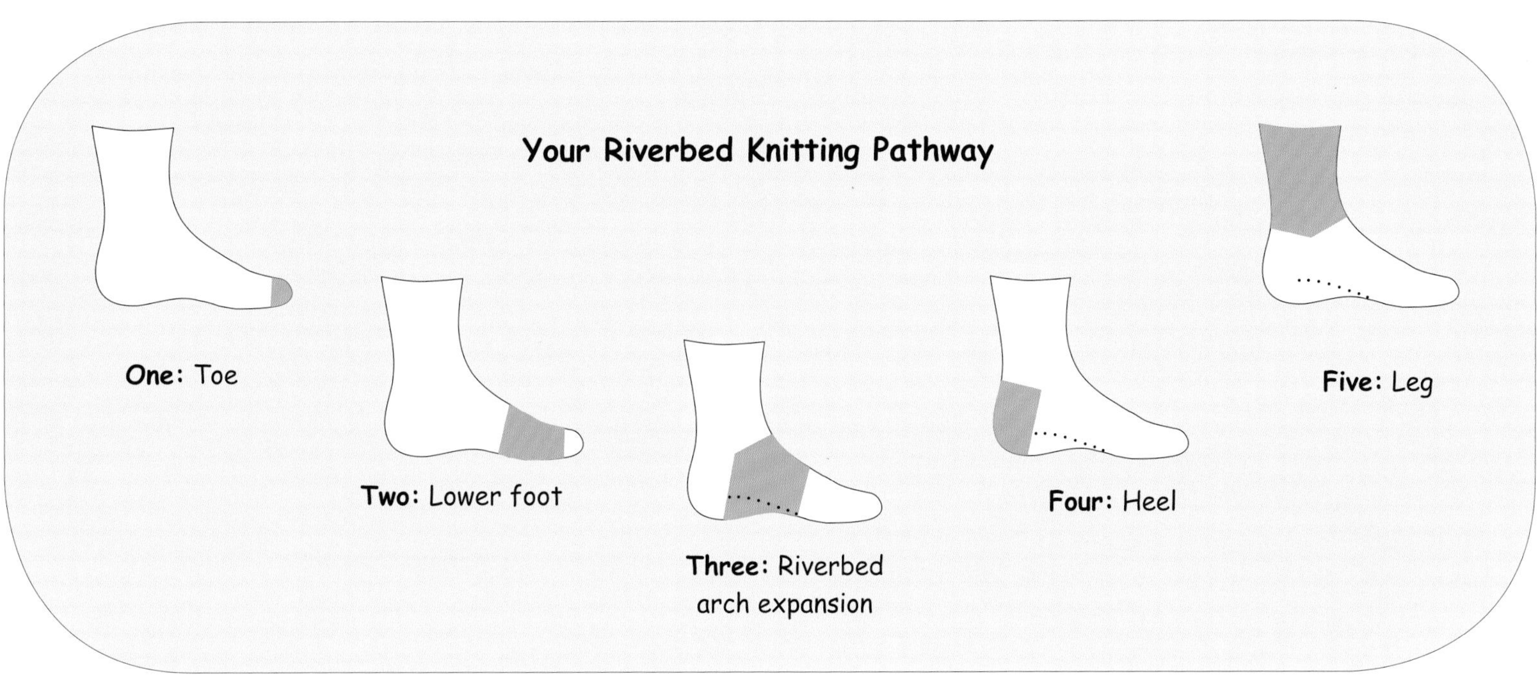

Rushing Rivulet Chart

Rushing Rivulet Socks

For the independent knitter: Follow Master Riverbed pattern (page 91), incorporating the Rushing Rivulet stitch pattern *(see chart and use a multiple of 4 sts around leg)* everywhere but toe, sole, and heel, and ending with a Picot Hem *(when sock is tall enough, repeat *yo, k2tog* to end, k about .75" or 2 cm, bind off loosely, fold to inside on yo line, and gently sew edge to inside).*

Yarn: Mountain Colors Weaver's Wool (100% wool, 100 g / 350 yds), 1 skein Sagebrush.

Rowan Margaret's Silken Slippers

I designed this two-layer slipper in honor of Rowan Margaret Dempsey LaPointe, newly born to Fleece Artist's Emily Dempsey in Nova Scotia. The merino outer sock holds a Sea Silk inner sock, to keep Rowan's small feet cozy and cuddly even when chilly winds rush across the North Atlantic.

Yarn: Fleece Artist Merino 2/6 (100% merino, 115 g/ 325 m), 1 skein Raspberry, and Handmaiden Sea Silk (70% silk, 30% Seacell®, 100 g/ 500 m), 1 skein Moss

Needles: size 3 (3.25 mm) for Merino, or size you need to get gauge, and 1 size smaller for Sea Silk®.

Gauge: in Merino, 7.5 sts = 1" (2.5 cm)

Size: newborn - 3 months

Markers: A, B, C, and D

Sole is starting ndl (ndl in left hand). Make 2 merino socks on larger ndls, and 2 silk socks on smaller ndls.

Toe

Make Standard Toe (page 126), starting with cast-on of 8 sts to each parallel ndl, finishing with total st count of 28. Knit 4 rnds.

Arch expansion - picture ①

Rnd 1: Knit 6, k1f&b, k to end. (29 sts)

Rnd 2: Knit 6, place A, k3, place B, k to end.

Arch Expansion Companion Rounds

  Rnd 3: K to A, k1, LLinc, k to 1 st before B, LRinc, k to end.

  Rnds 4 and 5: Knit.

Repeat companion rnds 3-5 another 5 times. (41 sts)

Work rnd 3 once more. (43 sts)

Move A 1 st to the *left* and B 1 st to the *right (toward each other)*. Knit to B, k1, repeat **LRinc, k2** 3x, k to end of instep, repeat **k2, LLinc** 3x, k1, stopping at A. (49 sts)

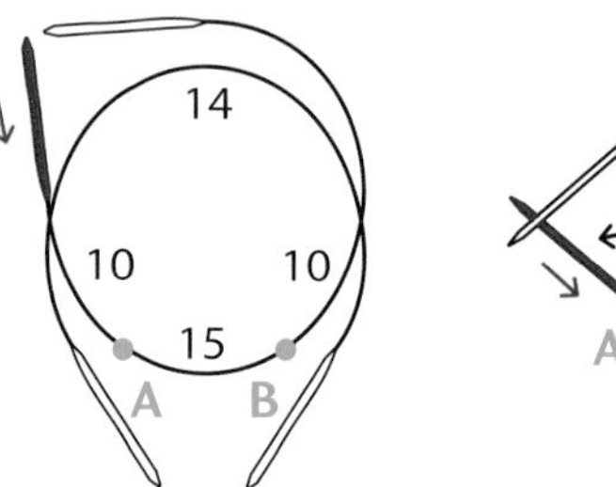

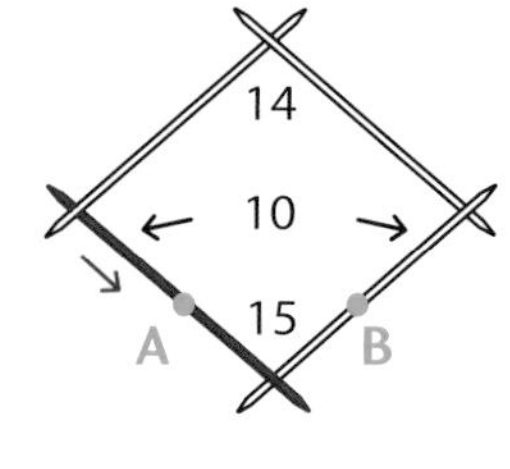

① Stitch distribution at end of arch expansion.

Heel

Work plain heel (page 122), beginning with step 3, keeping all heel sts on 1 circ or 2 dpn's. Yarn is at A. As you follow heel turn instructions, A and B will represent ends of sole ndl, even though there are 10 wing sts at either end. Use 3 for **I**. In step 4, the 10 wing sts (**H**) are already in place. Ignore **J**. Replace A *with* C and B *with* D. In step 5, repeat companion rows 3-4 until *only 4 sts* rem on outer sides of gaps (instead of the usual 2). Work a row 3, but do not turn after the ssk. Instead, resume knitting in the rnd: (rest of sole) k3, (instep) k14, (sole again) k3, k2tog, k15. Total sts: 33 - 14 instep and 19 sole

Leg

Instep is starting needle. Knit 2 rnds. Next rnd: LRinc, k7, stop. Total sts: 34. Rearrange sts on ndls so sock folds in half, from center of instep to center of back, with 17 sts in each half. *Do not bind off - set aside until all 4 socks reach this point. Yarn is at center front.*

Veil Chart 

Rose box shows 6-st pattern repeat of rnd 2, with additional edge sts. Alternate rows are purled.

Join socks and knit veil

Push merino sock inside silk sock with wrong sides together (weave in all loose ends first - you will not have access to them again). Cut tail of merino. With silk sock facing you as you work, use silk and larger ndls to join socks by knitting tog 1 st from each sock's ndls (like a 3-ndl bind-off, without the binding off) until only 1 set of 34 sts remains. *Yarn is at center front.*

Rnds 1-3: Knit.
Rnd 4: Repeat **k2tog, yo** to end.
Rnds 5-13: Knit.
Rnds 14-23: Repeat rnds 4-13 once more.
Rnd 24: Repeat **k2tog, yo** to end.
Rnds 25-26: Knit.
Rnd 27: Repeat **LRinc, k1** to end. (68 sts)
Rnd 28: Knit.
Rnd 29: Repeat **k17, LRinc** 3x, k to end. (71 sts)
Veil Companion Rows:
(Knitting continues in *rows*, with center front as turn point.)
Row 1: Purl.
Row 2: Knit 3, repeat **yo, k1, cdd, k1, yo, k1** 11x, k2.

Repeat companion rows 1 and 2 another 6 times. Bind off and weave in all ends. Push silk sock inside merino sock. Make 16" (40 cm) merino I-cord tie (cast on 3, k3, repeat **return 3 sts to left ndl, k3** until long enough). Use tapestry ndl to thread tail through remaining 3 sts and secure end inside I-cord. Fold cuff at middle line of eyelet holes, so first and third lines of holes meet. Weave the I-cord in and out of lined-up eyelets, starting at center front. Tie ends in a bow.

Clematis Vine

I would have liked to fill this book with two-handed knitting - it is one of my favorite things to do. If you've never knit with one color in each hand, try it - once you get the hang of it, your whole body responds with a feeling of well-being and brightness. I suspect the harmonious interaction of the hands is deeply nourishing to the nervous system. Anyway - only this sock made it in, but I encourage you to design your own! What we have here is basic Riverbed architecture, with everything worked in alternating columns of color, except for the panel of Clematis flowers. You could fill the panel with anything you like . . .

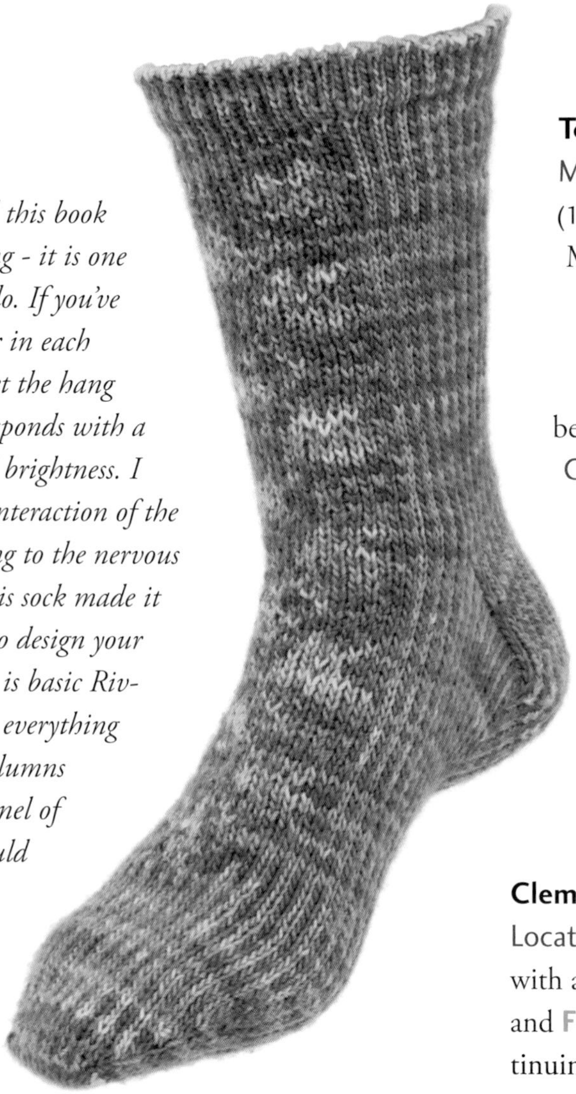

Yarn: Blue Moon Fiber Arts® Inc. Socks That Rock® Lightweight (100% merino, 4.5 oz / 360 yds), 1 skein Blue Brick Wall (main color - MC) and 1 skein 24 Karat (contrast color - CC)
Needles: size 2 (3 mm), or size you need to get gauge
Gauge: (working chart 1) 8.5 sts = 1" (2.5 cm)
Sizes: midfoot 7.5 (8, 8.5, 9)" or 19 (20, 21, 23) cm
Markers: A, B, C, D, E and F
Sole is starting ndl (ndl in left hand).

Toe - charts 1 and 2
Make Standard Toe (page 126), starting with MC and 9 (13, 15, 17) sts on each of 2 parallel ndls. Knit 1st rnd with MC, then begin working from Chart 1 with both colors.

Chart 1

Follow this color rule for toe increases: If increase is between 2 same color sts, work increase in other color. If increase is between a MC and a CC st, work increase in MC.
Continue with toe until there is a total of 54 (58, 62, 66) sts. Work 1 rnd without increases, then work a LRinc at end of instep and at end of sole - adding 1 st to each (total sts 56 (60, 64, 68). When toe is about 2" (5 cm) long, use 42 (46, 50, 54) for D to determine how long to knit toe section (see page 112). Knit toe to this length and then begin arch expansion. Begin Clematis Vine design on instep sometime before beginning arch expansion.

Clematis Vine - picture ①, chart 2 (see page 87)
Locate the 17 center sts on instep, beginning and ending with a MC st (you will be off-center by 1 st). Place E *before* and F *after* the 17 sts. Follow Chart 2 between E and F, continuing to alternate MC and CC as established around the rest of the foot.

Arch expansion
Place A before and B after the 2 center sole sts.
Rnd 1: *Work increases with MC, otherwise keeping to established columns of colors.* Knit to A, k1, LLinc, LRinc, k to end.

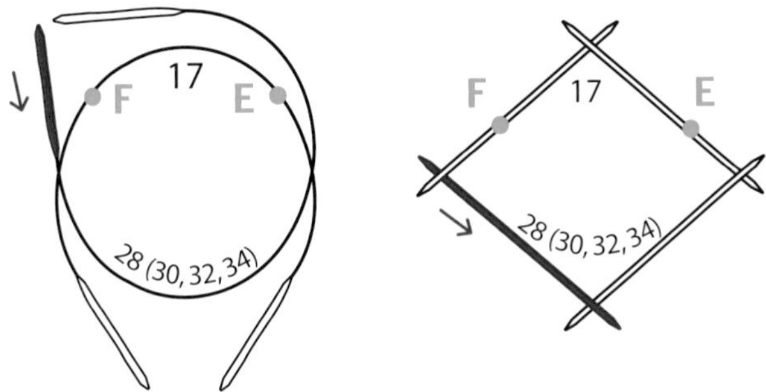

① Stitch and marker distribution as you begin the Clematis Vine. The number of instep sts before E and after F is 5 (6, 7, 8) on one side and 6 (7, 8, 9) on the other.

Generating fresh stitch patterns

The majority of stitch patterns are written for rows in sets of two, with changes made on right side rows. The New Pathways arch expansion formula, which uses rounds in sets of three, may inspire you to transform existing stitch patterns.

Try browsing through stitch dictionaries, looking for patterns that change every second round, with 1 plain round in between. Simply work 2 plain rounds in between change rounds. The design will stretch vertically and may take on a surprisingly different character, often more beautiful than before. An example is the braid in the Cables & Corrugations Sock in this chapter (page 88). I modified a traditional braid (which changed every second round) to change every third round. The result is a perfect, plump braid - something not possible with one plain round (the braid would be tight) or three (the braid would be thin).

It's handy to coordinate your stitch pattern's change round with the increase round in the arch expansion. This way you have one "pay attention" round, followed by two restful plain rounds.

Before continuing, move A and B as necessary so they mark the beginning and end of the 3 consecutive MC sts. As you work the section between A and B, do not introduce colors during the rnd 2's. Work the LLinc and LRinc in rnd 3 the 1st time with CC, the 2nd time with MC, the 3rd time with CC, etc. Maintain alternating color columns once they are established. (In this design, increases are worked every 2nd rnd instead of every 3rd rnd because of the compressed gauge.)

Arch expansion companion rounds

Rnd 2: Knit.

Rnd 3: K to A, k1, LLinc, k to 1 st before B, LRinc, k to end.

Repeat companion rnds 2-3, stopping after a completed rnd 3 when total stitch count reaches 84 (90, 96, 102). There are 29 (31, 33, 35) sts between A and B. The number of sts between the beginning of the sole and A and between B and the end of the sole is not equal - 1 side has 1 extra st. Move this extra st to adjacent end of instep. There are now 55 (59, 63, 67) sole sts and 29 (31, 33, 35) instep sts. Knit to A and stop.

Heel

Work plain heel (page 122), beginning with step 3, keeping all heel sts on 1 circ or 2 dpn's. Yarn is at A. As you follow heel turn instructions, A and B will represent ends of sole ndl, even though there are wing sts at either end. Use 7 (8, 9, 10) for I. In step 4, the 13 (14, 15, 16) wing sts (H) are already in place (ignore J). Replace A with C and B with D. Total sts after heel is finished: 58 (62, 66, 70) *Note: If you have 2 same color sts side by side when the heel is finished, work a LLinc or LRinc in between them in the other color. This will add to your stitch count, which is not a problem.*

Leg and cuff

If you'd like to add width to the leg, *begin to work increases partway up as follows: In between 2 sts, work a LLinc and a LRinc, working these increases with the opposite color to that of the borrowed leg. Distribute the pairs of increases on the back of the leg about every 6 rnds or so - first in the center, then in the middle of each side, then again in the center, etc., until desired width is reached. Photo to the left shows result.*

Follow Chart 2, adding repeats to reach 1" (2.5 cm) less than desired leg height at a completed rnd 37. Knit 1" (2.5 cm) of Chart 1 (alternating colors). Picot hem: With CC, repeat **k2, yo** to end, then k 1" (2.5 cm) with CC alone. Bind off with EZ's sewn bind-off (page 130), fold at picot line, and sew to inside.

Weave in all ends.

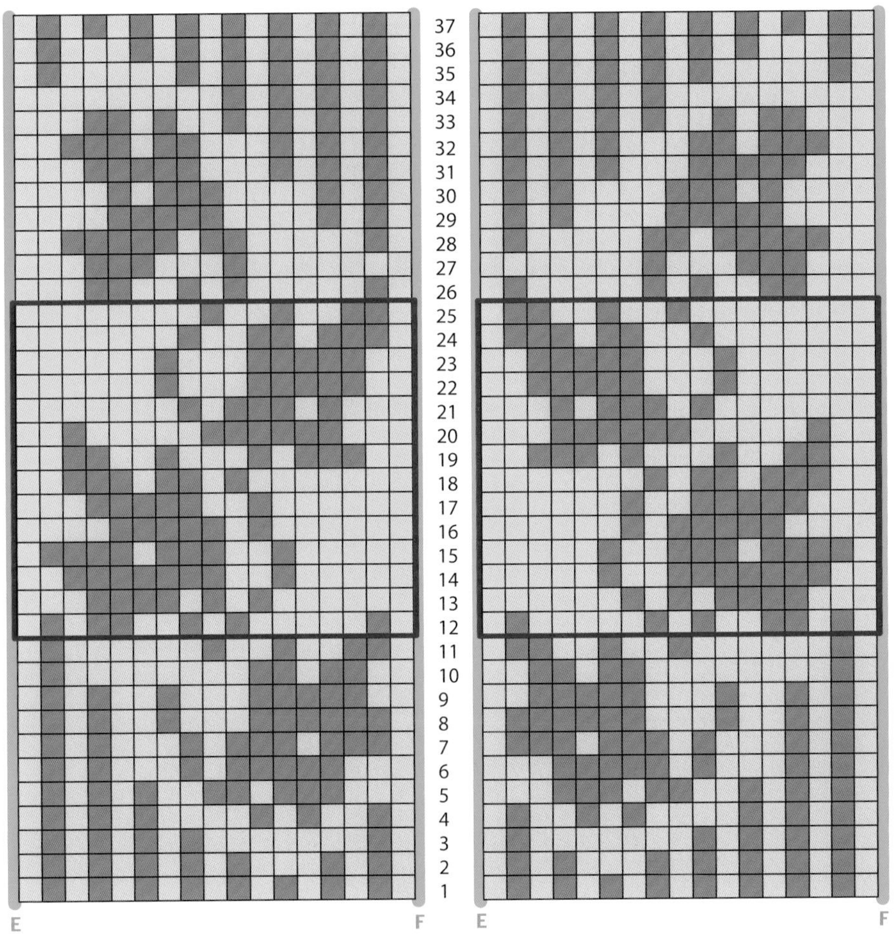

Chart 2 - Clematis Vine

Use left chart for one sock and right chart for other sock, to make a reflecting pair. Section in red box is repeated as many times as you like, depending on how high you make the leg.

Abbreviations and a list of technique lessons can be found on pages 134-136.

Cables & Corrugations

Yarn: Fleece Artist Merino 2/6 (100% merino, 115 g / 325 m), 1 skein Mellow Yellow
Needles: size 1 (2.5 mm), or size you need to get gauge
Gauge: 8.5 sts = 1" (2.5 cm)
Size: midfoot 7.5 (8.5)" or 19 (21) cm
Markers: A, B, C, and D
Sole is starting ndl (ndl in left hand).

Toe

Make Moccasin Toe (page 128), starting with a cast-on of 8 sts to each parallel ndl, finishing with total st count (D) of 56 (64). When toe is about 2" (5 cm) long, use D to determine length of toe section (page 112). Knit toe to this length.

Foot

Knit 13 (15), place A, k1f&b, k1, place B, k to end of rnd. Total sts: 57 (65) - 3 sts between A and B.

Riverbed arch expansion - chart 1 and picture ①

Rnd 1: Knit to A, k1, LLinc, k to 1 st before B, LRinc, k to end.
Rnd 2: Knit.
Rnd 3: Knit 31 (35), (small size) p1, k6, repeat **LRinc, k5** 4x, p1, (large size) p1, k6, LRinc, repeat **k6, LRinc** 3x, k6, p1.
Total sts 63 (71) - 31 (35) sole sts and 32 (36) instep sts.

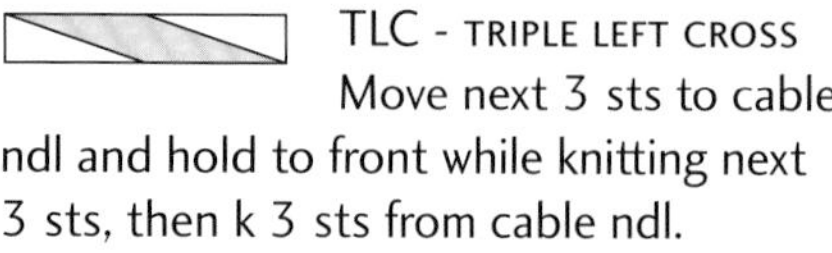

TLC - TRIPLE LEFT CROSS
Move next 3 sts to cable ndl and hold to front while knitting next 3 sts, then k 3 sts from cable ndl.

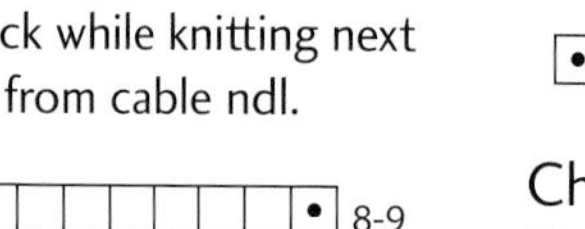

TRC - TRIPLE RIGHT CROSS
Move next 3 sts to cable ndl and hold to back while knitting next 3 sts, then k 3 sts from cable ndl.

☐ Knit

⊡ Purl

Chart 1
Companion rounds 4-9 (only instep sts are shown). Small size skips blue section.

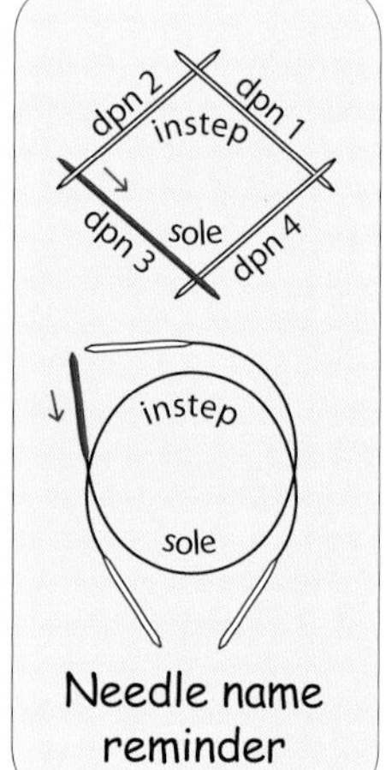

Needle name reminder

Companion rounds - chart 1

Rnd 4: Knit to A, k1, LLinc, k to 1 st before B, LRinc, k to end of sole, p1, k3, TRC, p12 (16), TLC, k3, p1.

Rnds 5 and 6: Knit to end of sole, p1, k9, p12 (16), k9, p1.

Rnd 7: Knit to A, k1, LLinc, k to 1 st before B, LRinc, k to end of sole, p1, TLC, k3, p12 (16), k3, TRC, p1.

Rnds 8 and 9: Knit to end of sole, p1, k30 (34), p1.

Repeat companion rnds 4-9 six more times. Total sts: 91 (99)

Rnd 46: Knit to A, k3, repeat *sl1, k1* 14x, k to end of sole, p1, k3, TRC, p12 (16), TLC, k3, p1. (see picture ①)

Rnd 47: Knit to end of sole, p1, k9, p12 (16), k9, p1.

Rnd 48: Knit to A, k3, repeat *sl1, k1* 14x, k to end of sole, p1, k9, p12 (16), k9, p1.

Rnd 49: Knit to B, k1 (2), repeat *LRinc, k2* 2x, LRinc, k1, repeat *LRinc, k2* 3x, LRinc, k1 (2), p1, TLC, k3, p12 (16), k3, TRC, p1 (stop at end of instep). Total sts: 98 (106)

Abbreviations and a list of technique lessons can be found on pages 134-136.

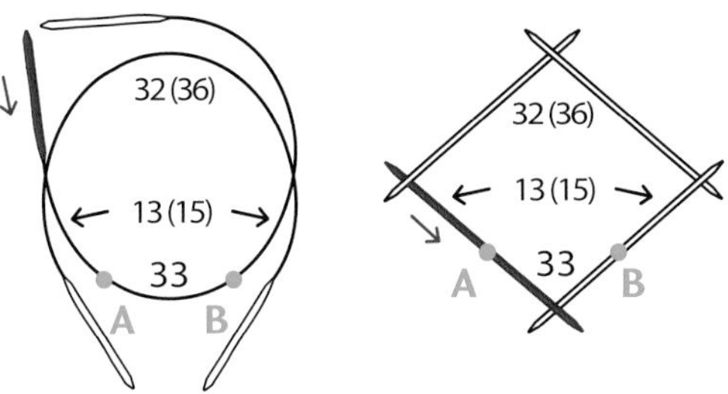

① Stitch distribution after completing rnd 46.

Heel - picture ② (see next page)

Row 1: Knit 1 (2), repeat *LLinc, k2* 2x, LLinc, k1, repeat *LLinc, k2* 3x, LLinc, k1 (2), (A), k3, repeat *sl1, k1* 14x, w&t. (see picture ② on next page) Total sts: 105 (113)

Follow reinforced heel directions (page 124), beginning with row 2 of step 3, using 8 (9) for **I**. Keep all sole sts on 1 circ or 2 dpn's. As you follow heel turn instructions, A and B will represent ends of sole ndl. In step 4, the 20 (22) wing sts (**H**) are already in place. Replace A *with* C and B *with* D. Total sts after heel is finished: 65 (69) - 33 sole sts and 32 (36) instep sts.

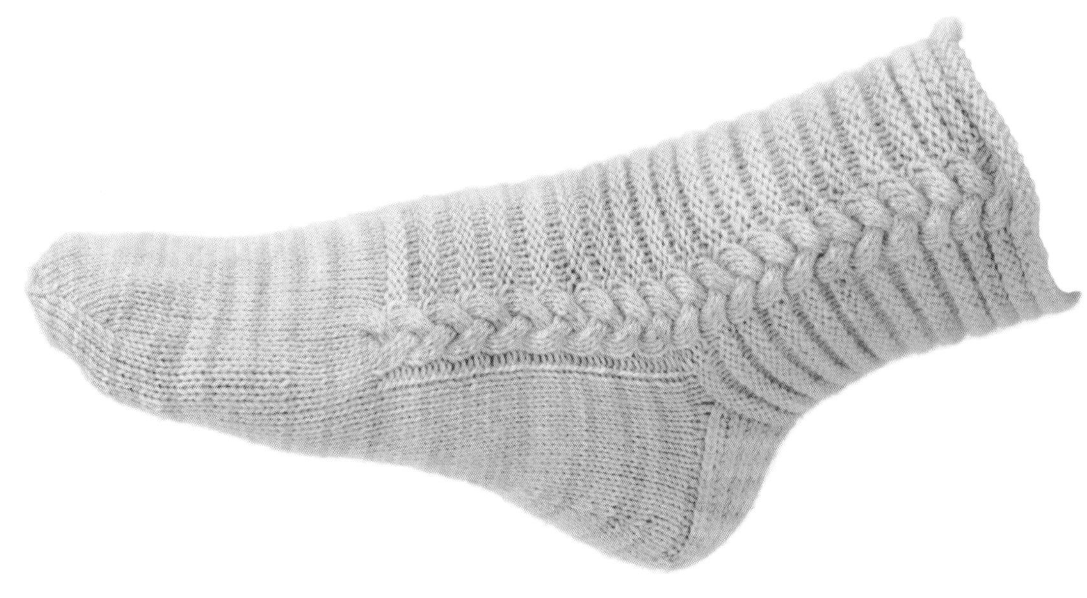

Leg

Instep is now starting ndl (ndl in left hand).

Rnd 1: Knit.

Companion rounds:

Rnd 2: Purl 1, k3, TRC, p12 (16), TLC, k3, p13, TLC, k3, p12.

Rnds 3 and 4: Purl 1, k9, p12 (16), k9, p13, k9, p12.

Rnd 5: Purl 1, TLC, k3, p12 (16), k3, TRC, p13, k3, TRC, p12.

Rnds 6 and 7: Knit.

Repeat companion rnds 2-7 another 10x.

Cuff

Purl 3 rnds. Bind off with EZ's sewn bind-off (page 130), and weave in all ends.

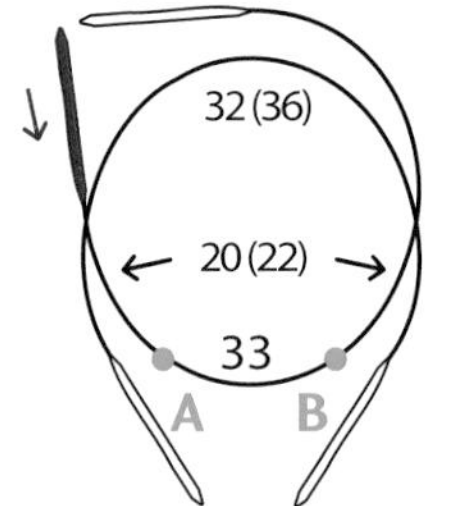

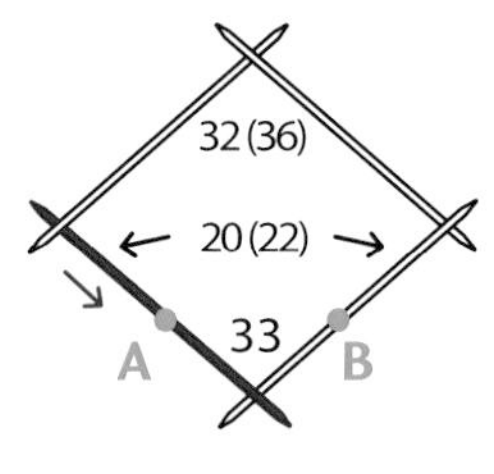

② Stitch distribution after completing row 1 of heel. After w&t at end of row 1, working yarn comes from the wrapped st. You have 1 unworked st and the wrapped st between **B** and the ndl tips, and are about to purl back.

See lesson on "A cable needle you may already have," page 95.

Chart 2

Leg companion rounds 2-7. Small size skips blue section.

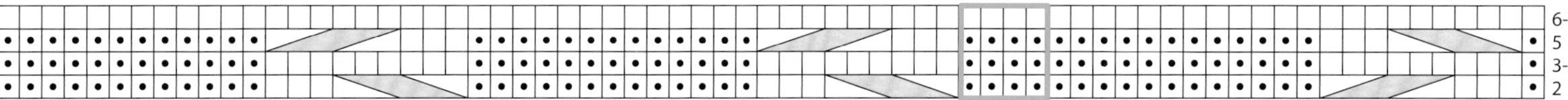

Riverbed Master Pattern

Find your Master numbers on pages 109-119.

Riverbed Master pattern, worked in Lana Grossa Meilenweit Fantasy color 4760

Markers: A, B, C and D
Sole is starting ndl (ndl in left hand).

Complete any toe (page 126). Knit toe E inches long.

Riverbed arch expansion

Marker placement if G is even - picture ①
Locate 4 center sts on sole. Place A before and B after the 4 center sts.
Marker placement if G is odd - picture ②
Locate center st on sole. Place A before and B after the 3 center sts.

Arch expansion companion rounds
Rnd 1: K to A, k1, LLinc, k to 1 st before B, LRinc, k to end.
Rnds 2 and 3: Knit.
Repeat companion rnds 1-3, stopping after a completed rnd 1 when total stitch count reaches F.
Remove markers.

Complete heel (page 120), leg, and cuff (page 130).

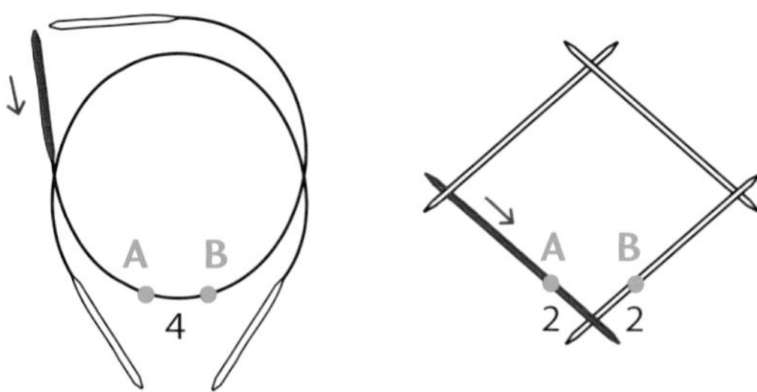

① If G is even, place A before and B after the 4 center sts.

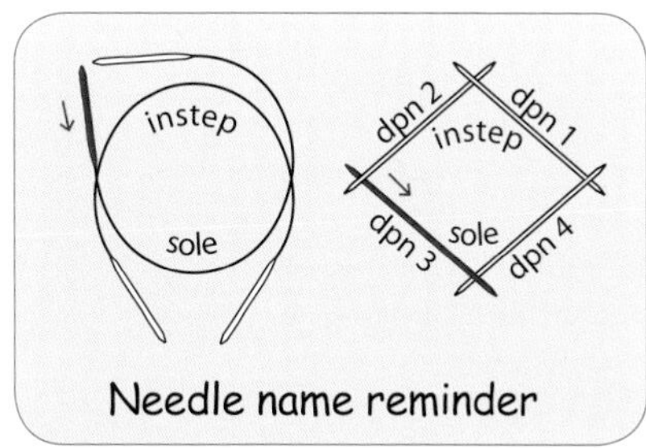

Needle name reminder

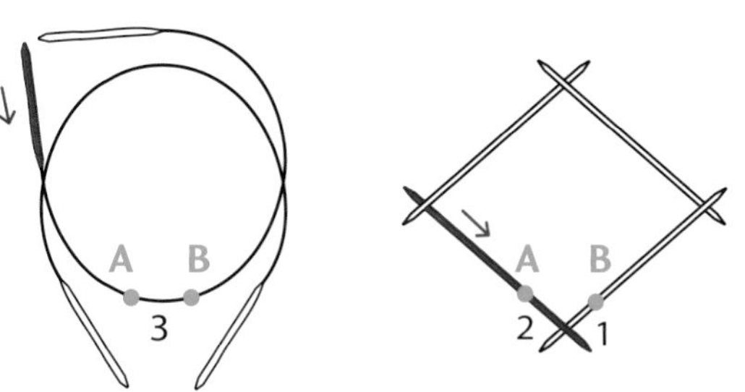

② If G is odd, place A before and B after the 3 center sts.

Abbreviations and a list of technique lessons can be found on pages 134-136.

Chapter 8 - Ridgeline Sock Architecture

Picture a mountain range, with streams falling away on either side of the ridgeline. The socks in this chapter mimic this natural form, with knitting spreading out from a ridgeline of increases over the mountain slope of your instep. The ridgeline may be plain, with increases organized along both edges, or a cable, a narrow panel of lace – any design that wants to run in a line. The ridgeline stitches clothe the part of your foot and leg that compresses vertically when you bend your ankle forward. Stitches with vertical compression, like slipped stitch patterns or garter stitch variations, are well-suited to this pathway.

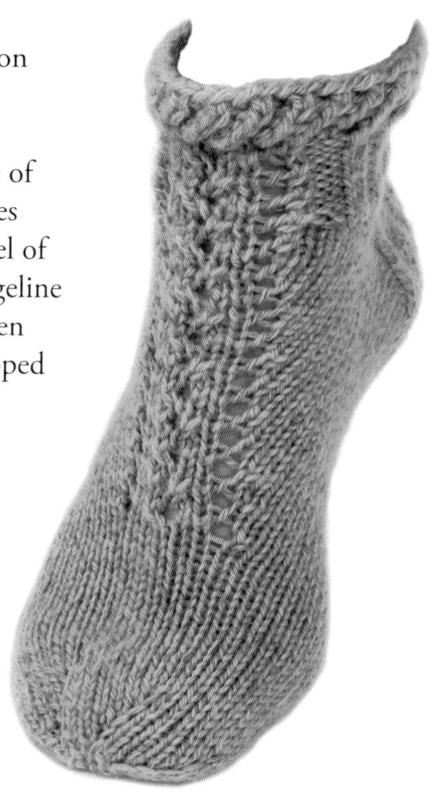

On a baby, the ridgeline can be quite wide, like the little cable on Charlie's Wiggle Socks. This cable compresses both vertically and horizontally, so the instep adds extra stitches to compensate. The cable also starts near the toe, because an infant's sock doesn't need to fit into shoes, and the bit of bumpiness won't be a problem.

The sock on this page is knit in a wonderful yarn of linen and merino, which you may not have considered for a sock before. I imagine a basket of them in all colors and sizes beside the door so shoes can be slipped off and these slipped on for comfort year round.

Joys of Ridgeline Architecture

- The increases fan out from a center ridgeline, inviting a vertical design
- The sides of the foot are free for designs
- The instep panel does well with vertically compressed stitches
- Learn this pathway, and you're ready for Upstream, Riverbed, and Sidestream architectures

Chart 1

Arch expansion - plain rnds 2-3 and 5-6 not shown.

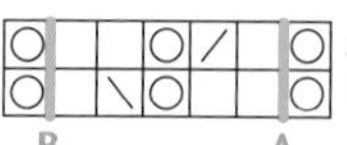

Chart 2

Ribbing and plain rnds 2-3 and 5-6 not shown.

4
1
B A

k2tog
ssk
k1
yo

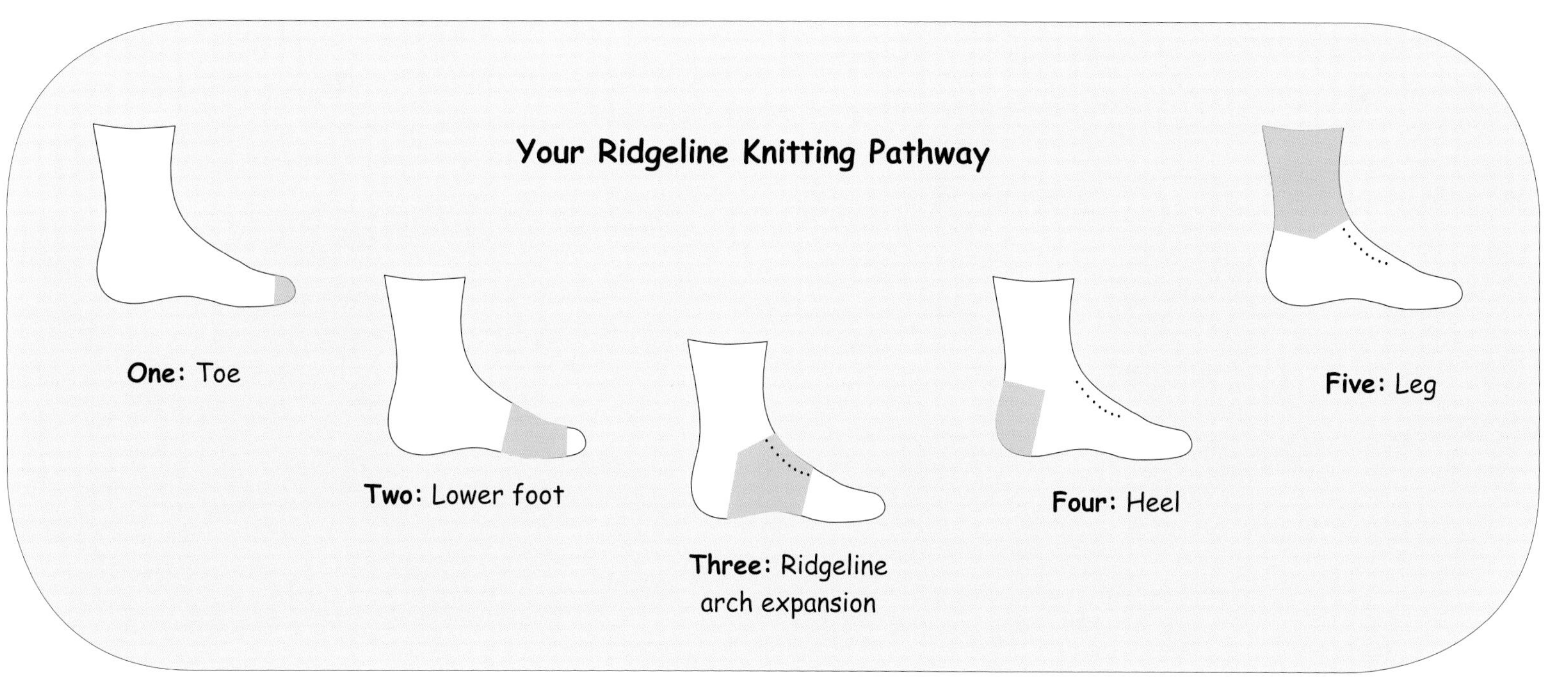

Home & Hearth Eyelet Anklets

For the independent knitter: Louet Merlin (70% merino, 30% linen, 100 g / 190 yds), 2 skeins Willow. My gauge was 6 sts = 1" (2.5 cm). You're in charge, though … so choose any yarn, needles, and gauge you wish. Follow Ridgeline Master pattern (page 99), replacing arch expansion with this set-up rnd: Place **A** *before* and **B** *after* the center 5 instep sts (if instep doesn't have an odd number of sts, add 1), followed by these companion rounds: Repeat rnds 1-6 of chart 1 (charts on page 92), knitting all sts not shown in chart. When heel is complete, repeat **work k2p2 ribbing to 2 sts before* **A**, work chart 2, *work ribbing to end,** until ankle is 1" (2.5 cm) shorter than desired height. Cuff: Repeat **yo, k2tog to end of rnd** 5x. Bind off loosely.

Charlie's Wiggle Socks

These little socks have perfectly smooth sides and sole, with paired cables wiggling their way from toe to ankle along the top. They were inspired by images of umbilical cords.

Yarn: Claudia Hand Painted Yarns (100% merino, 100 g/ 225 yds), 1 skein Blue Sky or Honey
Needles: size 2 (3 mm), or size you need to get gauge, cable needle
Gauge: 8 sts = 1" (2.5 cm)
Sizes: premie, (newborn, 3-6 months, 6-12 months)
Markers: A, B, C and D
Instep is starting ndl (ndl in left hand).

Toe

Make Wiggle Room Baby Toe (page 128), starting with 7 (9, 11, 13) sts on each of 2 parallel ndls, and finishing with a total of 22 (26, 30, 34). Knit until toe is 0.5" (1 cm) long.

Arch expansion (see chart)

Place A at beginning and B at end of 9 center instep sts.
LLinc's are made right *before* A and LRinc's right *after* B.
Companion Rounds:

Rnd 1: Knit to A, LLinc, DRC, k1, DLC, LRinc, k to end.
Rnds 2-3 and 5-6: Knit.
Rnd 4: Knit to A, LLinc, DLC, k1, DRC, LRinc, k to end.

Repeat companion rnds 1-6 another 2 (3, 4, 5) times.
On final rnd 6, stop at end of instep - *do not knit across sole.*
Stitch total: 34 (42, 50, 58) Move A 3 (4, 5, 6) sts to the right and B 3 (4, 5, 6) sts to the left. There are now 15 (17, 19, 21) sts between A and B.

Side socks are Blue Sky, in center is Honey

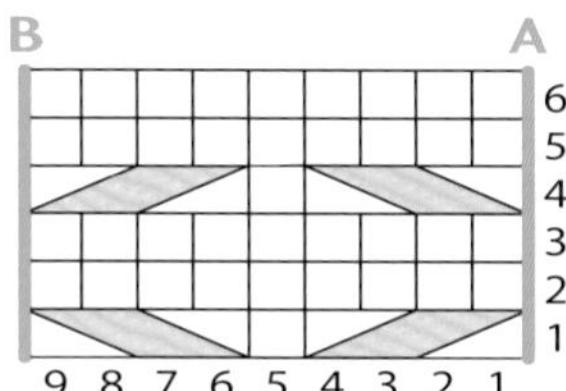

Arch expansion rnds 1-6. Work a LLinc right before passing A, and a LRinc right after passing B.

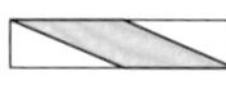
DLC - double left cross - move next 2 sts to cable ndl and hold to front while knitting next 2 sts, then k 2 sts from cable ndl.

DRC - double right cross - move next 2 sts to cable ndl and hold to back while knitting next 2 sts, then k 2 sts from cable ndl.

knit

Abbreviations and a list of technique lessons can be found on pages 134-136.

Heel

Work plain heel (page 122) on sole alone, beginning with step 3 (A and B are already in place), using 3 (4, 5, 6) for I and 4 (6, 8, 10) for H. No J is needed. Total sts after heel is finished: 26 (30, 34, 38) - 15 (17, 19, 21) instep and 11 (13, 15, 17) sole

Leg and cuff

Knit 1 rnd - (for 3-6 months size, LRinc at start of sole and at start of instep; for premie and 6-12 months, LRinc at start of sole only). Stitch total: 27 (30, 36, 39) Knit 1 rnd. Cuff rnds: Repeat **k2, p1** to end. Repeat until cuff is 2" (5 cm). Bind off loosely with EZ's sewn bind-off (page 130). If you'd like to add an ankle tie, see page 26.

A cable needle you may already have

If you're using 2 circs, one needle is always at work while the other dangles unused. That idle needle makes a splendid cable needle. It's always handy (and won't fall to be swallowed by the sofa), and works really well. Just pull up an unused end and insert the tip through the cable stitches that are to be held to the front or back. Slide the held stitches onto the needle's cord so the end is out of the way (unlike a cable needle, which remains awkwardly close). Knit the next stitches in line, then transfer the held stitches back to the working needle and let the "cable needle" dangle again.

Soft-Hearted Socks

These soft alpaca socks use a very simple method of outlining a contrast-color shape while knitting in the round - and you can use it in garments as well. Wear them with care - alpaca is not as durable as dedicated sock yarns.

Yarn: Frog Tree Sport Weight Alpaca (100% alpaca, 50 g / 130 yds), 2 skeins Chocolate, 1 skein Rose

Needles: size 1 (2.5 mm), or size you need to get gauge

Gauge: 8 sts = 1" (2.5 cm)

Sizes: midfoot 6 (6.5, 7.5, 8.5)" or 15 (16, 19, 21) cm

Markers: A, B, C and D

Instep is starting ndl (ndl in left hand).

Toe

Make Standard Toe (page 126), with Rose, starting with 9 (11, 12, 13) sts on each of 2 parallel ndls. When total sts reaches 34 (38, 44, 50), continue with toe instructions, alternating 2 rnds of Rose and 2 rnds of Chocolate. When total sts (D) reaches 42 (46, 52, 58), knit all rnds. When toe is 2" (5 cm) long, use D to determine how long to knit toe section (page 112) before beginning arch expansion. Knit toe to this length, continuing with Chocolate alone after 5 completed Rose stripes. Begin heart panel (see next section) once you have 7 completed Chocolate rnds.

Heart panel

Panel continues up foot until complete. Place A at beginning and B at end of central 11 instep sts. Work heart motif a total of 3x inside A and B as follows: Use middle of a 35" (90 cm) strand of Rose to k the single Rose st in rnds 1 and 2. After this, use each side of Rose strand to work that side's Rose sts. In rnd 11, when a center st is needed, use a 10" (25 cm) strand as you did the first one, starting with its center and then using its sides. Knit 7 plain rnds after each heart.

Arch expansion

Arch expansion begins once toe section is complete. Work heart panel between A and B.

Companion rounds:

Rnd 1: Knit to 1 st before A, LRinc, k to 1 st past B, LLinc, k to end.

Rnds 2 and 3: Knit.

Repeat companion rnds 1-3 until total sts reaches 62 (68, 78, 86) during a rnd 1. Stop at end of instep - do not knit across sole.

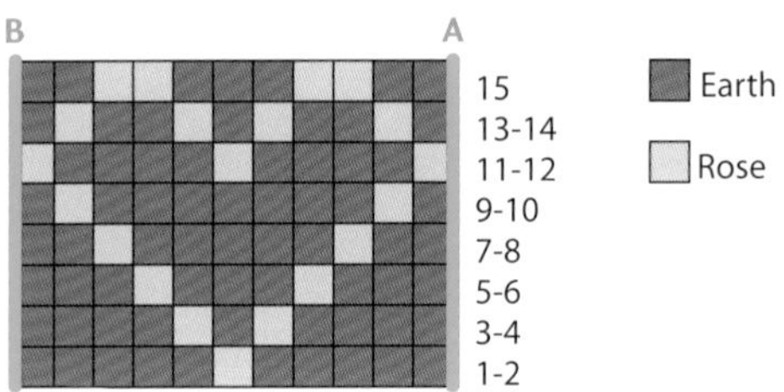

Heel

Work reinforced heel (page 120), beginning with step 1, using 21 (23, 26, 29) for Ⓖ, 10 (11, 13, 14) for Ⓗ, 4 (4, 5, 5) for Ⓙ, and 6 (6, 7, 8) for Ⓘ.

Total sts after heel is finished: 42 (46, 53, 58)

Leg and cuff

When 3rd heart motif (followed by 7 Chocolate rnds) is complete, work alternating sets of 2 Rose rnds and 2 Chocolate rnds until 5 Rose rnds are completed. (3rd size only - work a LRinc in the next rnd so st total is 54.) Knit 9 Chocolate rnds.

Next rnd: Repeat **k2tog, yo** to end. Knit 8 Rose rnds. Bind off with EZ's sewn bind-off (page 130), then fold hem to inside along yo rnd and sew gently (to guarantee elasticity) to inside.

Weave in all ends.

Abbreviations and a list of technique lessons can be found on pages 134-136.

Sometimes two different needle sizes make a "matched" pair

I'll bet that all your knitting life you've worked with a matched pair of needles. Guess what? Only one needle determines your gauge. Stop for a moment and see if you can figure out which one. I'll bet you can. It's just that you may never have thought about it before. Yes, it's the needle in your right hand. The passive left needle merely delivers loops to the active right needle, which manufactures new stitches. The gauge - the diameter of the new stitch - is born and bred entirely on the right needle. So if you purl more loosely than you knit - which shows up in a sock as a loose heel (because you are working in **rows** instead of rounds) - you can use a smaller needle just on the purl side. This unmatched pair of needles can really improve the durability and appearance of your heel. Another option: read page 135 to learn a method of purling more tightly.

Woven Ridge Socks

The woven (linen) stitch in the ridgeline panel distributes handpaint colors in short contrasting segments for a beautiful effect. Notice how muted the stripes are in this section. The handsome braided edge is simply a double-stranded bind-off.

Yarn: Artyarns Handpaint Stripes (100% wool, 100 g / 188 yds), 2 skeins color 105
Needles: size 2 (3 mm), or size you need to get gauge
Gauge: 6 sts = 1" (2.5 cm)
Sizes: midfoot 7 (8.25, 9.5) or 18 (21, 24) cm
Markers: A, B, C and D
Instep is starting ndl (ndl in left hand).

Toe

Make Standard Toe (page 126), starting with 7 (7, 9) sts on each of 2 parallel ndls, and completing toe with a total of 38 (46, 54) sts. When toe is about 2" or 5 cm long, use D to determine how long to knit toe section (page 112). Knit toe to this length.

Arch expansion - Chart 1

Sl1wyif *(slip 1 with yarn in front)* - Move yarn to front before slipping next st tip-to-tip (purlwise), then move yarn to back. Place A at beginning and B at end of central 7 instep sts. LLinc's are made right *before* A and LRinc's right *after* B.

Chart 1

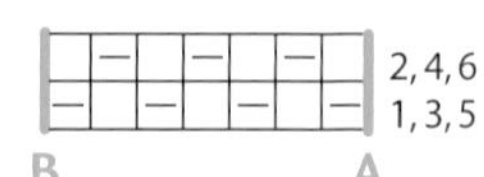

☐ knit ⊟ sl1wyif

Companion rounds:

Rnd 1: Knit to A, LLinc, repeat **sl1wyif, k1** 3x, sl1wyif (B), LRinc, k to end.
Rnds 2 and 6: Knit to A, k1, repeat **sl1wyif, k1** 3x, (B), k to end.
Rnds 3 and 5: Knit to A, repeat **sl1wyif, k1** 3x, sl1wyif (B), k to end.
Rnd 4: Knit to A, LLinc, k1, repeat **sl1wyif, k1** 3x, (B), LRinc k to end.

Repeat companion rnds 1-6 until st count reaches 58 (70, 82) during a rnd 4, stopping at end of instep - do not knit across sole. Remove A and B.

Heel

Work reinforced heel (page 120), beginning with step 1, using 19 (23, 27) for G, 10 (12, 14) for H, 4 (5, 5) for J, and 5 (6, 7) for I. Stitch total after heel is finished: 38 (46, 54)

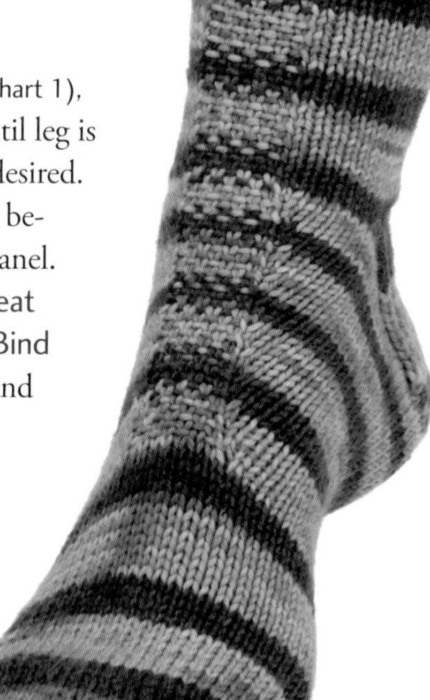

Leg and cuff - chart 1

Continue 7-st panel (chart 1), knitting all other sts, until leg is 2.5" (6 cm) shorter than desired. Next rnd, work a LLinc before and a LRinc after panel. Total sts: 40 (48, 56) Repeat **k3, p1** for 2.5" (6 cm). Bind off with double strand and weave in all ends.

Ridgeline Master Pattern

Find your Master numbers on pages 109-119.

Markers: A, B, C and D
Instep is starting ndl (ndl in left hand).

Complete any toe (page 126). Knit toe **E** inches long.

Ridgeline arch expansion
Ridgeline width works well with a number of sts between **A** and 2 times **A**. Choose an even number of sts if **G** is even, or an odd number if **G** is odd.

Marker placement - picture ①
Center ridgeline sts on instep. Place A before 1st ridgeline st, and B after final ridgeline st. (If **G** is odd, and you are using dpn's, one instep dpn will have 1 more st than the other.)

Arch expansion companion rounds
LLinc's are worked right *before* A and LRinc's right *after* B.
  Rnd 1: Knit to A, LLinc, k to B, LRinc, k to end.
  Rnds 2 and 3: Knit.
Repeat companion rnds 1-3, stopping after a completed rnd 1 when total st count reaches **F**. Remove A and B.

Complete heel (page 120), leg, and cuff (page 130).

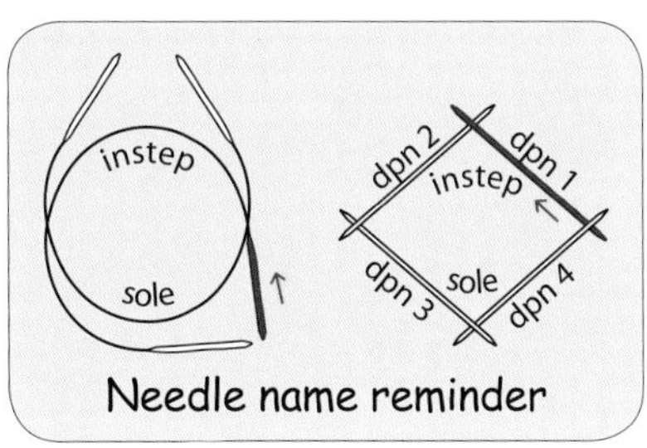

Needle name reminder

Home & Hearth Eyelet Anklet, page 93

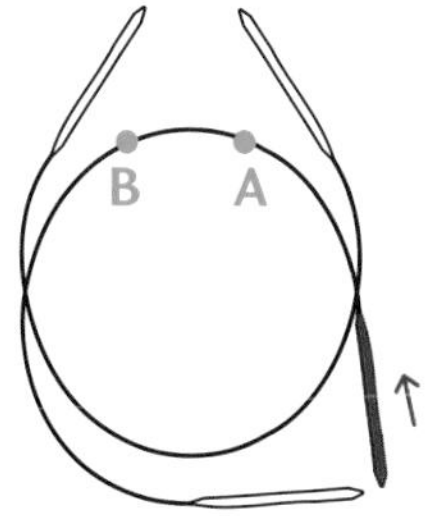

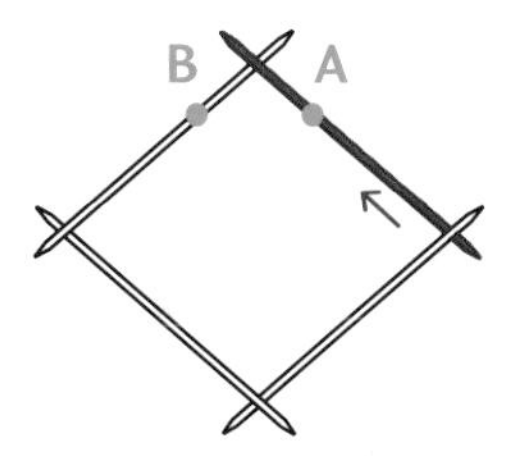

① The ridgeline sts are centered on instep circ or divided between dpns 1 and 2. A is placed *before* and B *after* ridgeline sts.

Abbreviations and a list of technique lessons can be found on pages 134-136.

Chapter 9 - Sidestream Sock Architecture

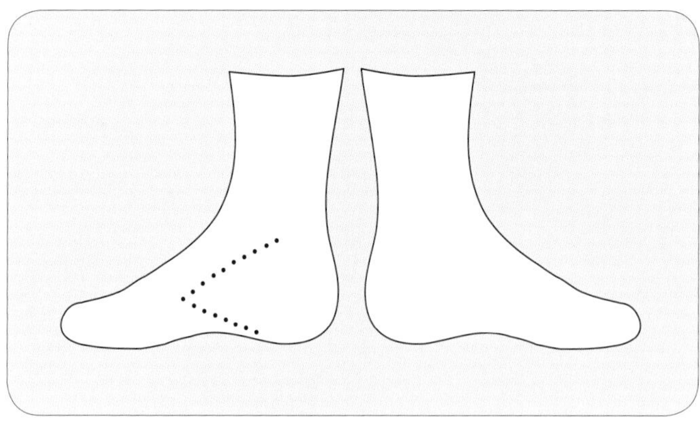

This sudden appearance of this architecture was what stunned me beside the lake in Indiana (as related in the introductory chapter). If it hadn't fit my foot - you can't argue with a foot - I never would have believed it possible that the entire arch expansion could be placed on one side of the foot without skewing the fit. See the illustration? One side is pure stockinette while the opposite side houses the entire expansion. Not long after accepting (although not understanding) what I saw on my foot, I began rotating the sock to see where else the expansion fit, and as you read in the introduction, it fit everywhere. I still think it's downright flabbergasting.

The Joys of Sidestream Architecture

- All increases are on one side, leaving the top and other side smooth and free for designs
- The enchantment of asymmetry
- Learn this pathway and you're ready for Upstream, Riverbed, and Ridgeline architectures

I hope you'll experiment with slight variations in rotation. If you start with a toe that can be rotated at whim (the Whirlpool Toe is ideal - see page 126) and try the sock on after finishing the arch expansion, you can decide just where you'd like to place the increase triangle. Once you decide, mark off the stitches over the instep (Ⓖ if using a Master pattern) and the same number for the sole, leaving the wing stitches (Ⓗ) in between. Work the heel and knit your way up the leg of your unique sock.

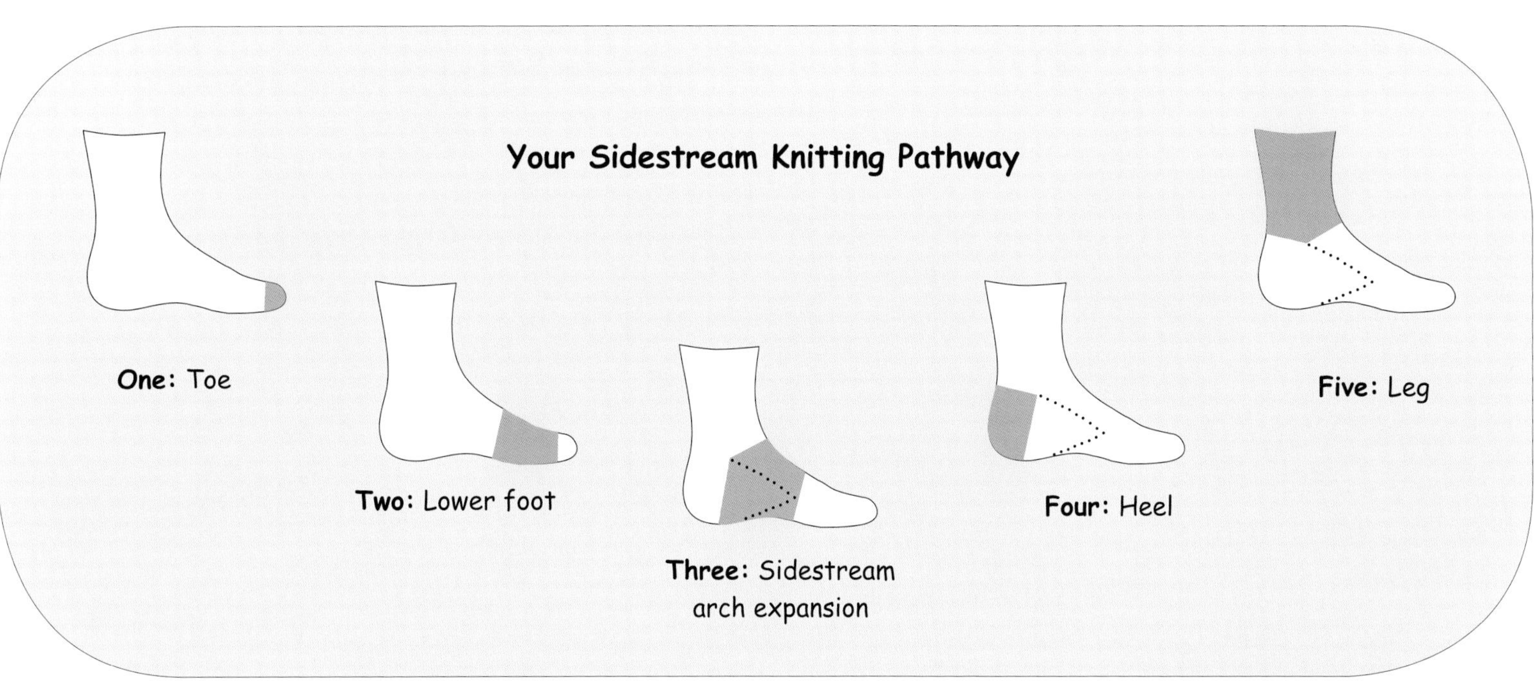

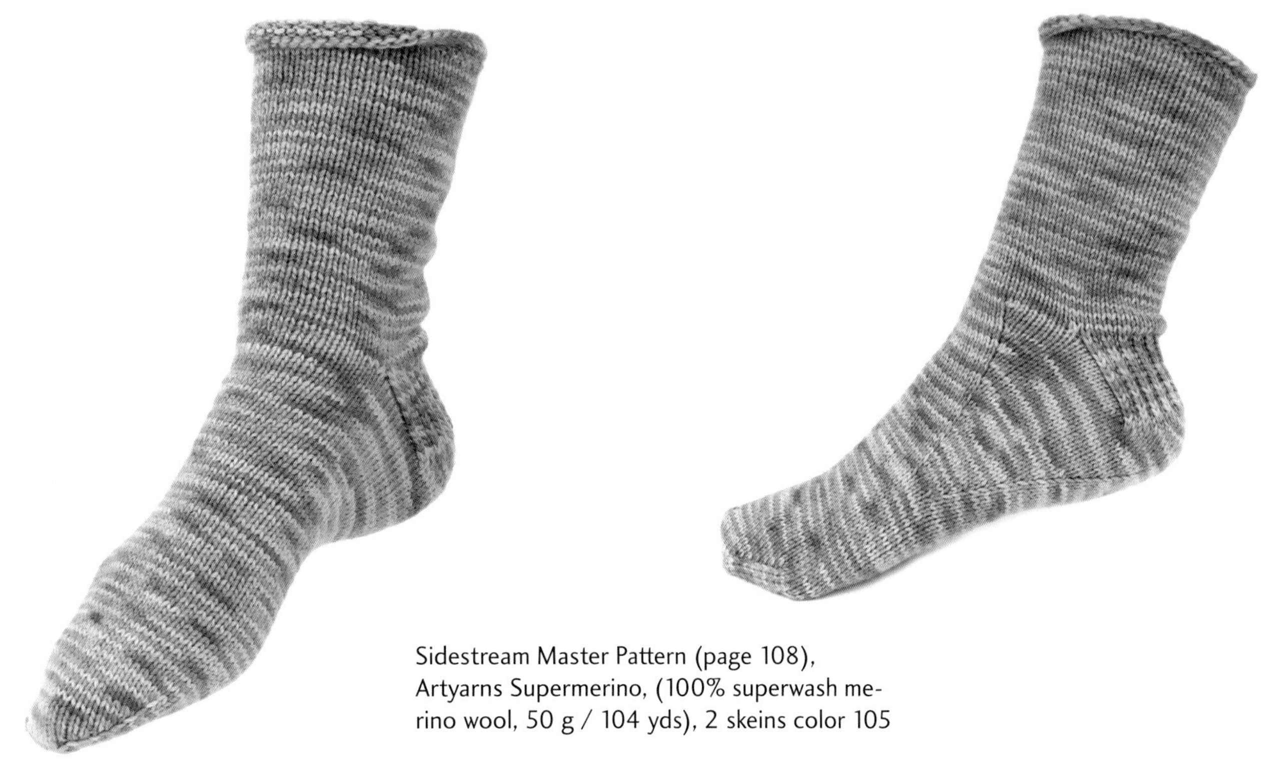

Sidestream Master Pattern (page 108), Artyarns Supermerino, (100% superwash merino wool, 50 g / 104 yds), 2 skeins color 105

Charlie's Sheriff Boat Socks

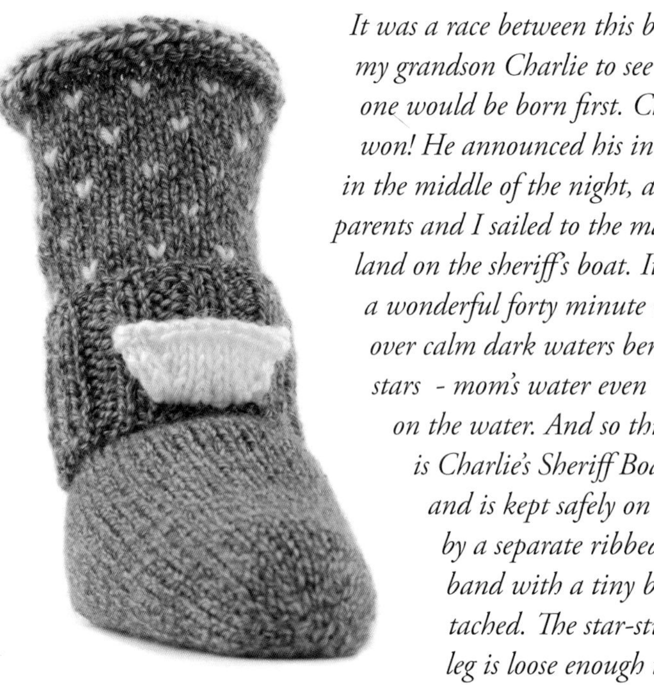

It was a race between this book and my grandson Charlie to see which one would be born first. Charlie won! He announced his intentions in the middle of the night, and his parents and I sailed to the mainland on the sheriff's boat. It was a wonderful forty minute voyage over calm dark waters beneath the stars - mom's water even broke on the water. And so this sock is Charlie's Sheriff Boat Sock, and is kept safely on little feet by a separate ribbed ankle band with a tiny boat attached. The star-studded leg is loose enough to get on and off wiggling feet.

Yarn: Crystal Palace Panda Wool (46% bamboo, 43% wool, 11% nylon, 50 g / 170 yds), 1 ball Bluebell, 1 ball Starlight
Needles: size 2 (3 mm), or size you need to get gauge
Gauge: 7 sts = 1" (2.5 cm)
Size: 0-3 (3-6, 6-9) months
Markers: A, B, C and D
Instep is starting ndl (ndl in left hand).

Toe

With Bluebell, make Whirlpool Toe (page 126), finishing with total st count of 24 (28, 32). Knit until toe measures 1 (1.5, 2)" or 2.5 (4, 5) cm long.

Arch expansion - pictures ① and ②

Rnd 1: Knit 1, place A, knit until 1 st before end of sole, place B, k1f&b. (3 sts between A and B) See picture ①.

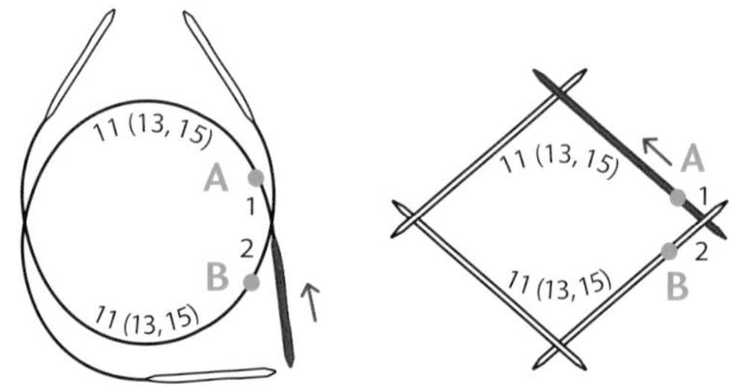

① Stitch distribution after rnd 1 of arch expansion.

Rnd 2: LRinc, k to 1 st past B, LLinc, k1. (5 sts between A and B)

Arch expansion companion rounds

Rnds 3-4: Knit.

Rnd 5: Knit to 1 st before A, LRinc, k to 1 st past B, LLinc, k to end.

Repeat companion rnds 3-5, stopping after a completed rnd 5 when total stitch count reaches 41 (47, 53). See picture ②.

Remove A and B.

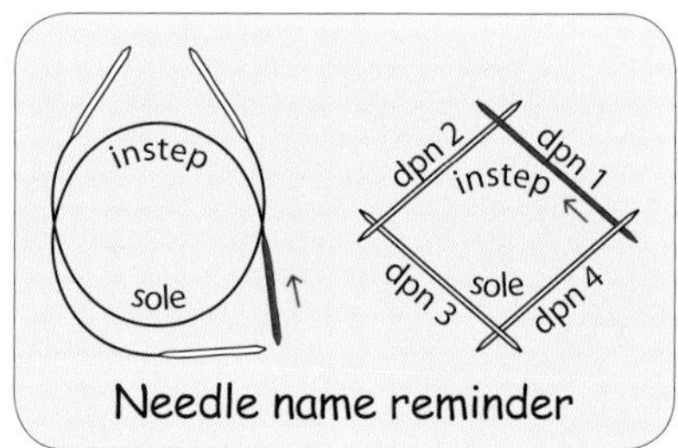

Second sock only - rotation: Knit to end of instep, then k1 from sole onto instep. *Now instep and sole switch identities – what was sole is now instep, and what was instep is now sole.*
Both socks: Instep has 20 (23, 26) sts and sole has 21 (24, 27) sts. Knit to end of instep. Knit next 8 (10, 10) sole sts onto instep. Instep now has 28 (33, 36) sts and sole has 13 (14, 17) sts.

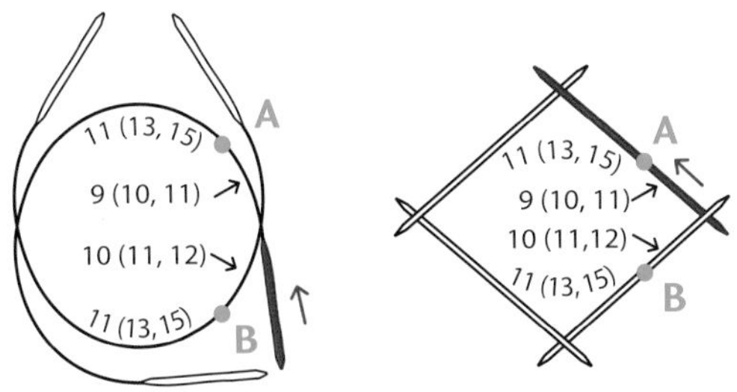

② Stitch distribution just before A and B are removed.

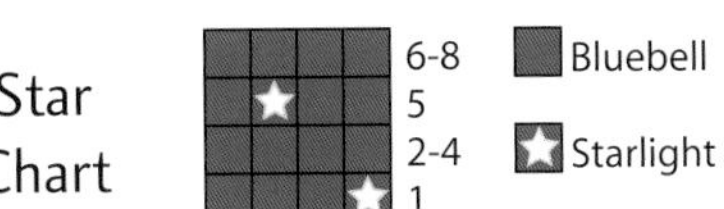

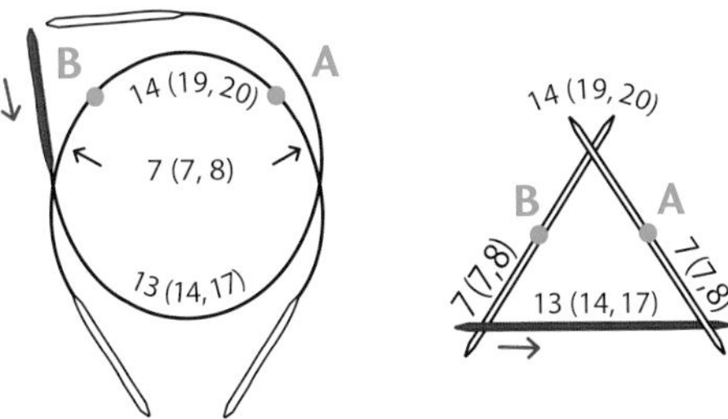

③ Stitch distribution as heel begins.

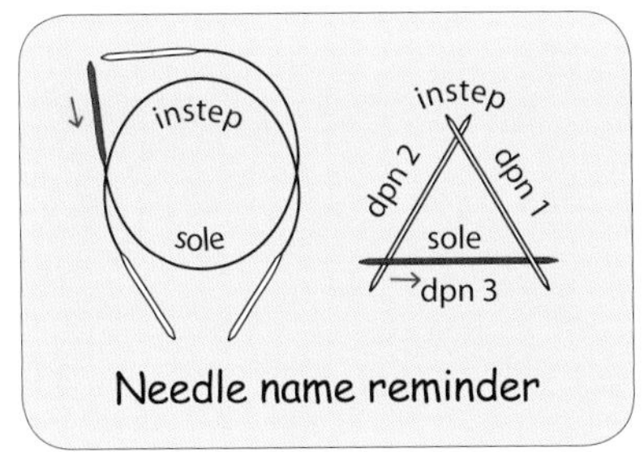

Place A 7 (7, 8) sts after start of instep and B 7 (7, 8) sts before end of instep. Next (starting) ndl is sole. *If using dpn's, put all sole sts on 1 dpn.*

Heel - see picture ③ as you begin
Work plain heel (page 122), starting at step 3. A and B are already in place. Use 3 (3, 4) for **I**, and 7 (7, 8) for **H**, and ignore **J**. Total sts after heel is finished: 27 (33, 37)

Leg and cuff
Knit 3 rnds. Next rnd: Include 9 (7, 11) evenly distributed LRinc's during this rnd. Total sts: 36 (40, 48) Continue knitting until leg measures 1 (1.5, 2)" or 3 (4, 5) cm above heel. Add Starlight and repeat the Star Chart's *rnds 1-8* twice, then *rnds 1-4* once more. Purl 1 rnd, k 1 rnd, then bind off with both yarns held together. Weave in ends.

Boat and ankle-band
Boat: With Starlight, follow directions for Standard Toe (page 126), starting by casting on 5 sts to each parallel ndl, and finishing with total st count of 18. Knit 1 rnd. Bind off and weave in ends.
Ankle-band: With Bluebell, cast on 24 (28, 32), join, and work k2, p2 ribbing for 1.5" (3 cm). Bind off using EZ's sewn bind-off (page 130). Sew boat to ankle-band.

Sunrise Socks

By now you may have noticed that I like to use Trekking double-stranded to blend the colors. Here's another example, this one with a garter stitch toe, garter arch expansion, and a reversible cuff.

Yarn: Zitron Trekking XXL (75% wool, 25% nylon, 100 g / 459 yds), 1 skein 105 Sunrise, and Fortissima Socka (75% wool, 25% nylon, 100 g / 420 yds), 1 skein 2048 Oatmeal

Needles: size 6 (4 mm), or size you need to get gauge

Gauge: (using 2 strands together) 6 sts = 1" (2.5 cm)

Size: midfoot 5 (6.5, 8, 9.5)" or 13 (16, 20, 24) cm

Markers: A, B, C and D

Yarn is used double-stranded at all times.

Instep is starting ndl (ndl in left hand).

Toe

With Oatmeal, make Garter Toe (page 127), casting on 6 (8, 10, 12) sts to each parallel ndl, and finishing with total st count (D) of 24 (32, 40, 48). Knit 1 rnd. Change to Sunrise. When toe is about 2" (5 cm) long, use D to determine length of toe section (page 112). Knit toe to this length.

Arch expansion - picture ①

Rnd 1: Knit 5 (7, 9, 11), place A, k1f&b, k1, place B, k to end.

Total sts: 25 (33, 41, 49)

Rnd 2: Knit.

Rnd 3: Knit to A, k1, LLinc, p1, LRinc, k to end.

Total sts: 27 (35, 43, 51)

Arch expansion companion rounds

- Rnds 4 and 8: Knit.
- Rnds 5 and 7: Knit to A, k1, p to 1 st before B, k to end.
- Rnd 6: Knit to A, k1, LLinc, k to 1 st before B, LRinc, k to end.
- Rnd 9: Knit to A, k1, LLinc, p to 1 st before B, LRinc, k to end.

Repeat companion rnds 4-9, stopping after a completed rnd 6 or 9 when total stitch count reaches 37 (49, 61, 73). If completed rnd was a rnd 6, work a rnd 7 before continuing. See picture ①. Remove A and B. *Yarn is at start of instep.* Rotate first sock: Knit 13 (17, 21, 25), and stop - these sts are now sole. *If using dpn's, put all sole sts on 1 dpn.* Knit next 24 (32, 40, 48) sts with other circ or next 2 dpn's - these sts are now instep. *Yarn is at start of sole.*

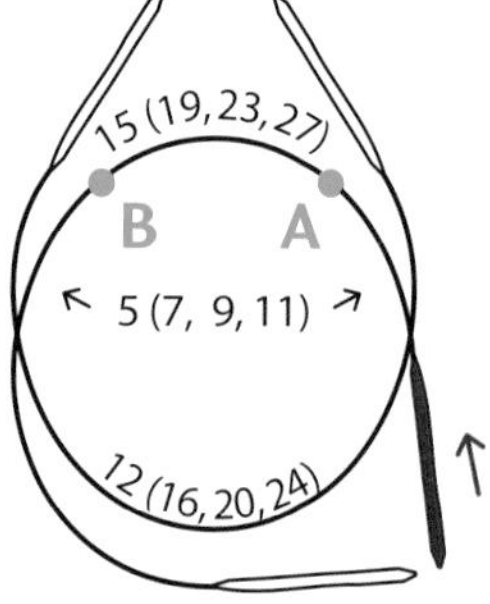

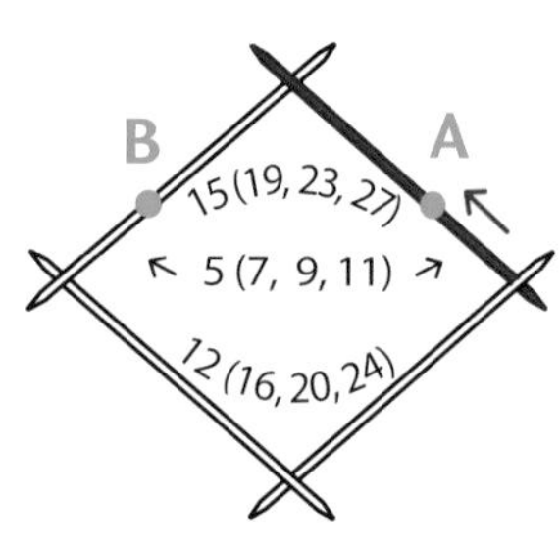

① Stitch distribution before removing A and B.

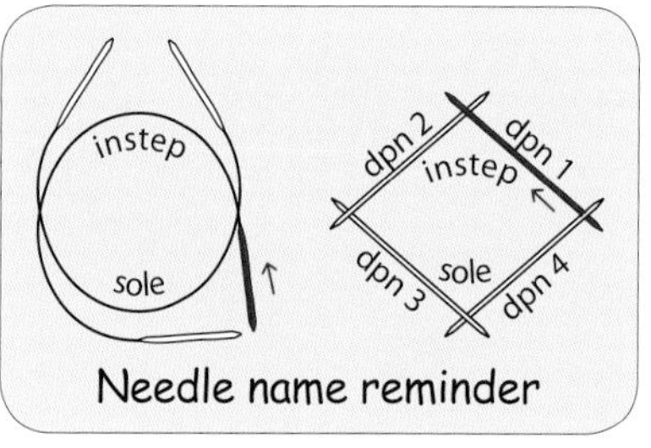

Rotate second sock: Use sole ndl to k12 (16, 20, 24) sts *from* instep *onto* sole ndl. Leave next 13 (17, 21, 25) sts on other circ or 1 dpn - these sts are now sole. Remaining 24 (32, 40, 48) sts (on 1 circ or 2 dpn's) are now instep. *Yarn is at start of sole.* Both socks: Place A 6 (8, 10, 12) sts *after start* of instep and B 6 (8, 10, 12) sts *before end* of instep. See picture ②.

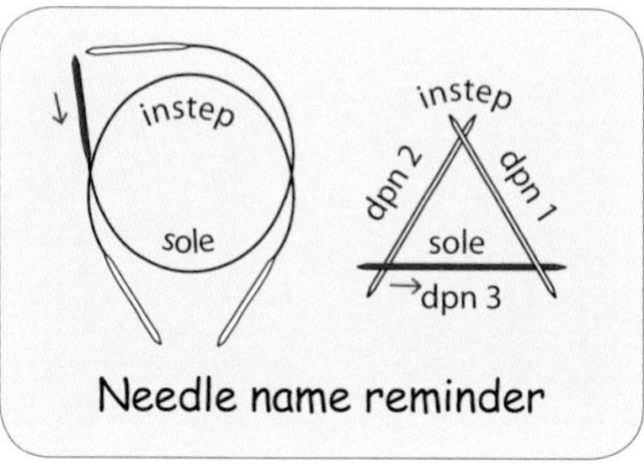

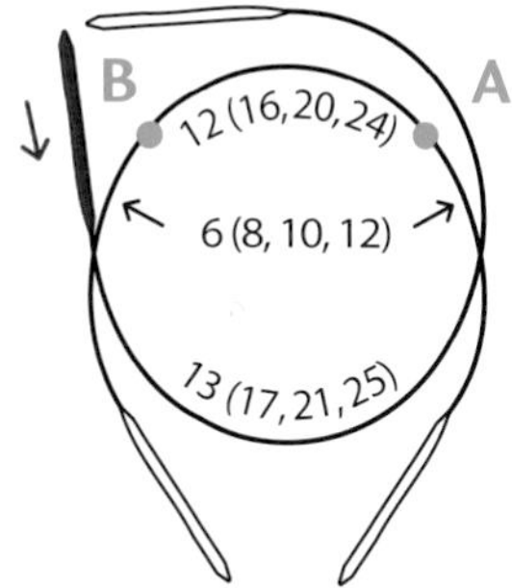

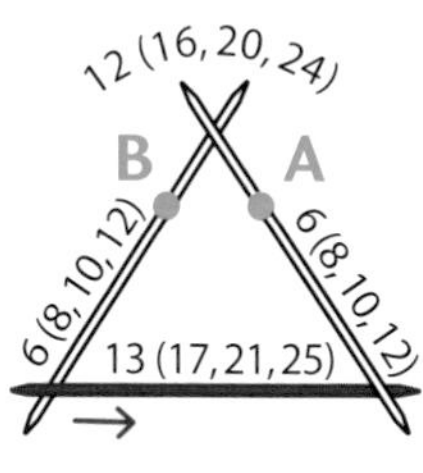

② Stitch distribution as heel begins.

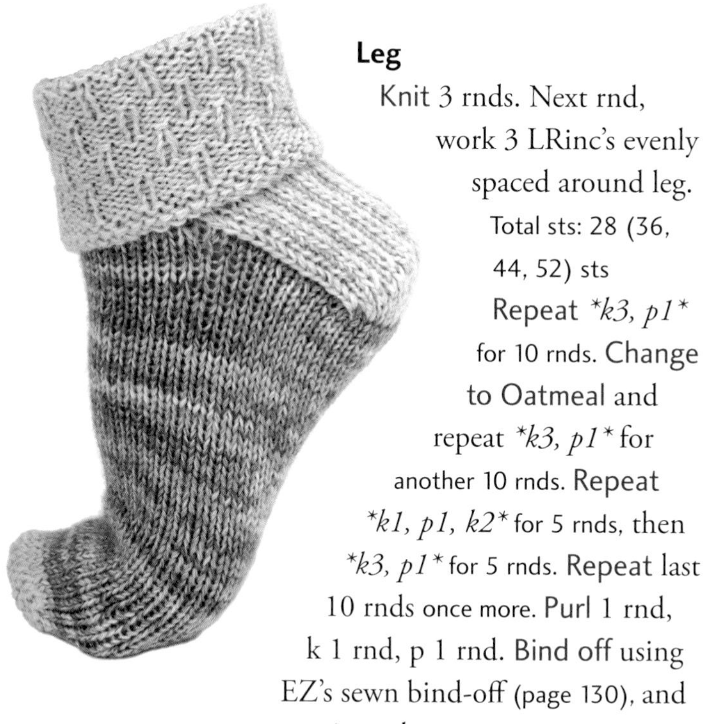

Leg

Knit 3 rnds. Next rnd, work 3 LRinc's evenly spaced around leg.
Total sts: 28 (36, 44, 52) sts

Repeat **k3, p1** for 10 rnds. Change to Oatmeal and repeat **k3, p1** for another 10 rnds. Repeat **k1, p1, k2** for 5 rnds, then **k3, p1** for 5 rnds. Repeat last 10 rnds once more. Purl 1 rnd, k 1 rnd, p 1 rnd. Bind off using EZ's sewn bind-off (page 130), and weave in ends.

Heel - see picture ② as you begin

With Oatmeal, make reinforced heel (page 120) beginning with step 1. A and B, G, and H are already in place. Use 6 (8, 10, 12) for H, 4 (5, 6, 7) for I, and 3 (3, 4, 5) for J. At end of step 5, change to Sunrise after the ssk and before working the k1, just before you resume knitting in the rnd.
Total sts: 25 (33, 41, 49)

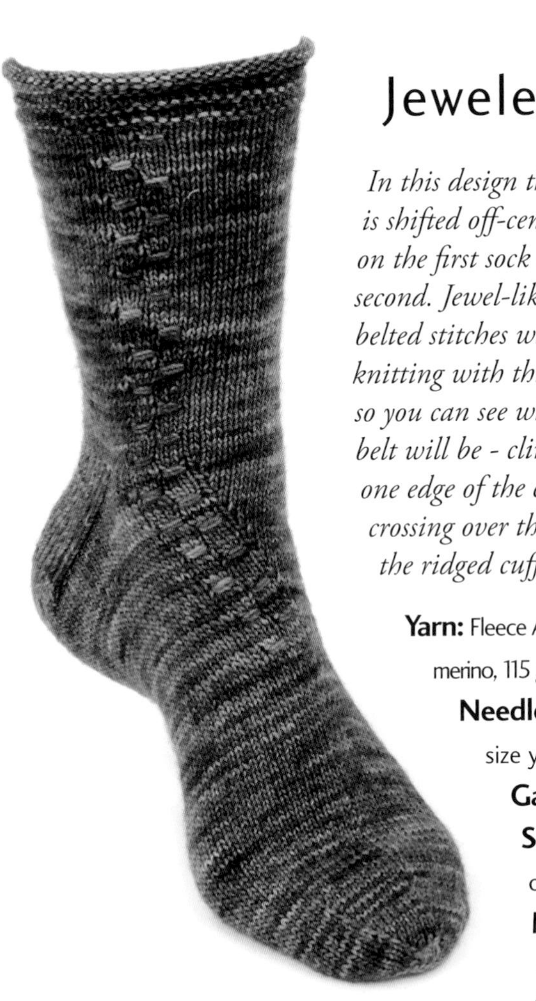

Jeweled Steps

In this design the expansion triangle is shifted off-center in one direction on the first sock and the other on the second. Jewel-like lozenges - sets of belted stitches which tempt you to keep knitting with this handpainted yarn so you can see which color the next belt will be - climb like footsteps up one edge of the expansion triangle, crossing over the instep and rising to the ridged cuff.

Yarn: Fleece Artist Merino 2/6 (100% merino, 115 g / 325 m), 1 skein Parrot
Needles: size 1 (2.5 mm), or size you need to get gauge
Gauge: 8 sts = 1" (2.5 cm)
Sizes: midfoot 7 (8, 9)" or 18 (20, 23) cm
Markers: A, B, C and D
Instep is starting ndl (ndl in left hand).

Toe
Make Whirlpool Toe (page 126), finishing with total st count (D) of 48 (56, 64). When toe is about 2" (5 cm) long, use D to determine length of toe section (page 112). Knit toe to this length.

Arch expansion - chart
Rnd 1: (instep) Knit 23 (27, 31), place A, k1f&b, (sole) k1, place B, k 23 (27, 31). (3 sts between A and B) Total sts: 49 (57, 65)
Rnd 2: Knit.
Rnd 3: Knit to A, k1, LLinc, k1, LRinc, k 24 (28, 32).

Arch expansion companion rounds
Rnds 4 and 5: Knit.
Rnd 6: Knit to A, k1, LLinc, k to 1 st before B, LRinc, k to end.
Repeat companion rnds 4-6, working Jeweled Steps (see chart) on 6 sts to left of B *for first sock,* or on 6 sts to right of A *for second sock* as follows: On first repeat of rnd 6, work rnd 1 (k3, wrap 3 sts twice, k3) of Jeweled Steps. On next repeat of rnd 6, work rnd 4 (wrap 3 sts twice, k6 *(first 3 are the wrapped sts)*) of Jeweled Steps. Continue alternating between rnds 1 and 4 of Jeweled Steps each time you work a rnd 6. Continue until total st count is 71 (83, 95), after a completed rnd 6.
First sock: Move A 10 sts and B 9 sts to the *left.*
Second sock: Move A 9 sts and B 10 sts to the *right.*

Rotate, and place instep markers
Knit to 11 (13, 15) sts past B and stop. The next 25 (29, 33) sts need to be on 1 circ or dpn, with all other sts on other circ or on 2 dpn's. Rearrange sts as described. *This ndl with* 25 (29, 33) sts *is now sole* (and will be used for working the heel) and other(s) are *instep.* See picture ① for result. *Yarn is at start of sole.*

Heel - pictures ① and ②
Work reinforced heel (page 124), starting at step 1 - A and B are already in place. As you begin step 3, see picture ②. Use 24 (28, 32) for the instep G and 25 (29, 33) for the sole G, 4 (5, 6) for J, 11 (13, 15) for H, and 7 (9, 10) for I. Total sts after heel is finished: 49 (57, 65)

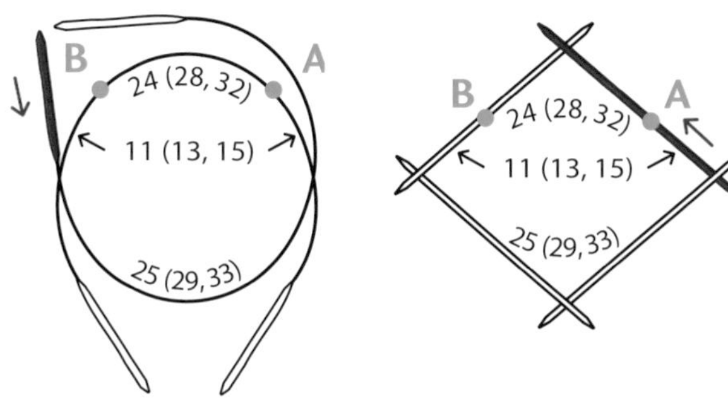

① Stitch distribution as step 1 of heel begins.

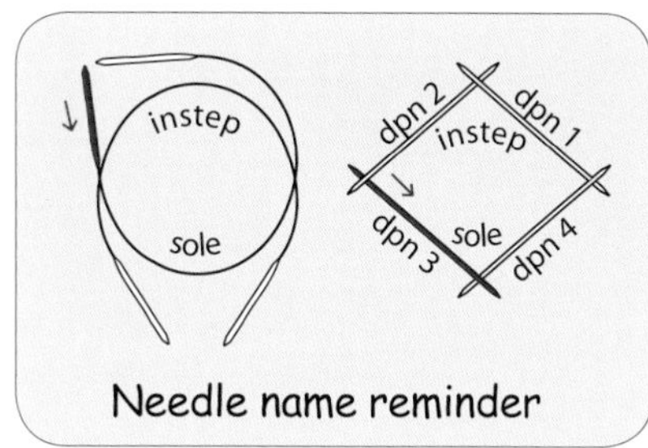

Needle name reminder

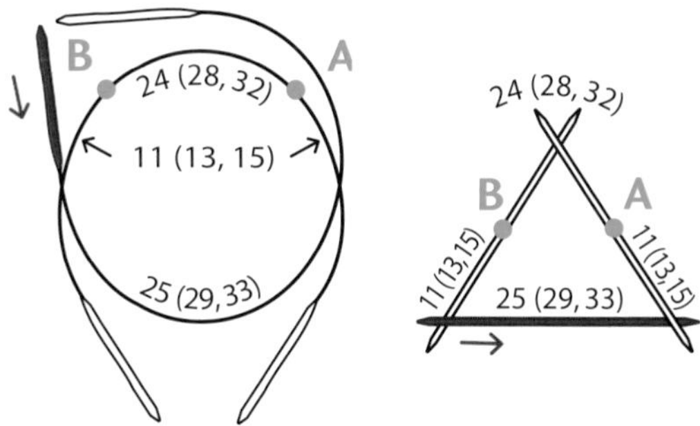

② Stitch distribution as step 3 of heel begins.

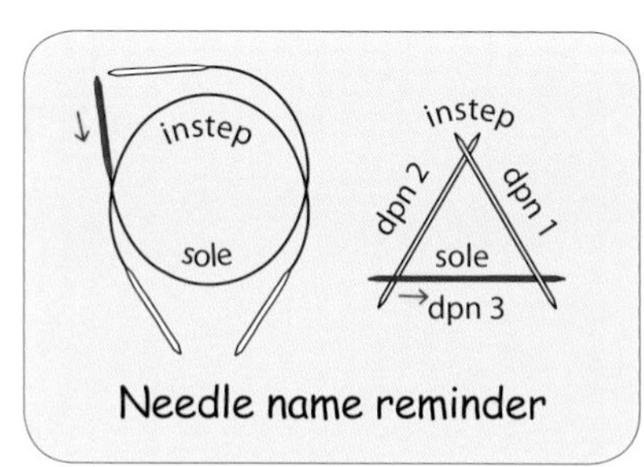

Needle name reminder

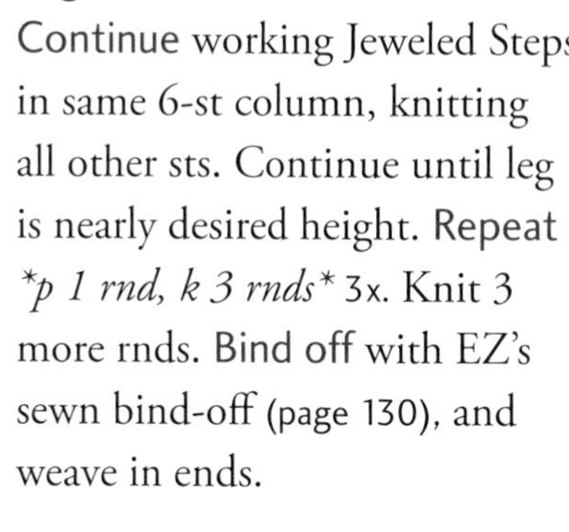

Leg and cuff

Continue working Jeweled Steps in same 6-st column, knitting all other sts. Continue until leg is nearly desired height. Repeat **p 1 rnd, k 3 rnds** 3x. Knit 3 more rnds. Bind off with EZ's sewn bind-off (page 130), and weave in ends.

Jeweled Steps Chart

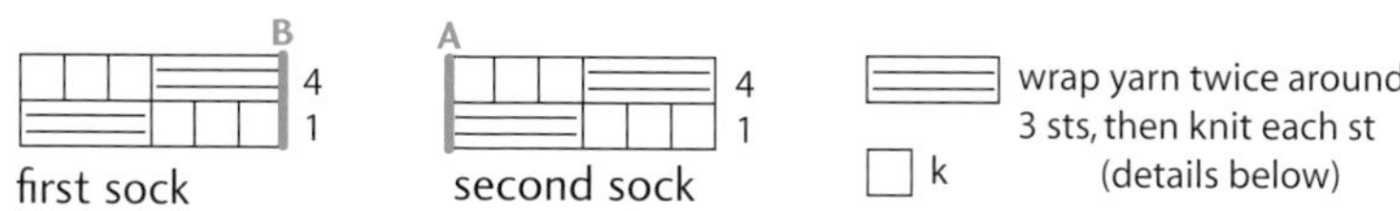

Wrap yarn twice around 3 sts, then knit them: Repeat **slip next 3 sts tip-to-tip to right ndl, bring yarn between ndls to front, return 3 slipped sts to left ndl, bring yarn across front and between ndls to back** 2x. Knit the 3 wrapped sts, being careful the wraps are not too tight. Rnds 2-3 and 5-6 are plain knit rnds, and are not shown in the chart.

Abbreviations and a list of technique lessons can be found on pages 134-136.

Master Sidestream Pattern

Find your Master numbers on pages 109-119.

Artyarns Supermerino, (100% superwash merino wool, 50 g / 104 yds), 2 skeins color 105

Markers: A, B, C and D
Instep is starting ndl (ndl in left hand).

Complete any toe (page 126). Knit toe E inches long.

Sidestream arch expansion - picture ①

Marker placement if G is an even number
Knit 1, place A, knit until 1 st before end of sole, place B, k1f&b.

Marker placement if G is an odd number
Knit 1, place A, knit until 2 sts before end of sole, place B, k2.

Arch Expansion Companion Rounds

Rnd 1: Knit to 1 st before A *(on first repetition only, there is only 1 st before A)*, LRinc, k to B, k1, LLinc, k to end.
Rnds 2 and 3: Knit.

Repeat companion rnds 1-3, stopping after a completed rnd 1 when total stitch count reaches F. Remove markers.

Rotation for second sock only: Knit to end of instep. *Instep and sole just switched identities – what was sole is now instep, and what was instep is now sole. Next circ or next 2 dpn's are now instep.*

Complete heel (page 120), beginning with step 1 (if G was even, the instep G will have 1 extra st *(for the first sock)* or the sole G will have 1 extra st *(for the second sock)* in step 1 of the heel), then complete leg, and cuff (page 130).

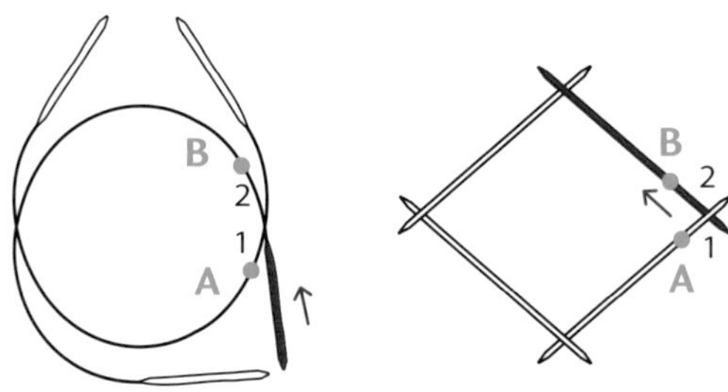

① There are 3 sts between A and B when the arch expansion companion rounds begin.

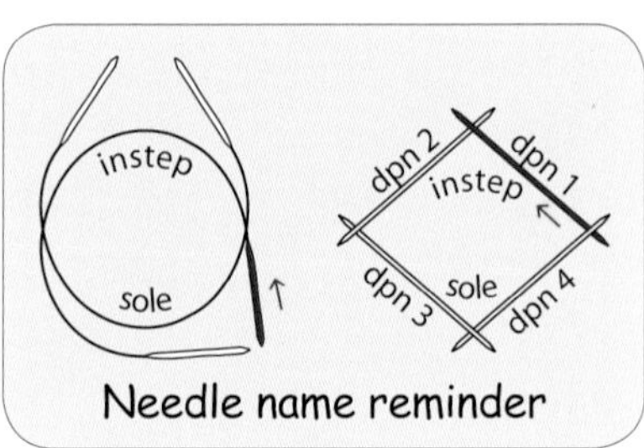

Needle name reminder

Abbreviations and a list of technique lessons can be found on pages 134-136.

Master Sock Numbers

________ Ⓐ stitches-per-inch gauge

________ Ⓑ foot length

________ Ⓒ midfoot circumference

________ Ⓓ midfoot stitch count

________ Ⓔ length of first section of a toe-up sock

________ Ⓕ stitch count after arch expansion

________ Ⓖ stitch count for heel and instep sections

________ Ⓗ stitch count for each set of wing stitches

________ Ⓘ stitches to wrap on each side of heel turn

________ Ⓙ custom instep adjustment number

Recipient ________________________________ Date ________________

Yarn ____

Gauge ________ stitches per inch/ 2.5 cm and ________ rounds per inch/ 2.5 cm

Needles (type and size) ________________________________

Sock description ________________________________

____

Notes ____

____

____

____

Chapter 10 - The Freedom of Master Numbers

This chapter empowers you to knit socks to fit *anyone* using your favorite needles, yarn, and gauge. After some practice, I hope you won't even need the book anymore.

To get started, you'll need a piece of paper (or make a copy of the form on the previous page), a pencil, a tape measure, and a calculator. During the next few minutes you'll gather a custom number to match each letter. Then you're set to plug those numbers into a master pattern for any style of sock architecture in these pages - and to create your own unique socks.

It's worthwhile to keep a record of master numbers for each sock you knit, along with information on the yarn, needles, and gauge used. If you do, you'll have a reliable resource for future use. The reproducible form on page 109 is designed for this purpose. You might add a photo and a snippet of yarn in the space in the right corner.

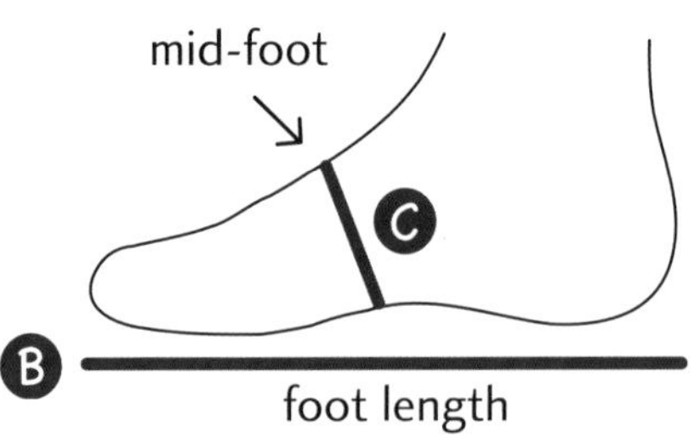

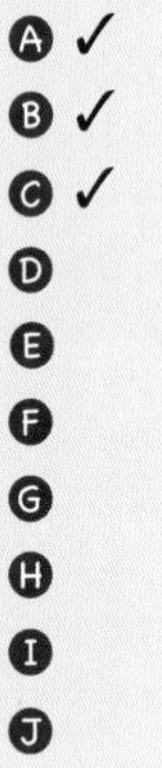

On each page of this chapter you'll find a checklist to make sure you don't miss anything. The first three letters are already checked, because the first three numbers are found on this page. Write them down before continuing on.

A is your stitches-per-inch/2.5 cm gauge

Read page 9 and follow the directions for an honest stitches-per-inch/ 2.5 cm gauge. If necessary, round the result to the nearest whole number or whole-and-a-half (for example, 6 or 6.5).

B is your foot length

Place a ruler on the floor, with its zero end against the wall. Stand on the ruler with your heel against the wall. The spot where your toes end is your foot length.

C is your mid-foot circumference

Wrap a tape measure around the middle of your foot to find the circumference.

Socks that fit well in shoes

You might assume that multiplying your mid-foot measurement by your stitches-per-inch/ 2.5 cm gauge would give you the correct number of stitches to use around your mid-foot. But this is not so. A "matching" fit results in loose socks that will not fit smoothly into shoes. A good general rule is to subtract about 10% to make the fit work well. This has already been done for you in the Master Number charts.

is the number of stitches around the mid-foot.

Find your D in Table 1 below.

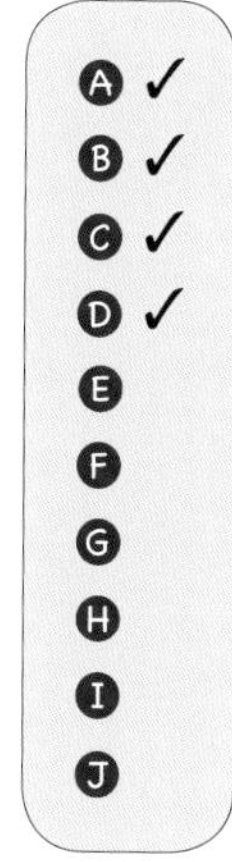

For inquiring minds...

Usually this is the same number of stitches as around the ankle and leg.

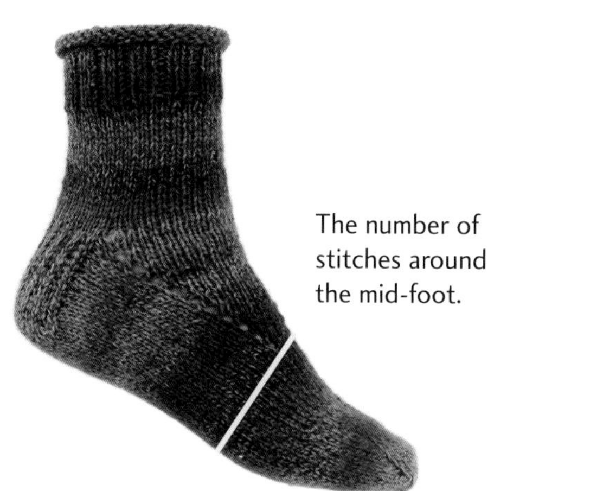

The number of stitches around the mid-foot.

Table 1 — Number of stitches around the mid-foot

C – Circumference mid-foot	A – Stitches per inch (2.5 centimeters): 4.5	5	5.5	6	6.5	7	7.5	8	8.5	9	9.5
4” (10 cm)	18	20	22	24	26	28	30	32	34	36	38
5” (12.5 cm)	20	22	24	26	28	30	32	36	38	40	42
5.5” (14 cm)	22	24	26	30	32	34	36	40	42	44	46
6” (15 cm)	24	26	28	32	36	38	40	42	44	48	50
6.5” (16 cm)	26	30	32	36	38	40	42	46	48	52	56
7” (17.5 cm)	28	32	34	38	42	44	48	50	52	56	60
7.5” (19 cm)	30	34	36	40	44	48	50	54	58	60	64
8” (20 cm)	32	36	40	42	46	50	54	56	60	64	68
8.5” (21 cm)	34	38	42	46	50	54	58	62	64	68	72
9” (22.5 cm)	36	40	44	48	52	56	60	64	68	72	76
9.5” (24 cm)	38	42	48	52	56	60	64	68	72	76	80
10” (25 cm)	40	44	50	54	58	62	68	72	76	80	84
10.5” (26 cm)	42	48	52	56	60	66	70	76	80	86	90
11” (28 cm)	44	50	56	60	66	70	76	80	84	90	94
11.5” (29 cm)	48	52	58	62	68	72	78	82	86	92	98

 is the length to knit the 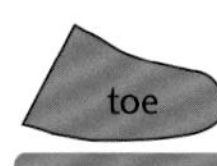 toe of a toe-up sock.

A ✓
B ✓
C ✓
D ✓
E ✓
F
G
H
I
J

Skip this page if you are making a top-down sock.

Step 1- Knit
Knit the toe until it's 2" (5 cm) or taller, unless you are making a baby sock - then you may take a measurement at 1" (2.5 cm).

Step 2 - Measure
Measure a 2" (5 cm) high column of stitches, then divide by 2 to get your rounds-per-inch/ 2.5 cm gauge (RPI). If you measured just 1" (2.5 cm), then that is your RPI.

Step 3 - Divide

D (midfoot stitch total) ÷ RPI = **length of heel & arch section.**

Step 4 - Subtract

B (foot length) - **length of heel & arch section** = E

E is the length to knit the toe section of your toe-up sock.

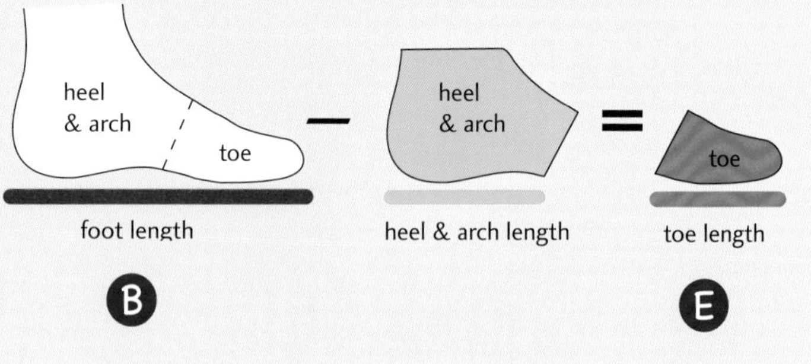

Elusive RPI

A rarely mentioned and important fact is that individual knitters achieving the same stitches-per-inch gauge do not necessarily share the same rounds-per-inch gauge (RPI). I asked a group of volunteers to knit swatches in the round with the same yarn, using any size needle that gave them 6 stitches-per-inch. Although everyone's stitches-per-inch gauge was 6 stitches-per-inch, their RPI's ranged from 7 to 8 stitches per inch! I cannot explain the mystery of round variability, but it did motivate me to figure out a system allowing sock knitters to measure and use their actual RPI to achieve the desired foot length.

is the number of stitches you'll have after completing all arch expansion increases, just before beginning the heel.

Find F in Table 3 below.

A ✓
B ✓
C ✓
D ✓
E ✓
F ✓
G
H
I
J

For inquiring minds…

The arch expansion total is nearly always equal to the midfoot total plus half the midfoot total. Sometimes a pattern repeat or another factor changes that by a stitch or two.

Table 3 — Stitch count after arch expansion

A – Stitches per inch (2.5 centimeters)

C – Circumference mid-foot

STS/ INCH (2.5 cm)	4.5	5	5.5	6	6.5	7	7.5	8	8.5	9	9.5
4" (10 cm)	28	30	34	36	40	42	46	48	52	54	58
5" (12.5 cm)	30	34	36	40	42	46	48	54	58	60	64
5.5" (14 cm)	34	36	40	46	48	52	54	60	64	66	70
6" (15 cm)	36	38	42	48	54	56	60	62	66	72	74
6.5" (16 cm)	38	44	48	54	56	60	62	68	72	78	84
7" (17.5 cm)	42	48	50	56	62	66	72	74	78	84	90
7.5" (19 cm)	44	50	54	60	66	72	74	80	86	90	96
8" (20 cm)	48	54	60	62	68	74	80	84	90	96	102
8.5" (21 cm)	50	56	62	68	74	80	86	92	96	102	108
9" (22.5 cm)	54	60	66	72	78	84	90	96	102	108	114
9.5" (24 cm)	56	62	72	78	84	90	96	102	108	114	120
10" (25 cm)	60	66	74	80	86	92	102	108	114	120	126
10.5" (26 cm)	62	72	78	84	90	98	104	114	120	128	134
11" (28 cm)	66	74	84	90	98	104	114	120	126	134	140
11.5" (29 cm)	72	78	86	92	102	108	116	122	128	138	146

is the number of stitches to mark off for the instep and the sole before working the heel.

Find G in Table 4 below.

A ✓
B ✓
C ✓
D ✓
E ✓
F ✓
G ✓
H
I
J

For inquiring minds...

The instep and heel sections are usually one half of the midfoot total. Occasionally a stitch pattern or other factor means that one or the other will be off by a stitch or two.

Table 4 — Number of stitches for instep and heel turn sections

A – Stitches per inch (2.5 centimeters)

C – Circumference mid-foot

STS/ INCH (2.5 cm)	4.5	5	5.5	6	6.5	7	7.5	8	8.5	9	9.5
4" (10 cm)	9	10	11	12	13	14	15	16	17	18	19
5" (12.5 cm)	10	11	12	13	14	15	16	18	19	20	21
5.5" (14 cm)	11	12	13	15	16	17	18	20	21	22	23
6" (15 cm)	12	13	14	16	18	19	20	21	22	24	25
6.5" (16 cm)	13	15	16	18	19	20	21	23	24	26	28
7" (17.5 cm)	14	16	17	19	21	22	24	25	26	28	30
7.5" (19 cm)	15	17	18	20	22	24	25	27	29	30	32
8" (20 cm)	16	18	20	21	23	25	27	28	30	32	34
8.5" (21 cm)	17	19	21	23	25	27	29	31	32	34	36
9" (22.5 cm)	18	20	22	24	26	28	30	32	34	36	38
9.5" (24 cm)	19	21	24	26	28	30	32	34	36	38	40
10" (25 cm)	20	22	25	27	29	31	34	36	38	40	42
10.5" (26 cm)	21	24	26	28	30	33	35	38	40	43	45
11" (28 cm)	22	25	28	30	33	35	38	40	42	45	47
11.5" (29 cm)	24	26	29	31	34	36	39	41	43	46	49

is your 'wing stitch' number - the stitches on each side in between the G instep stitches and the G sole stitches you just identified in the previous step.

A ✓
B ✓
C ✓
D ✓
E ✓
F ✓
G ✓
H ✓
I
J

For inquiring minds...

Each set of wing stitches is usually equal to half the number of increases made during the arch expansion.

Table 5 — Number of wing stitches on each side

A – Stitches per inch (2.5 centimeters)

G – Circumference mid-foot

STS/ INCH (2.5 cm)	**4.5**	**5**	**5.5**	**6**	**6.5**	**7**	**7.5**	**8**	**8.5**	**9**	**9.5**
4" (10 cm)	5	5	6	6	7	7	8	8	9	9	10
5" (12.5 cm)	5	6	6	7	7	8	8	9	10	10	11
5.5" (14 cm)	6	6	7	8	8	9	9	10	11	11	12
6" (15 cm)	6	6	7	8	9	9	10	10	11	12	12
6.5" (16 cm)	6	7	8	9	9	10	10	11	12	13	14
7" (17.5 cm)	7	8	8	9	10	11	12	12	13	14	15
7.5" (19 cm)	7	8	9	10	11	12	12	13	14	15	16
8" (20 cm)	8	9	10	10	11	12	13	14	15	16	17
8.5" (21 cm)	8	9	10	11	12	13	14	15	16	17	18
9" (22.5 cm)	9	10	11	12	13	14	15	16	17	18	19
9.5" (24 cm)	9	10	12	13	14	15	16	17	18	19	20
10" (25 cm)	10	11	12	13	14	15	18	18	19	20	21
10.5" (26 cm)	10	12	13	14	15	16	18	18	20	21	22
11" (28 cm)	11	12	14	15	16	17	18	20	21	22	23
11.5" (29 cm)	12	13	14	15	16	18	19	20	21	23	24

is the number of stitches to wrap on each side as you work the short rows of the heel turn.

Find I in Table 6 below.

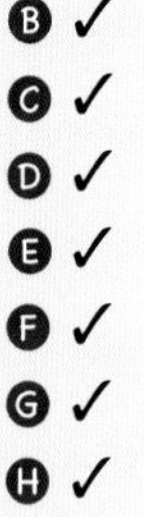

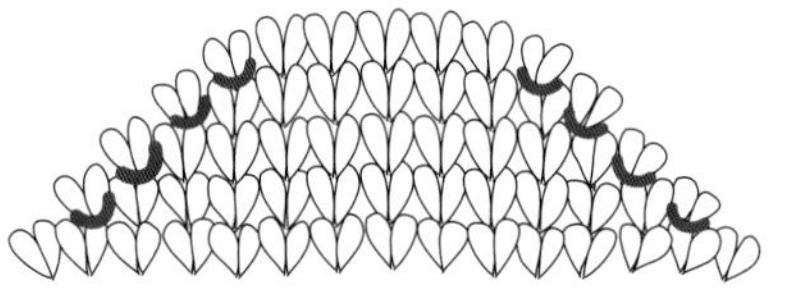

In this example there are 4 wraps on each side of the heel turn.

For inquiring minds…

You usually wrap a few less than a third of the total sole stitches. For a deeper heel, you can wrap more.

Table 6 — Number of wraps on each side of heel turn

A – Stitches per inch (2.5 centimeters)

C – Circumference mid-foot / STS/ INCH (2.5 cm)	4.5	5	5.5	6	6.5	7	7.5	8	8.5	9	9.5
4" (10 cm)	3	3	3	3	3	3	4	4	5	5	5
5" (12.5 cm)	3	3	3	3	3	4	4	5	6	6	6
5.5" (14 cm)	3	3	3	4	4	5	5	6	6	6	6
6" (15 cm)	3	3	3	4	5	5	6	6	6	7	7
6.5" (16 cm)	3	3	4	5	5	5	6	6	7	7	8
7" (17.5 cm)	3	4	4	5	6	6	7	7	7	8	8
7.5" (19 cm)	3	4	5	6	6	7	7	7	8	8	9
8" (20 cm)	4	5	6	6	6	7	7	8	8	9	9
8.5" (21 cm)	5	5	6	6	7	7	8	8	9	9	10
9" (22.5 cm)	5	6	6	7	7	8	8	9	9	10	11
9.5" (24 cm)	5	6	7	7	7	8	9	9	10	11	11
10" (25 cm)	6	6	7	8	8	9	11	11	11	12	13
10.5" (26 cm)	6	6	7	8	8	9	11	11	11	12	13
11" (28 cm)	6	7	8	8	9	10	11	12	12	12	13
11.5" (29 cm)	7	7	8	8	9	10	11	12	12	12	13

 **invites you to custom-fit the instep of a toe-up sock.**

Skip this page if you are making a top-down sock.

A ✓
B ✓
C ✓
D ✓
E ✓
F ✓
G ✓
H ✓
I ✓
J ✓

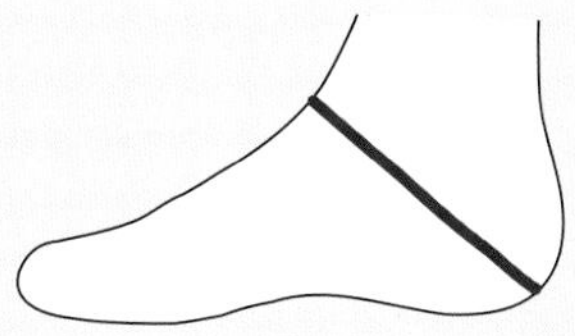

First measure from the top of your arch around the base of your heel and back to the top.

Now divide the measurement by (C) (use a calculator). Keep only the first two numbers after the decimal point (for example, 1.4165361 would become 1.41) **Use the shortened number** to determine your instep type below, and to find your (J).

If the shortened number is less than 1.32, you have a lower than average instep. (For a plain heel, divide by the number in parentheses.)

For a lower than average instep, divide: (H) ÷ 3 (4)= (J)

If the shortened number is between 1.32 and 1.42, you have an average instep. (For a plain heel, divide by the number in parentheses.)

For an average instep, divide: (H) ÷ 2.4 (3.2)= (J)

If the shortened number is greater than 1.42, you have a higher than average instep. (For a plain heel, divide by the number in parentheses.)

For a higher than average instep, divide: (H) ÷ 1.7 (2.4)= (J)

Round off your (J) to the nearest whole number, and write it down.

See next page for standard foot measurements.

For inquiring minds...

Knit stitches are short and wide, like Corgi dogs. Tip those stitches on their sides (or ask a Corgi to stand) and they become tall and narrow. When the short wide stitches of the heel meet the tall, narrow wing stitches, the dogs don't match. So you add dogs (uh, stitches) to the wings to make the dimensions match. Because a reinforced heel, worked with slipped stitches, is even shorter, you need a greater number of additional stitches than when working a plain heel.

Foot Dimensions

The table to the right correlates average measurements with age (from birth up to 36 months) or shoe size (from a child's 9 to adult). I had a fascinating discussion with my podiatrist, Dr. Regina Currier, about the inconsistency of actual measurements and shoe sizes, which became obvious as I collected and analyzed foot measurements from about 300 individuals in my research for this book. There are many variables beyond the obvious ones (such as the measurements in this table) that affect the fit of a shoe, and there is no reliable sizing among manufacturers. So if you have a chance to measure the foot you are knitting for, don't depend on shoe size. But if you cannot measure the foot, this table will steer you in the right general direction. After all, knitted socks tend to be stretchy and forgiving.

The generalities I note below (from my collected data) may or may not apply to you or the actual feet you are knitting for, but are interesting nevertheless.

Babies and toddlers up to 5.5"/ 14 cm foot length:
Midfoot and ankle circumferences are usually larger than foot length.

Child or adult up to 9" / 22 cm foot length:
Midfoot and ankle circumferences, and foot length are all usually very close to equal.

Adult foot length between 9-10"/ 22-25 cm:
Midfoot circumference is usually about 95% of foot length, and equal to ankle circumference.

Adult foot length greater than 10"/ 25 cm:
Midfoot circumference is usually about 90% of foot length, and equal to ankle circumference.

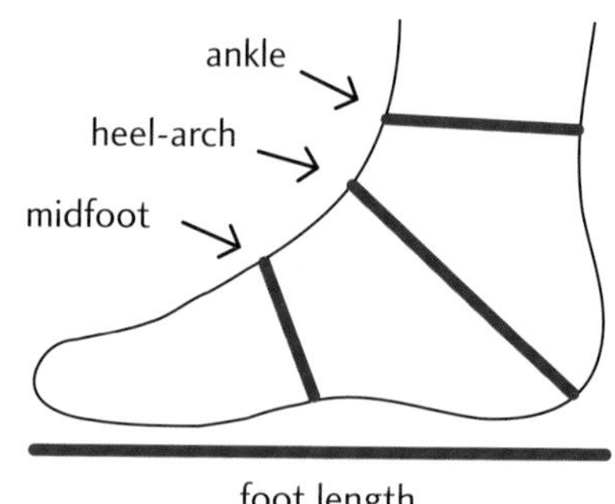

Age or shoe size	Foot length	Midfoot	Heel /arch	Ankle
newborn	3.5"	3.75"	5.5"	4.25"
3-6 months	3.75"	4"	5.75"	4.5"
6-9 months	3.75"	4.25"	6"	4.5"
9-12 months	4"	4.25"	6"	4.75"
12-18 months	4.5"	4.75"	6.25"	5"
18-24 months	4.75"	5"	6.5"	5.25"
24-30 months	5"	5.25"	6.75"	5.25"
30-36 months	5.75"	5.75"	7.5"	6"
Child's 9	6"	6"	8"	6"
Child's 10	6.5"	6.25"	8,25"	6.25"
Child's 11	6.75"	6.75"	8.75"	6.75"
Child's 12	7.25"	7"	9"	7"
Child's 13	7.5"	7.5"	9.5"	7.5"
Woman's 3	8"	8"	10"	8"
Woman's 4	8.25"	8.25"	10.5"	8.25"
Woman's 5	8.5"	8.5"	12"	8.5"
Woman's 6	9"	9"	12.25"	9"
Woman's 7/ Man's 6	9.25"	9"	12.25"	9.25"
Woman's 8/ Man's 7	9.75"	9.25"	12.5"	9.75"
Woman's 9/ Man's 8	10"	9.5"	13"	10"
Woman's 10/ Man's 9	10.25"	9.5"	13"	10.25"
Woman's 11 / Man's 10	10.75"	9.75"	13.25"	10.75"
Woman's 12/ Man's 11	11"	10"	14"	11"
Man's 12	11.25"	10"	14"	11.25"
Man's 13	11.75"	10.5"	14.5"	11.75"
Man's 14	12"	10.75"	15"	12"
Man's 15	12.25"	11"	15.5"	12.25"

Fitting Plump or Thin Feet

In traditional sock patterns, the foot and leg use the same number of stitches. If this has worked for you before, skip this page. If your feet are plump or thin overall, the Master Numbers chapter already has your correct numbers, so you can also skip this page. But if you have a foot which suddenly narrows or widens at the ankle or leg, you'll find adjustments here to give you a custom fit.

Determining the fitting requirements of an individual
Measure the leg at cuff level and also just above the ankle bone.
Add these numbers together.

Divide the answer by your midfoot circumference, Ⓒ (see page 110).

For example:

Benjamin's cuff is 13", his ankle is 10", and his midfoot is 10.5".
Add: 13 + 10 = 23
Divide: 23 ÷ 10.5" = 2.1904761
Shorten the decimal: 2.19~~04761~~

If your answer is less than 2.00, you have thinner than average ankles and/or legs.

The simplest adjustment for you is to use smaller needles for the cuff, leg and instep.

Or, for a toe-up sock, include a few extra instep stitches in the number of wing stitches consumed by the heel, thus decreasing the number of ankle and leg stitches.

Or, for a top-down sock, start with fewer leg stitches and increase to the normal number during arch expansion.

In Germany it's common to work an inch or two of ribbing around the ankle, with a decorative pattern above. This technique is well-suited for snugging up a sock around narrow ankles without making other adjustments.

If your answer is between 2.00 and 2.6, you have average ankles and/or legs. *Make no adjustments.*

If your answer is greater than 2.6, you have plumper than average ankles and/or legs.

The simplest adjustment for you is to use larger needles for the cuff and leg.

Or, for a toe-up sock, when adding Ⓙ increases for instep adjustment (see heel step 1, page xx), work increases along the heel turn section as well (up to an increase every 3rd st). Proceed as usual, using heel stitch, not plain knitting for the heel. The heel stitch will initially absorb the extra width and then release it to give up to 15% more width around the ankle. Alternatively, or in addition, the arch expansion section can be steepened, by increasing 2 stitches every 2nd round instead of every 3rd. *(If you do this, count how many rounds you will eliminate, divide by your rounds-per-inch gauge, and add this measurement to the toe section, or the sock will be too short.)* By increasing 2 stitches every 2nd round, ankle (and leg) circumference could be increased up to 30%.

Or, for a top-down sock, start with more leg stitches, and increase to normal number during arch expansion. If only your leg is larger, use additional stitches around the cuff, tapering to the correct number lower on the leg.

Chapter 11 – Master Heels, Toes, & Cuffs

This is the "Parts Department" - where you'll find your Master Heel instructions (most of the patterns send you here for the heel, and after a while you will know the heel routines by heart) or to browse the Master Toes and Cuffs when designing your own socks. Heels begin here, toes start on page 126, and cuffs on page 130.

Overview of the Heel Process

Step 1, placing markers and maybe moving some stitches, sets you up to move smoothly through the remaining 4 steps. If you're making a toe-up sock, you'll also work some increases in the "wing" sections.

Step 2 is a personal decision: do you want a plain heel or a reinforced heel?

Step 3, the heel turn, is worked back and forth on the sole alone, in short rows. When done, you'll have 2 fewer stitches.

In step 4, the wing stitches move from each end of the instep to adjacent ends of the sole. This leaves the working yarn temporarily inaccessible, located between the first wing and the heel turn, so slide the far end of that circ (or a free dpn) through those wing stitches until both tips emerge where they belong.

In step 5, you work back and forth on the heel turn stitches, always stopping 1 stitch short of the gap to nibble up that stitch and the next one in an ssk or p2tog. When only 2 wing sts remain on each side, you'll resume knitting in the round, nibbling up 1 of each set of 2 remaining wing stitches in the first round. You've regained the 2 stitches lost in step 3, and are ready to begin the leg or foot.

Start with the set-up:

If there are *exactly* Ⓖ sts on your sole ndl(s), go to step 1. (If using dpn's, put all sole sts on 1 dpn before continuing.)

If there are *more* than Ⓖ sts on your sole ndl(s), locate the central Ⓖ sole sts. Then move the sole sts which are outside the central Ⓖ sts *from the sole ends to the adjacent ends of the instep*. You may have to knit or unknit some sts so the yarn ends up at an intersection of instep and sole. Now you have exactly Ⓖ sts on your sole ndl(s). (If using dpn's, put all sole sts on 1 dpn before continuing.) Go on to step 1.

Complete set-up on previous page before starting.

Step 1: Place markers for instep - picture ①
Place A at beginning and B at end of the central Ⓖ sts on instep, so there are Ⓗ wing sts to the right of A and Ⓗ wing sts to the left of B. There are Ⓖ sts on sole.

TOP-DOWN socks only
If you are not at the *start of the sole*, knit to the end of the instep, then go to step 2. See result in picture ①.

TOE-UP socks only
If you are not at the *start of the instep,* knit to the end of the sole. Now knit the first wing section of Ⓗ sts, including Ⓙ evenly distributed LRinc's in this section. Knit to B. As you knit the second wing section of Ⓗ sts, include Ⓙ evenly distributed LLinc's in this section. Stop at end of instep - do not knit across sole. See result in picture ①.

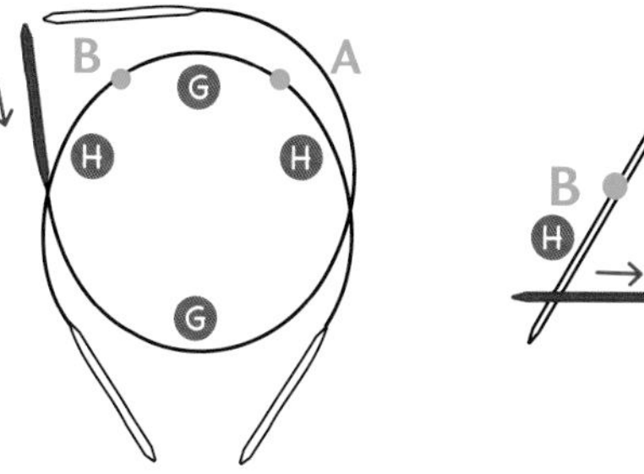

① A and B mark the beginning and end of the instep's central Ⓖ sts, with Ⓗ wing sts on each side of A and B, and Ⓖ sole sts below. For toe-up socks, Ⓙ sts have been added to each Ⓗ wing section. *Sole is starting ndl (ndl in left hand).*

Step 2: Choose a plain or reinforced heel. *You are at the start of the sole, with all sole stitches on 1 circ or dpn.* The remainder of the heel is worked back and forth in rows *on the sole needle alone.* Go on to step 3 for the heel you have chosen (page 122 for plain, page 124 for reinforced).

Left: plain heel; right: reinforced heel.

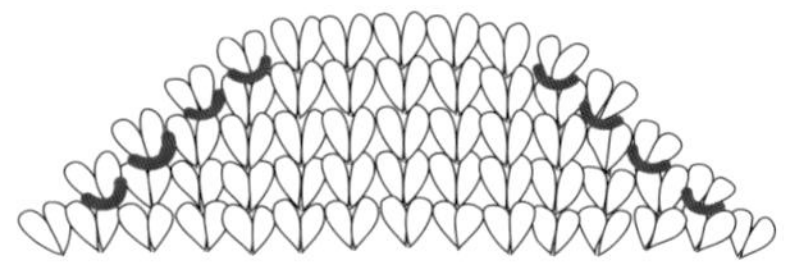

② SAMPLE HEEL TURN
Note the sequential wrapped stitches on each side, and the single unwrapped stitch at each end. The shape is the result of knitting increasingly shorter rows, always wrapping the yarn around a stitch before turning. Review page 14 for a detailed lesson on wrapping stitches.

③ CIRCS (step 4): After completing heel turn, move the H wing stitches from the ends of the instep to adjacent ends of the sole, placing C and D to separate the moved wing sts from the heel turn sts. After the move, yarn is at C.

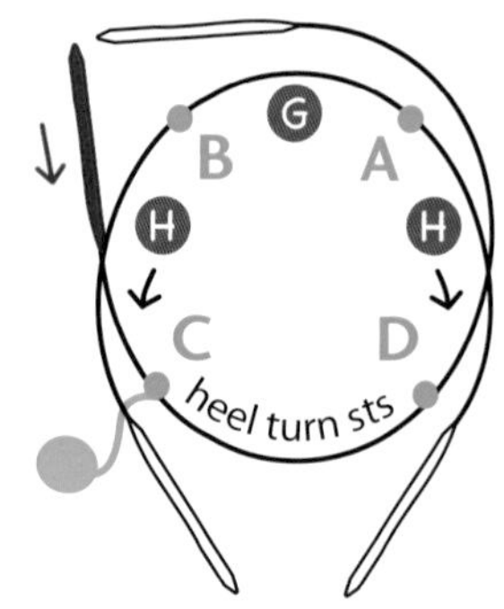

④ CIRCS (step 4): C and D mark the boundaries between wing sts and heel turn sts. Yarn is temporarily inaccessible because it is coming from the middle of a needle (see previous picture), so slide the other end of the sole circ through the wing sts (end at C). Remove C. Begin step 5, which begins with a slipped st - the st with the yarn, which is the first st on the starting ndl (ndl in left hand).

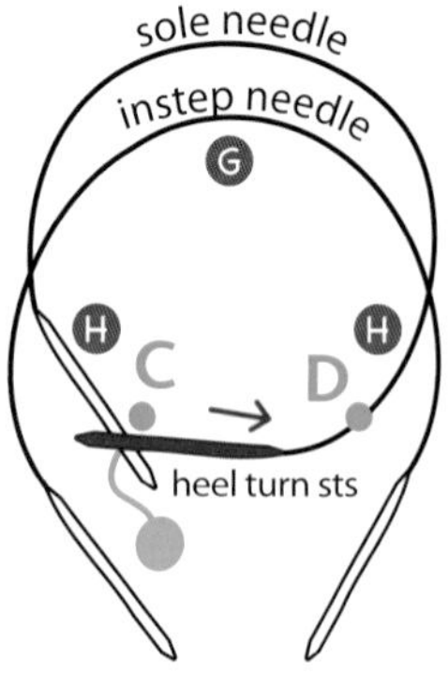

Master Plain Heel

Be sure all sole stitches are on 1 circ or on dpn 3, and all instep stitches are on the other circ or divided between dpn's 1 and 2. *Yarn is at start of sole.* You may want to review w&t, cw, and cw/ ssk and cw/ p2tog (pages 14-15) before continuing. Heel is worked back and forth in rows on sole needle only.

Step 3: Heel turn - picture ②

"Ndl" refers to sole ndl - since it is the only ndl in use.

Row 1: (RS) Knit until 2 sts before end of ndl, w&t.

Row 2: (WS) Purl until 2 sts before end of ndl, w&t.

Companion rows:

Row 3: (RS) Knit until 3 (next row, 4, following row 5, then 6, etc.) sts before end of ndl, w&t.

Row 4: (WS) Purl until 3 (next row, 4, following row 5, then 6, etc.) sts before end of ndl, w&t.

Repeat companion rows 3-4, *always adding 1 to the number of sts that remain before end of ndl* after each set of companion rows. Continue repeating companion rows until I sts are wrapped on each side (see picture ② for view of sequential wrapped sts on each side of heel turn, before the wraps are concealed). Last row completed is a row 4, a (WS) purl side row.

Final 2 rows of heel turn:

(RS) Knit up to 1st wrapped st. Repeat **cw** until only 1 wrapped st rem, cw/ssk, turn.

(WS) Slip 1, purl to 1st wrapped st on purl side. Repeat **cw** until only 1 wrapped st rem, cw/p2tog. You now have 2 fewer sts on the sole than you had when beginning the heel turn. If using dpn's, before continuing, add dpn 4 again and divide sole sts between dpn's 3 and 4.

Step 4: Move stitches - pictures ③ and ④

For CIRCS, *see pictures on previous page, and for* DPN's *see pictures on on this page.*

(See picture ③) Move both sets of H *(for toe-up socks, this includes the* J *sts you added to* H *earlier)* wing sts to adjacent ends of sole, placing C and D in front of wing sts to separate them from heel stitches. Put away A and B. Yarn is now at C and is temporarily inaccessible because it is coming from the middle of a needle.

(See picture ④) Slide other end of the sole circ or free dpn through the wing sts that end at C, where the yarn is. Remove C. Now 2 needle tips are at C, with yarn coming from the starting needle.

Step 5: Work back of heel - picture ⑤

Row 1: (RS) Slip 1, k until 1 st before D, ssk, removing D, turn.
Row 2: (WS) Slip 1, p until 1 st before C, p2tog, removing C, turn.
Heel companion rows:
Row 3: (RS) Slip 1, k until 1 st before gap, ssk, turn.
Row 4: (WS) Slip 1, p until 1 st before gap, p2tog, turn.
Repeat companion rows 3-4 until only 2 sts rem on outer sides of gaps. Next row: (RS) Slip 1, k until 1 st before gap, ssk, k1. *Resume knitting in the round.* (instep) Knit to end of instep. (sole) Knit 1, k2tog, k to end of sole. Leg or foot rnds may now begin (if following a master pattern, knit leg or foot until desired length to start of cuff or toe). *Instep is starting needle.*

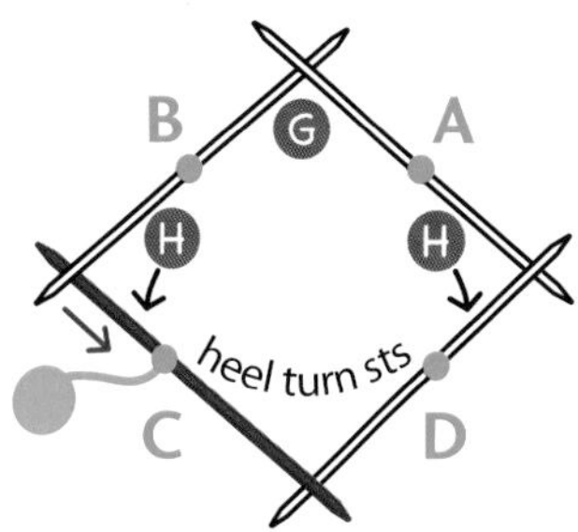

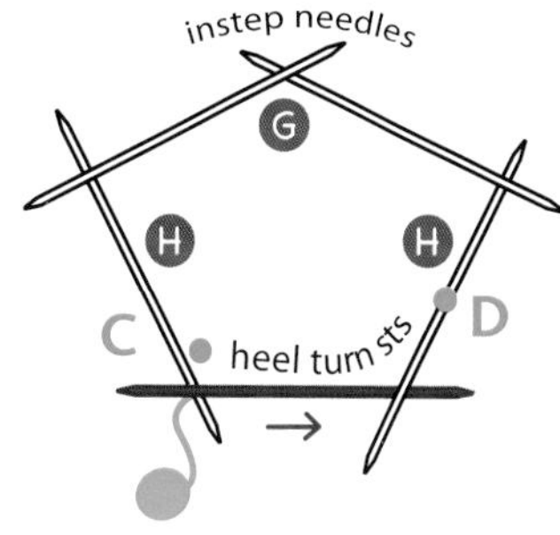

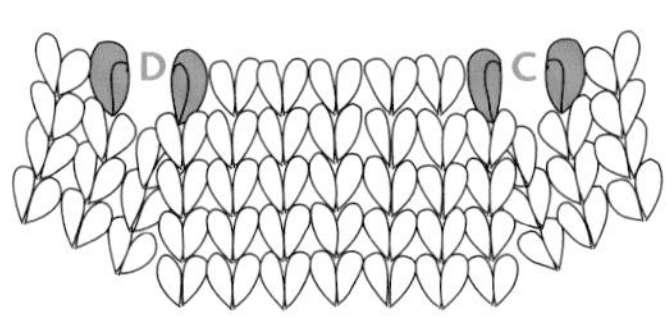

See page 125 for help if you have trouble seeing the wraps or lifting them.

③ DPN'S (step 4): After completing heel turn, move the H wing stitches from the ends of the instep to adjacent ends of the sole, placing C and D to separate the moved wing sts from the heel turn sts. After the move, yarn is at C.

④ DPN'S (step 4): C and D mark the boundaries between wing sts and heel turn sts. Working yarn is temporarily inaccessible because it is coming from the middle of a needle (see previous picture), so slide a free dpn through the wing sts that end at C. Remove C. Begin step 5, which begins with a slipped st - the st with the yarn, which is the first st on the starting ndl (ndl in left hand).

⑤ BACK OF HEEL
(same for circs & dpn's)
As you remove C and D, visible gaps are left behind. During heel turn companion rows, always pause 1 st before the gap. The next st and the st on the other side of the gap are worked together as an ssk or a p2tog before turning around to work back.

Master Reinforced Heel

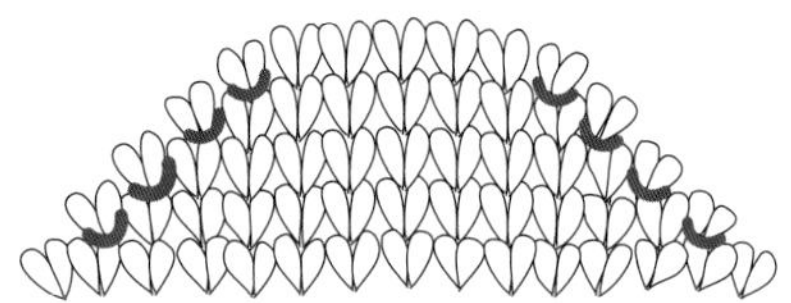

② SAMPLE HEEL TURN

Note the sequential wrapped stitches on each side, and the single unwrapped stitch at each end. The shape is the result of knitting increasingly shorter rows, always wrapping the yarn around a stitch before turning. Review page 14 for a detailed lesson on wrapping stitches. (Note: heel pictured is a plain heel.)

Handling wraps easily

After wrapping the required number of stitches on each side of the heel turn, and before concealing the wraps, try clipping a safety-pin style marker on each wrap. Now you see exactly where each wrap is, and when concealing wraps (cw), can use each marker to lift its wrap up and over the stitch it wraps, dumping it to the left of that stitch on the left needle.

Be sure all sole stitches are on 1 circ or on dpn 3, and all instep stitches are on the other circ or divided between dpn's 1 and 2. *Yarn is at start of sole.* You may want to review w&t, cw, and cw/ ssk and cw/ p2tog on pages 14-15 before continuing. Heel is worked back and forth in rows on sole needle only.

Step 3: Heel turn - picture ②

"Ndl" refers to sole ndl - since it is the only ndl in use.

Row 1 if total number of sole sts is *even*: (RS) Knit 1, LRinc, k1, repeat **sl1, k1** until 2 sts before end of ndl, w&t.

Row 1 if total number of sole sts is *odd*: (RS) Knit 3, repeat **sl1, k1** until 2 sts rem before end of ndl, w&t.

Row 2: (WS) Purl until 2 sts rem before end of ndl, w&t.

Companion Rows:

Row 3: (RS) Repeat **k1, sl1** until 3 (next row, 5, following row 7, then 9, etc.) sts before end of ndl, w&t.

Row 4: (WS) Purl until 3 (next row, 5, following row 7, then 9, etc.) sts before end of ndl, w&t.

Row 5: (RS) Repeat **sl1, k1** until 4 (next row, 6, following row 8, then 10, etc.) sts before end of ndl, w&t.

Row 6: (WS) Purl until 4 (next row, 6, following row 8, then 10, etc.) sts before end of ndl, w&t.

Repeat companion rows 3-6, *always adding 1 to the number of sts that remain before end of ndl* after each pair of companion rows. (For instance, the next repeat of rows 3-4 will work until 5 sts before end of ndl, the next repeat of rows 5-6 will work until 6 sts before end of ndl, etc.). Continue repeating companion rows 3-6 as described until ❶ sts are wrapped on each side.

(See picture ② for view of sequential wrapped sts on each side of heel turn, before the wraps are concealed.) Last row completed is a row 4 or 6, a (WS) purl side row.

Final 2 rows of heel turn: (RS) Knit k sts and slip slipped sts up to 1st wrapped st. Repeat **cw** until only 1 wrapped st rem, cw/ssk, turn. (WS) Slip 1, purl to 1st wrapped st on purl side. Repeat **cw** until only 1 wrapped st rem, cw/p2tog. You now have 2 fewer sts on the sole than you had when beginning the heel turn. If using dpn's, before continuing, add dpn 4 again and divide sole sts between dpn's 3 and 4.

Step 4: Same as for plain heel (page 123).

Step 5: Work back of heel

Row 1: (RS) Repeat **sl1, k1** until 1 st before D, ssk, removing D, turn.

Row 2: (WS) Slip 1, p until 1 st before gap, p2tog, turn.

Heel Companion Rows:

Row 3: (RS) Repeat **sl1, k1** until 1 st rem before gap, ssk, turn.

Row 4: (WS) Sl1, p until 1 st rem before gap, p2tog, turn.

Repeat companion rows 3-4 until only 2 sts rem on outer sides of gaps. (RS) (sole) Repeat **sl1, k1** until 1 st before gap, ssk, k1. *Resume knitting in the round.* (instep) Knit to end of instep. (sole) Knit 1, k2tog, k to end of sole. Leg or foot rnds may now begin (if following a master pattern, knit leg or foot until desired length to start of cuff or toe). *Instep is starting ndl (ndl in left hand).*

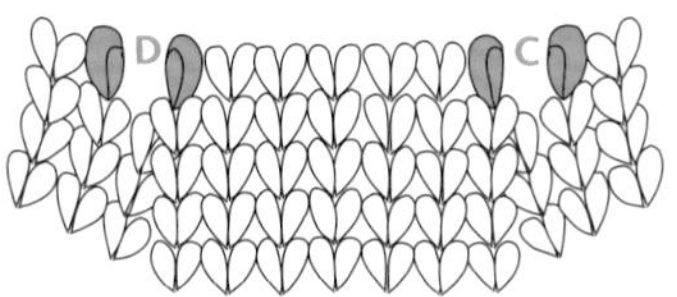

⑤ BACK OF HEEL (same for circs & dpn's)

As you remove C and D, visible gaps are left behind. During heel turn companion rows, always pause 1 st before the gap. The next st and the st on the other side of the gap are worked together as an ssk or a p2tog before turning around to work back. (Note: heel pictured is a plain heel.)

Combination Heels

Feel free to combine a reinforced heel turn with a plain back of heel - or vice versa. Steps 3 and 5 for each style of heel are completely interchangeable.

Slipping stitches on right side rows, commonly known as heel stitch, is what make the reinforced heel denser than a plain heel. The fabric compresses both vertically and horizontally and shows a lovely corrugated surface.

To make the heel even thicker, turn the finished sock inside out and run strands of yarn up and down through the columns of horizontal bars formed by the slipped stitches.

Master Toe-up Toes

Standard Toe

To determine cast-on number: Divide Ⓓ by 6. If Ⓖ is *odd*, round answer to closest *odd* whole number, or to closest *even* whole number if Ⓖ is *even*. Cast on required number of sts to each of 2 parallel ndls using Judy's Magic Cast-On (page 22) and knit to end of round (all sts), then knit another half-round (half the sts).

Instep is starting ndl (ndl in left hand).

Companion rounds:

Rnd 1: Repeat **Knit 1, LRinc, k until 1 st rem, LLinc, k1** once on instep and once on sole.

Rnd 2: Knit.

Repeat companion rounds 1 and 2, stopping after a completed rnd 1 when total st count reaches Ⓓ. Knit until foot is Ⓔ inches long.

Standard Toe

Knitting flows over the toe and smooth increase columns expand along the sides. This traditional style is worked toe-up, with no grafting.

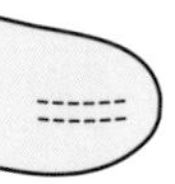

To make a toe longer and more pointed, add rounds between increase rounds, or begin a standard toe with fewer stitches (for a wider toe, begin with more stitches).

Whirlpool Toe - picture ⑥

Use figure-8 method (page 17) to cast on 3 sts to each of 2 parallel ndls, knitting initial round and a half as instructed on same page.

Instep is starting ndl (ndl in left hand).

Rnd 1: Repeat **LRinc, k1** 6x. (12 sts total)

Rnd 2: Knit, placing A, B, C, and D as shown in picture ⑥.

Companion rounds:

Rnd 3: LRinc, k to A, LRinc, k to B, LRinc, k to end of instep, LRinc, k to C, LRinc, k to D, LRinc, k to end of sole.

Rnd 4: Knit.

Repeat companion rnds 3-4 until total st count is within 6 sts of Ⓓ. If 6 more sts are needed to reach Ⓓ, repeat rnd 3 once more. If fewer than 6 sts are needed, distribute necessary number of LRinc's at established increase points (markers and ndl beginnings). Remove markers. Knit until toe is Ⓔ inches long.

Whirlpool Toe

This toe is a refined version of the top-down Star Toe. Its center is a smooth bit of knitting, whereas the Star Toe relies on a purse-string closure.

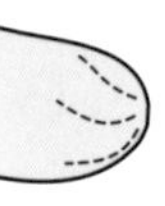

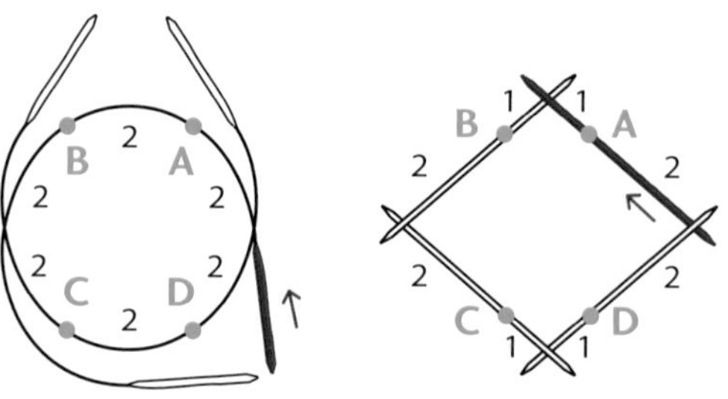

⑥ Whirlpool Toe marker arrangement after rnd 1.

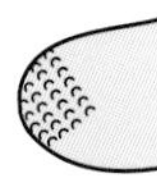

Garter Toe
This simple toe is surprisingly beautiful and curves into a lovely diamond shape, with points centered top, bottom, and sides.

Cast on to 2 parallel ndls.

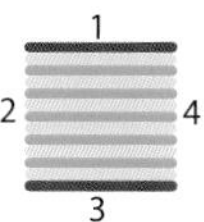

When number of purl ridges equals cast-on number, pick up and knit same number of sts along side 2. Knit across sts on side 3. Pick up and k same number of sts on side 4.

Garter Toe
Cast on ¼ (or as close to ¼ as possible) of Ⓓ sts to each of 2 parallel ndls using Judy's Magic Cast-On (page 22). Turn needles so purl side is up, and working in rows on top ndl only, knit until number of purl ridges on each side equals cast-on number. Slide other end of same circ (or free dpn) through edge of each purl ridge on adjacent side, picking up same number of sts as cast-on number - 1 for each purl ridge. Knit across picked-up sts (with same circ or another dpn). Now knit across next ndl (with other end of same ndl if using circs, or with another dpn). Pick up and knit same number of sts along remaining edge in same manner. Needles now hold Ⓓ sts. If necessary, distribute a few k1f&b's to add stitches. Knit until foot is Ⓔ inches long. Toe forms a diamond shape when worn.

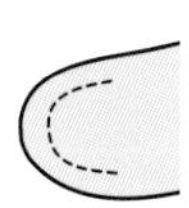

Pontoon Toe
An even band of knitting streams over the toe while side panels widen to create the toe shape.

Pontoon Toe - picture ⑦
Determine cast-on number: If half of Ⓓ is *odd*, divide Ⓓ by 6 and pick the closest *odd* number. If half of Ⓓ is *even*, divide Ⓓ by 6 and pick the closest *even* number. Cast on this number of sts to each of 2 parallel ndls using Judy's Magic Cast-On (page 22). Working in rows on 1 ndl (think of other ndl as a stitch holder for now), repeat **k 1 row, p 1 row** 2x, then k 1 row. Now knit in the round:

Rnd 1: Use other end of most recently working circ (or free dpn) to pick up 4 sts along short side of rectangle beside yarn. Knit those 4 sts with same circ or another dpn. Switch to "stitch holder" ndl, k to its end, pick up and k 4 sts along 2nd short side of rectangle as for 1st side.

Rnd 2: Shift final 2 sole sts to instep and final 2 instep sts to sole. Knit, placing **A** 2 sts *after start* and **B** 2 sts *before end* of instep, and **C** 2 sts *after start* and **D** 2 sts *before end* of sole. (see picture ⑦)

Companion rounds: (LLinc right *before* and LRinc right *after* marker)

Rnd 3: Knit to **A**, LLinc, k to **B**, LRinc, k to **C**, LLinc, k to **D**, LRinc, k to end.

Rnd 4: Knit.

Repeat companion rounds 3 and 4, stopping after a completed rnd 4 when total st count reaches Ⓓ. Remove markers. Knit until foot is Ⓔ inches long.

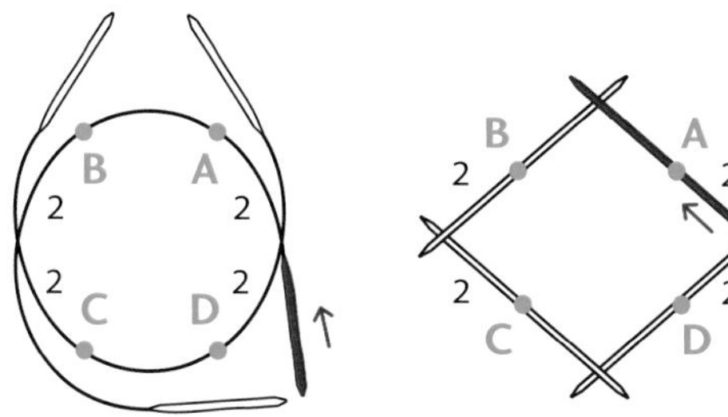

⑦ Pontoon Toe marker arrangement after rnd 2, ready to begin companion rounds.

Find Master Numbers on pages 109-119, and a list of abbreviations and techniques on pages 134-136.

Moccasin Toe

Follow instructions for Pontoon Toe (page 127).
When done, rotate toe by moving half the instep sts to sole, and half the sole sts to instep. Knit until foot is Ⓔ inches long.

Moccasin Toe
Rotating the Pontoon Toe cups your toes with a horizontal band of knitting.

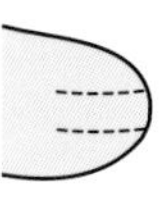

Wiggle Room Baby Toe

Subtract 8 from Ⓓ. Divide the answer by 2.
This is the number of sts to cast on to each of 2 parallel ndls using Judy's Magic Cast-On (page 22). Knit 1 rnd (all cast-on sts). Knit across 1 circ or 2 dpn's. Next circ or next 2 dpn's are now instep. Repeat once on instep and once on sole: **k1, LLinc, LRinc, k until 1 st rem, LLinc, LRinc, k1**. Total sts now = Ⓓ. Knit until foot is Ⓔ inches long.

Wiggle Room Baby Toe
A wide toe and gently rounded corners promise fat little feet plenty of wiggle room.

Master Top-Down Toes

Star Toe - picture ⑧

Step 1: Divide Ⓓ by 6. If 6 divides evenly into Ⓓ, use that answer now in step 2. If not, eliminate extra sts (the remainder after dividing) by working **k5, k2tog** a number of times equal to the extra sts, then knit to end. Count sts, divide by 6 again, and use the answer in step 2. See picture ⑧.
Step 2: Place markers A, B, C, and D to divide the sock into 6 equal sections (number from step 1), as shown in picture 3. To determine length toe will add, multiply the number of sts in each section by 2, subtract 6 from the result, and measure the height of that many rnds in your sock.
Companion rounds:

Rnd 1: Knit to 2 sts before A, k2tog. Repeat with (B, *end of instep,* C, D, *end of sole).* Rnd 2: Knit.

Repeat companion rnds 1 and 2 until only 12 sts remain. Repeat rnd 1 once more (6 sts rem). Cut tail and use tapestry needle to weave end through remaining sts, pull tight, and securely weave in all ends. For a more pointed toe, work additional knit rnds between decrease rnds.

Star Toe
This traditional and easy toe finishes with a purse-string closure.

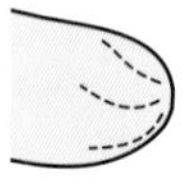

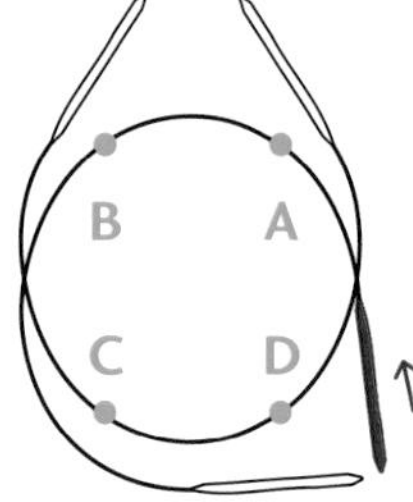

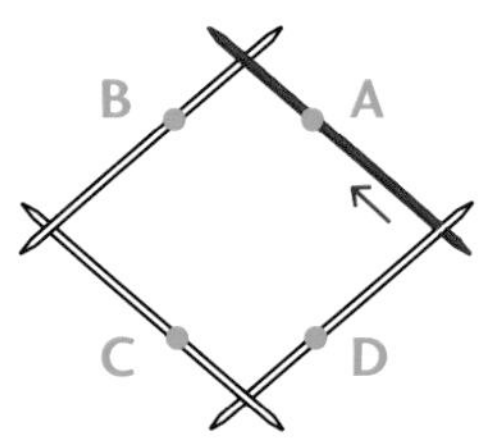

⑧ Star Toe - markers and start of instep and sole divide stitches into 6 even sections. K2tog decreases are worked at start of instep and sole and at each marker on each decrease rnd.

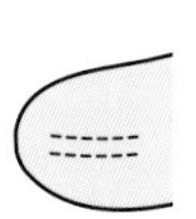

Standard Toe
The traditional grafted toe has been common for centuries and many variations exist.

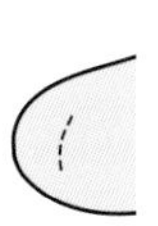

Boxy Baby Toe
This toe actually forms a soft little box for baby toes to slide into, and adds almost no length.

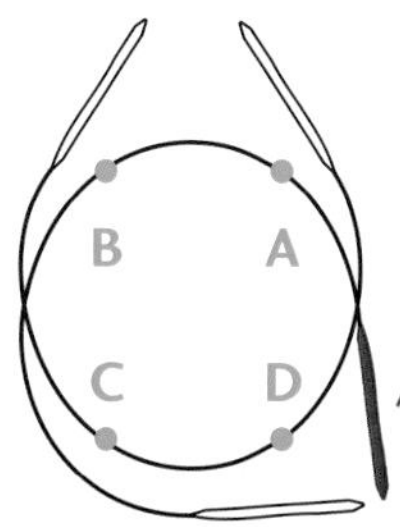

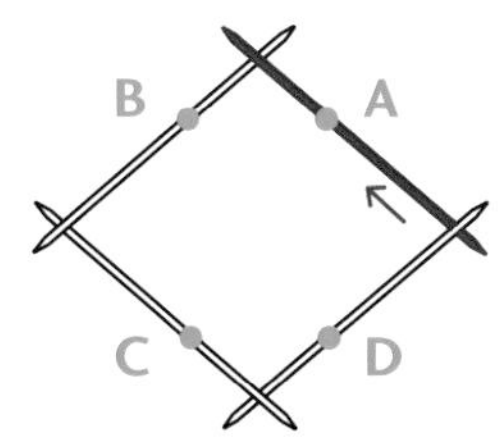

⑨ Boxy Baby Toe - 1/3 of D is between A and B, and 1/3 is between C and D.

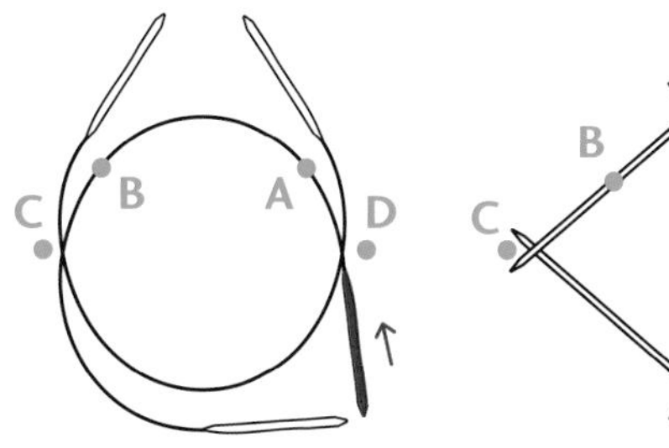

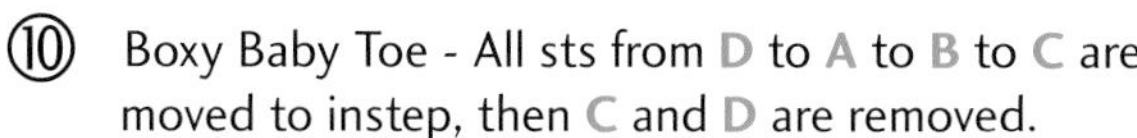

⑩ Boxy Baby Toe - All sts from D to A to B to C are moved to instep, then C and D are removed.

Standard Toe

If you don't have an equal number of instep and sole sts, rearrange them evenly, or if there is 1 extra, decrease it away before beginning. To determine length toe will add, divide D by 3. Measure height of that many rnds in your sock.

Companion rounds:

Rnd 1: Repeat **Knit 1, ssk, k until 3 sts rem, k2tog, k1** once on instep and once on sole.

Rnd 2: Knit.

Repeat companion rnds 1 and 2 until about ⅓ of original sts remain. Graft remaining sts closed.

Boxy Baby Toe - pictures ⑨ and ⑩

This toe adds almost no length. Divide D by 3. Round off answer to a whole number if necessary. Identify that number of sts in the center of instep and in the center of sole, then place markers A, B, C, and D as shown in picture ⑨. If the number of sts between B and C is not equal to the number between A and D, decrease away the extra st on the next rnd. Knit 1 rnd, stopping at D. Arrange sts so all sts from D to A to B to C are on 1 circular ndl or 2 dpn's, as shown in picture ⑩. Put away C and D.

Row 1: (RS) Knit to 1 st before B, remove B, ssk, turn.

Row 2: (WS) Slip 1, p to 1 st before A, remove A, p2tog, turn.

Companion rows:

Row 3: (RS) Knit to 1 st before gap, ssk, turn.

Row 4: (WS) Slip 1, p to 1 st before gap, p2tog, turn.

Repeat companion rows 3 and 4 until all side sts are decreased away. Graft remaining sts closed (page 22).

Find Master Numbers on pages 109-119, and a list of abbreviations and techniques on pages 134-136.

Master Toe-Up Cuffs

Elizabeth Zimmermann's sewn bind-off

The top of a sock must be elastic enough to pass over the largest part of the foot. A bind-off that never fails is Elizabeth Zimmermann's sewn bind-off, referred to here as EZ's sewn bind-off. I've added a refinement to smoothly join beginning and end.

Clip a safety pin through 1st st on left needle. Cut a tail of yarn (about 10 times the unstretched circumference of sock) and thread it through a tapestry needle. Insert tapestry needle into first 2 sts on left needle as if to purl. Pull yarn through. Now insert it through 1st st (closest to left tip) as if to knit, pull yarn through, and pull that st off needle. Repeat: **2 as if to purl, 1 as if to knit and off**, until all sts but 1 are gone. Now use the safety pin to lift the st it holds onto the left needle, followed by the single remaining st (2 sts on left needle). Repeat "2 as if to purl, 1 as if to knit and off" once more, and weave in ends. The result is perfect, unless you pull the yarn too tightly.

Corn on the Cob Cuff (a purled rolled edge)

Variation 1: Purl 3 rnds, bind off with EZ's sewn bind-off. Edge will roll inward. Variation 2: Purl 7 rnds, bind off with EZ's Sewn Bind-Off, and sew to inner rnd at start of the 7 purl rnds. This variation may be considered the toe-up version of the top-down Cobblestone Cuff.

A Double-Stranded Cuff on this Upstream sock's shows off the beauty of the hand-painted yarn. The sock begins with a Pontoon Toe.

This Spiraling Coreolis sock has a Whirlpool Toe and an I-Cord edge which begins right after the final Coreolis band stitch. Cast on 3 sts and work modified applied I-Cord (see I-Cord Cuff instructions on next page). When all edge stitches are consumed, make a 3" (7 cm) long tail of free I-cord (see I-Cord Cuff), weave in the end, knot the cord at its base, then sew knot to edge as shown.

The small yellow socks follow Master patterns and demonstrate various toes and cuffs. They're knit with Artyarns Ultramerino 4, (100% superwash merino wool, 50 g / 191 yds), color 134.

This Riverbed sock has a Moccasin Toe and ends with a simple k2, p1 ribbing, bound off with EZ's sewn bind-off for elasticity.

This Foxglove sock starts with a Whirlpool Toe and swims upward to end in a Sea Anenome Cuff.

Double-Stranded Cuff

Bind off with a double strand of yarn. This results in a more elastic fit as well as a handsome braided effect.

I-Cord Cuff

Experiment a bit to find the right formula for your sock. First try this: Cast on 3 sts with waste yarn to a free ndl and k 2 rnds. Place the 3 waste yarn sts on left tip of "real" ndl. Begin (using sock yarn) modified applied I-Cord: **Repeat **k2, ssk, return 3 sts to left ndl** 3x. *Knit 3, return 3 sts to left ndl.*** Repeat everything between ** and ** 3x. Examine the edge by tugging at it. If it has the elasticity of the knitting beneath it, it's what you want. If not, unravel and try this: **Repeat **k2, ssk, return 3 sts to left ndl** 2x. *Knit 3, return 3 sts to left ndl.*** Repeat everything between ** and ** 3x. Examine it again. Continue experimenting with different proportions of applied I-cord (rnds *with* an ssk, which consumes an edge st) and free I-cord (rnds *without* an ssk, which add length without consuming an edge st). When you find the best proportion, use it. At the end, remove the waste yarn, place the freed sts on a ndl, and graft the ends together (page 22).

Sea Anenome Cuff

This cuff has elasticity already built in, and adds the height of about 9 rnds to the leg. Grains of sand (purls) swirl around the cuff with sea anenome fingers above. Work final 6 rnds of leg as follows (requires 5-st-multiple): Repeat **k4, k1f&b** to end. Knit 1 rnd. Repeat **p1, k2** to end. Knit 1 rnd. Repeat **k1, p1, k1** to end. Knit 1 rnd. Repeat **k2, p1** to end. Knit 1 rnd. Begin edge: Repeat **k1 but do not remove st from left ndl, return new st to left ndl** 3x, followed by **bind off 6 sts,** until no sts remain. Cut tail and weave in all ends.

Find Master Numbers on pages 109-119, and a list of abbreviations and techniques on pages 134-136.

Master Top-Down Cuffs

Always start with a stretchy cuff

The top of a sock must be elastic enough to pass over the largest part of the foot. You may use any cast-on you prefer, but as you cast on, elongate the yarn that runs between cast-on stitches (it's quite logical - the running yarn determines the length of the edge). This simply takes careful attention and a gentle touch. Another method is to cast on with a doubled strand of yarn, which makes the edge longer as well as stronger. Carol Breitner's first book, to be published in 2008, **The Sock Divide - Knitting Socks That Fit**, offers a terrific method for stretchy cuffs. Whatever strategy you choose, always test the cuff early on, to be sure it really is stretchy enough.

This Sidestream sock starts with a garter stitch toe and ends with a purled rolled edge. The cuff is shaped by working a cdd in the center of each side, and a LLinc, k1, LRinc at the center of the front and back, alternating with rounds of plain knit.

Rolled Edge Cuff

Cast on Ⓓ sts. Join (page 10) and knit 3 rnds. This edge rolls to the *outside*. For an edge that rolls to the *inside*, purl 3 rnds.

Cobblestone Cuff

Use Judy's Magic Cast-on (page 22) to cast on Ⓓ stitches to each of 2 parallel circs or 2 dpn's (long dpn's). Knit 3 (or more) rnds. Fold knitting lengthwise with *purl side out*, ndls parallel. Use a dangling circ end or free dpn to k tog 1 st from each ndl until the 2 sets of sts become 1 set (reduced to same number as were cast on to each ndl), now all on 1 ndl. Divide this wonderfully elastic "caterpillar" of sts among 2 circs or 4 dpn's, join (page 10) and begin knitting in the rnd. (Use tail to weave ends closed later.)

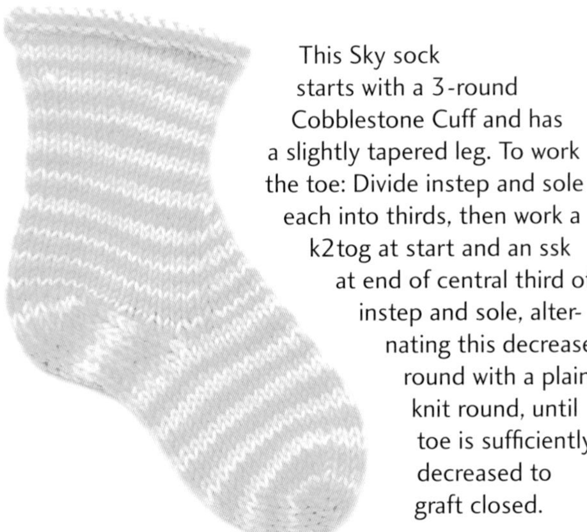

This Sky sock starts with a 3-round Cobblestone Cuff and has a slightly tapered leg. To work the toe: Divide instep and sole each into thirds, then work a k2tog at start and an ssk at end of central third of instep and sole, alternating this decrease round with a plain knit round, until toe is sufficiently decreased to graft closed.

The small yellow socks follow Master patterns and demonstrate various toes and cuffs. They're knit with Artyarns Ultramerino 4, (100% superwash merino wool, 50 g / 191 yds), color 134.

This Cedar Sock begins with Hansel's Cuff and ends with a Star Toe, to light up the breadcrumbs he drops so he and Gretel can find their way home.

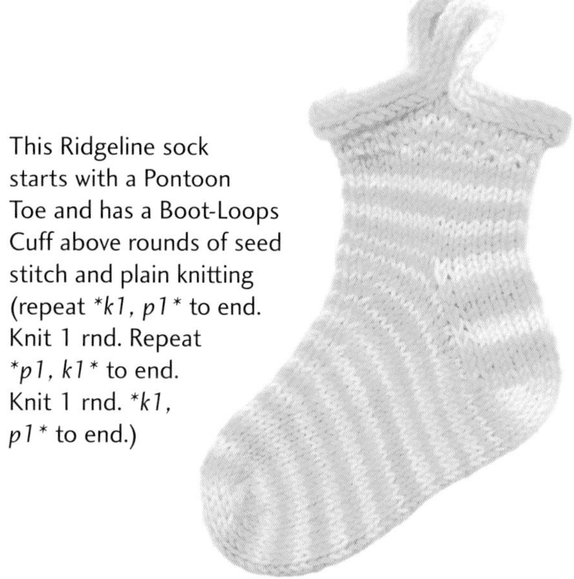

This Ridgeline sock starts with a Pontoon Toe and has a Boot-Loops Cuff above rounds of seed stitch and plain knitting (repeat *k1, p1* to end. Knit 1 rnd. Repeat *p1, k1* to end. Knit 1 rnd. *k1, p1* to end.)

Hansel's Cuff

This cuff is worked similarly to the Cobblestone cuff and shares its wonderfully elastic nature. It is smooth stockinette except for the edging of purl bumps - like the trail of bread crumbs Hansel left so he and his sister Gretel could find their way home in the fairy tale. Follow Cobblestone Cuff directions, but fold lengthwise with *knit* side out when joining the sts of 1 ndl with the other, and instead of knitting the sets of sts together, *purl* them together.

Pebble-Edge Cuff

Follow Cobblestone Cuff directions, with these changes: Turn ndls upside-down after cast-on, *so the purl ridge faces up.* This places the purl ridge along the cuff's outside top edge. When joining the sts of 1 ndl with the other, keep *knit side* (and purl ridge) out.

Boot-Loops Cuff

Cast on 3 sts with waste yarn and begin I-cord: repeat **k3, return 3 sts to left ndl** 2x. Cut tail of waste yarn and continue repetition with project yarn until I-cord reaches length required for cuff (if possible, try it on over widest part of foot, where it should stretch but pass), then record the length. Knit 2" (5 cm) additional I-cord for each boot-loop. When done, cut 6" (15 cm) tail, leaving sts on ndl. Remove waste yarn and place the 3 freed sts on another ndl. Making sure that I-cord is not twisted, hold ends together and graft (page 22) together, securing ends inside I-cord tube. Fold I-cord circle in half with a 1" (2.5 cm) tall boot-loop is at each end. Tie string around base of each boot-loop. To begin leg, pick up Ⓓ sts evenly distributed around the base of the I-cord cuff, leaving boot-loops free, and begin knitting leg in the rnd. Later, remove string and sew base of boot-loops to make them stand up.

Double-Stranded Cuff

Cast on with a double strand of yarn. This results in a more elastic fit as well as a handsome braided effect.

Resources

A huge thank you to each of the generous yarn companies … you kept my home filled with a tantalizing palette of colors and textures that fed the book each and every day.

Artyarns - *Supermerino (all the little yellow socks!), Handpaint Stripes* – artyarns.com

Blue Moon Fiber Arts® Inc. - *Socks That Rock®, Twisted* – bluemoonfiberarts.com

Cascade - *Cascade Fixation* – cascadeyarns.com

Chappy's Fiber Arts and Crafts - *Sock blockers & letter markers* – www.purrfectlycatchydesigns.com

Claudia Hand Painted Yarns - *Fingering and sport weight Merino* – claudiaco.com

Crystal Palace Yarns - *Bunny Hop, Panda Cotton, Panda Wool* – straw.com

Fleece Artist - *Merino 2/6, Sea Wool, Kid Aran* – fleeceartist.com

Hand Maiden - *Sea Silk, 4-ply Cashmere* – handmaiden.ca

Louet - *Gems Merino, Merlin* – louet.com

Mountain Colors - *Bearfoot, 4/8's Wool, Weaver's Wool* – mountaincolors.com

Nature's Palette - *Nature's Palette Plant-Dyed Merino Fingering™* – handjiveknits.com

Philosopher's Wool - *Philosopher's Wool* – philosopherswool.com

Russi Sales - *Heirloom Breeze* – russisales.com

Abbreviations

cdd - centered double decrease - slip next 2 sts tog as for a k2tog, k next st, pass 2 slipped sts over k st.
circ(s) - circular needle(s)- see page 8
cw - conceal wrap - see page 15
cw/ p2tog - conceal wrap / purl 2 together - see page 15
cw/ ssk - conceal wrap/ slip, slip, knit - see page 15
dpn(s) - double-pointed needle(s) - see page 8
k - knit
k1f&b - knit into front and back of same stitch - see page 11
k2tog - knit 2 stitches together from left to right - see page 11
LLinc - leaning left increase - see page 11
LRinc - leaning right increase - see page 11
p - purl
p1b&f - purl into back and front of same stitch - see page 11
p2tog - purl 2 sts together
rem - remain, remains, or remaining
rnd(s) - round(s)
RPI - rounds-per-inch (or per 2.5 cm) - see page 112
RS - right side
sl1 - slip 1 stitch (always slip tip-to-tip, also known as purl-wise - unless instructed to slip as if to knit - see page 10
sl1 wyif - slip next st purlwise with yarn in front
ssk - slip next 2 sts 1 at a time knitwise, then k together from right to left through the back loops - see page 11
ssp - slip, slip, purl - with yarn in back, slip next 2 sts knitwise 1 at a time. Return sts to left ndl. Insert right ndl through 2nd st before 1st st through back, and p sts tog.
st(s) - stitch(es)
starting ndl - starting needle - see page 7
WS - wrong side
w&t - wrap and turn - see page 14
wyif - with yarn in front
yo - yarn over - bring yarn over ndl from front to back

Skacel Collection - *Austermann Step, Fortissima, Trekking, and Addi Turbo needles, including the new Addi lace needles (fabulous for socks!), and Cat's Magical Markers (the ones you see here are a prototype). They can be popped over the cable or slid onto a needle, and are beautiful! A special thanks to Karin Skacel Haack (of Skacel) and Thomas Selter (of the Selter Company in Germany, who make Addi Turbo needles), who embraced my suggestion to produce the markers and with whom I have worked to perfect the design.* – skacelknitting.com

Tightening up loose purl stitches

Many knitters purl more loosely than they knit. When changing from rounds to rows, their gauge becomes looser (especially apparent in stockinette). A sock knitter who purls loosely will end up with looser-than-desirable heels.

One solution is to use a smaller needle to purl the wrong side rows of the heel. How much smaller? That varies from knitter to knitter and from yarn to yarn, but usually, dropping from one to three sizes does the trick.

A second solution is to purl with the yarn in back, as when knitting. This method is also ideal when working knit and purl stitches side-by side (like ribbing or cables) because it keeps neighboring knit stitches tidy as well. In some references this is known as the Norwegian or Icelandic Purl.

Here's how: With the **yarn** in back, poke the right tip under the **yarn** and up through the first **stitch** on the left needle. Stretch the **stitch** behind the **yarn** out to the right (picture shows this stage only). Now press the right tip down on the **yarn** and pull it down through the **stretched stitch**.

Remove the original **stitch** from the left needle as usual. The method feels awkward at first, but is well worth knowing. Note that the new purl stitch is mounted "backwards." Just be sure to work into the "winning leg" (page 10) when you meet it next.

Patterns

27 — Bartholomew's Tantalizing Socks
40 — Cedar Dancing Socks
54 — Charlie's Dragon Socks
26 — Charlie's Seeded Heart Socks
102 — Charlie's Sheriff Boat Socks
94 — Charlie's Wiggle Socks
88 — Cables & Corrugations
84 — Clematis Vine
73 — Dove Socks
70 — Etta Mae's Bootikins
66 — Fountain Foxgloves
93 — Home & Hearth Eyelet Anklets
106 — Jeweled Steps
62 — Marcelo's Seven-League Boots
49 — Master Cedar
57 — Master Coreolis (Simple)
58 — Master Coreolis (Spiral)
67 — Master Foxglove
99 — Master Ridgeline
91 — Master Riverbed
108 — Master Sidestream
33 — Master Sky
79 — Master Upstream
36 — Max's Springy Ring Socks
74 — Milkmaid's Stockings
42 — Ocean-Toes
72 — Philosopher's House Socks
30 — Robin Hood's Fireside Boots
32 — Robin Hood's Fireside Boots, Elf Toe variation
82 — Rowan Margaret's Silken Slippers
81 — Rushing Rivulet
48 — Slipstitch Rings
64 — Simple Socks with a Slant
96 — Soft-Hearted Socks
104 — Sunrise Socks
56 — Tibetan Coreolis
37 — Veil of Leaves
98 — Woven Ridge

Techniques

7 — Knowing your needles' names
7 — Sock parts
8 — Knitting with 2 circular needles
8 — Knitting with 5 double-pointed needles
8 — Knitting with 1 long circular needle
9 — Gauge really does matter
10 — Stitch mount
10 — Slipping stitches correctly
10 — Managing markers
10 — Joining in the round
11 — Increases - LRinc and LLinc, k1f&b, p1b&f
11 — Decreases - ssk and k2tog
12 — Moving stitches between circular needles
14 — Wrap and turn (w&t)
15 — Conceal wrap (cw, cw/ssk, and cw/ p2tog)
17 — Figure-8 cast-on
22 — Grafting, Kitchener stitch, weaving . . .
22 — Judy's Magic Cast-on
58 — Widening a simple Coriolis band
53 — Camel sense- avoid ladders between needles
65 — Yarn-over "Bubble Trails"
71 — Make a Button-bobble
85 — Generating fresh stitch patterns
97 — Sometimes 2 different needle sizes make a matched pair
95 — A cable needle you may already have
110 — Socks that fit well in shoes
112 — Length of toe-up toe section, and elusive RPI
118 — Foot proportions and shoe sizes
119 — Fitting plump or thin feet
119 — German ankle ribbing
120 — Overview of the heel process
124 — Handling wraps easily
125 — Combination heels
126 — To make a toe longer or more pointed
130 — Elizabeth Zimmermann's (EZ's) sewn bind-off
132 — Start with a stretchy cuff
135 — Tightening up loose purl stitches
136 — A very fine end, indeed

A very fine end, indeed

I only figured this out about a month before this book went to print, and it seemed to be such a miracle (and suddenly so obvious) that I immediately began teaching it in my workshops. I soon learned the following:

1. Embroiderers recognize this as a daisy stitch.

2. Both Lucy Neatby and Lily Chin have been teaching this finishing technique for years.

But in case you, like me, have been an ignorant fool, I shall show you how to join the end of a bind-off to its beginning, creating a continuous chain of stitches, a tiny thing of great beauty.

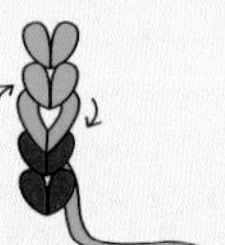

From right to left:

1. The **final bound off stitch** has had its tail cut and awaits its fate.

2. The knitter fearlessly pulls up one end of the **tail**.

3. After the **tail** is threaded on a tapestry needle, the knitter locates the base of the **first bound off stitch** and weaves the **tail** right through its **2 legs**, then back down through the **stitch** from which the **tail** had come.

4. The knitter tugs the **tail** until the chain of stitches is smooth, and weaves in the end. And it is a very fine end, indeed.